AF147341

Nedra

by

George Barr Mccutcheon

Nedra
by George Barr Mccutcheon

Copyright © 2024

All Rights reserved.

No part of this publication may be reproduced, stored in a retrieval system, or transmitted in any form or by any means, electronic, mechanical, photocopying or Otherwise, without the written permission of the publisher.
The author/editor asserts the moral right to be identified as the author/editor of this work.

ISBN: 978-93-64282-74-1

Published by

DOUBLE 9 BOOKS

2/13-B, Ansari Road
Daryaganj, New Delhi – 110002
info@double9books.com
www.double9books.com
Tel. 011-40042856

This book is under public domain

ABOUT THE AUTHOR

George Barr McCutcheon was an American novelist and playwright born on July 26, 1866, in Tippecanoe County, Indiana. He is best known for his popular "Graustark" series, a collection of romantic adventure novels set in a fictional Eastern European country. McCutcheon's work gained considerable popularity in the early 20th century, earning him a prominent place in American literature of the time. McCutcheon began his career as a journalist, working for newspapers in Lafayette, Indiana and later in Chicago. His transition to fiction writing brought him widespread acclaim with the publication of his first major novel, "Graustark: The Story of a Love Behind a Throne" in 1901. The success of this novel led to several sequels, including "Beverly of Graustark" and "Truxton King," which captivated readers with their tales of romance, political intrigue, and adventure. In addition to the Graustark series, McCutcheon wrote numerous standalone novels, many of which also achieved significant popularity. "Brewster's Millions," published in 1902, is one of his most famous works. The novel, which tells the story of a man who must spend a large inheritance within a short period to receive an even larger one, has been adapted into several films and stage productions. Despite his success as a novelist, McCutcheon remained humble and dedicated to his craft. He continued to write prolifically throughout his life, producing a substantial body of work that includes both novels and plays.

CONTENTS

CHAPTER I
THE INSPIRATION

A tall young man sped swiftly up the wide stone steps leading to the doorway of a mansion in one of Chicago's most fashionable avenues. After pushing the button sharply he jerked out his watch and guessed at the time by the dull red light from the panel in the door. Then he hastily brushed from the sleeve of his coat the telltale billiard chalk, whose presence reminded him that a general survey might be a wise precaution. He was rubbing a white streak from his trousers' leg when the door flew open and the butler admitted him to the hallway. This personage relieved him of his hat, coat and stick and announced:

"Miss Vernon is w'itin' for you, sir."

"How the devil did I happen to let eight o'clock strike nine before I knew it?" muttered the visitor. He was at the drawing-room door as he concluded this self-addressed reproach, extending both hands toward the young woman who came from the fireplace to meet him.

"How late you are, Hugh," she cried, half resentfully. He bent forward and kissed her.

"Late? It isn't late, dear. I said I couldn't come before eight, didn't I? Well, it's eight, isn't it?"

"It's nearly seventy minutes past eight, sir. I've been waiting and watching the hands on the clock for just sixty minutes."

"I never saw such a perfect crank about keeping time as that grandfatherly clock of yours. It hasn't skipped a second in two centuries, I'll swear. You see, I was playing off the odd game with Tom Ditton."

He dropped lazily into a big arm-chair, drove his hands into his pockets and stretched out his long legs toward the grate.

"You might have come at eight, Hugh, on this night if no other. You knew what important things we have to consider." Miss Vernon, tall and graceful, stood before him with her back to the fire. She was exceedingly pretty, this girl whom Hugh had kissed.

"I'm awfully sorry, Grace; but you know how it is when a fellow's in a close, hard game--especially with a blow-hard like Tom Ditton."

"If I forgive you again, I'm afraid you'll prove a begging husband."

"Never! Deliver me from a begging husband. I shall assert all kinds of authority in my house, Miss Vernon, and you'll be in a constant state of beggary yourself. You'll have to beg me to get up in the morning, beg me to come home early every night, beg me to swear off divers things, beg me to go to church, beg me to buy new hats for you, beg me to eat things you cook, beg me to--"

"I suppose I shall even have to beg you to kiss me," she cried.

"Not at all. That is one thing I'll beg of you. Lean over here, do, and kiss me, please," he said invitingly.

She placed a hand on each arm of the chair and leaned forward obediently. Their lips met in a smile.

"You lazy thing!" she exclaimed, her face slightly flushed. Then she seated herself on one of the big arms, resting her elbow on the back of the chair beside his head. For a few minutes both were silent, gazing at the bright coals before them, the smile remaining upon their lips. Hugh had been squinting between the toes of his shoes at a lonely black chunk in the grate for some time before he finally spoke reflectively.

"I can't afford to be lazy much longer, can I? Married men never have a minute's rest, you know."

"We're not married."

"No; but we're going to be, let me remind you. We are to--to announce it to-morrow night, are we not? It has come to that, you see." He did not look very cheerful, nor did she.

"Yes, I suppose it's imperative. That is why aunt is giving her reception,--just to tell everybody we're engaged."

"And then everybody will shake hands with us and say, 'Congratulations,' 'How lovely,' 'So surprised,' 'Howdy do,' and so forth, and we say 'Thanks,' 'How good of you,' and more so forth. It will be great!" Another silence and inspection of the fire, he taking an altered aim at the black chunk. "Say!" he exclaimed, "wouldn't it do just as well if I didn't put in an appearance to-morrow night? Your aunt can announce the thing, as agreed, and you can tell 'em that I have a sick uncle in Indianapolis, or have had my leg broken, or something like that. Now, there's a good girl."

"No," she said. "We fell in love because we couldn't help it, and this is the penalty--an announcement party."

"I'll never quite understand why *you* fell," said he dubiously.

"I think we were both too young to know," she responded. "It seems to me that we've been in love ever since we were babies."

"And it never hurts a baby to fall, you know," said he, with fine logic. "Of course it may cripple 'em permanently, but they don't know how it happened."

For some moments she caressed his brown hair in silence, the smile lingering on her lips after it had left her eyes. His eyes closed dreamily under the gentle touch of her fingers. "But, dear," she said, "this is no joking matter. We have been engaged for nearly three months and not a soul knows of it. We'll have to tell them how we managed to keep it a secret for so long, and why,--and all that. And then everybody will want to know who the bridesmaids are to be."

"I believe I'd like to know that myself, as long as I'm to walk out of the church ahead of them--provided I don't get lost."

"Helen Grossman is to be the maid of honor. I believe I'll ask Jean Robertson, Eloise Grant, Harriet Noble, Mayme McMurtrie, Ellen Boyland--"

"Are we to have no guests?"

"--and Effa Samuels. Won't it be a pretty set of girls?"

"Couldn't be prettier."

"And now, who is to be your best man?"

"Well, I thought I'd have Tom Ditton," a trifle confusedly.

"Tom Ditton! I thought you did not approve of him," she cried. "You certainly did not when he came to see me so frequently."

"Oh, he isn't such a bad sort, after all. I'd just as soon have him as any one. Besides, he's an expert at it. If it was left to me, I'd much rather sit behind the pulpit until it is all over. People won't miss me while they've got you to look at."

"We could be married so quietly and prettily if it were not for Aunt Elizabeth," pouted Miss Vernon. "She insists on the church wedding, the teas and receptions and--"

"All that sort of rot," he interjected, as if fearing she might not express herself adequately. "I like your Aunt Elizabeth, Grace, but she's--she's an awful--"

"Don't say it, Hugh. I know what you mean, but she can't help it. She lives for society. She's perfectly crazy on the subject. Aunt Elizabeth made up her mind we should be married in church. I have talked myself black in the face--for your sake, dear--but it was like trying to convert a stone wall. She is determined. You know what that means."

"No wonder she's a widow," growled Hugh Ridgeway sourly. "Your father served you a mighty mean trick, dear, when he gave you over to her training. She might have spoiled you beyond redemption."

"Poor father! He loathed display, too. I've no doubt that is why he left me in her care until I reached the age of discretion. She was not always like this. Father's money has wrought the change. Aunty was as poor as a church mouse until father's death put her at the head of my household--it was mine, Hugh, even if I was only six years old. You know we could live pretty well on forty thousand a year."

"You'll have a million or so when you're twenty-three, dear, and I'll venture to say your aunt has saved something in all these years."

"Oh, she had at least two hundred thousand dollars by the will. It has cost her nothing to live all these years as my guardian and trustee. We just had to do something with my income, you know."

"I don't see why you should let this fortune stand in the way, Grace," growled he. "Haven't I enough of my own to take its place?" Hugh Ridgeway had a million in his own right and he could well afford to be unreasonable. "The will says you are not to have your father's money until you are twenty-three years old. He evidently thought that was a discreet age. You are not to marry before you have reached that age. I've been waiting for two years, Grace, and there still remains two months--"

"One month and twenty-eight days, Hugh," she corrected.

"And in the meantime we have to stay here and face all this ante-nuptial wretchedness. It's sickening, Grace. We hate it, both of us. Don't we? I knew you'd nod your head. That's why I can't help loving you. You've got so

much real good hard sense about things. If your confounded Aunt Lizzie-
-Elizabeth, I should say--would let us get married as we want--Hang it
all, Grace, it's our affair anyhow, isn't it? Why should we permit her to
dictate? It's not her wedding. She's been married twice; why can't she let
well enough alone?"

"She loves me, Hugh, after all," gently.

"Well, so do I. I'm willing--not perfectly willing, of course--but
reasonably so, that we should wait until the twenty-third of May, but
I don't see why we should have the whole town waiting with us. Why
don't you assert yourself, dear, before it is too late? Once she pulls off this
announcement party, it's all off with peace of mind and contentment so far
as we are concerned. Of course, she'll be enjoying it, but what of us? Are
you afraid of her?"

"Don't bully me, Hugh," she pleaded. He was contrite at once and
properly so. "She has lived for this time in her life. She never has been
crossed. I can't--honestly I can't go to her now and--quarrel. That's what it
would mean--a quarrel. She would never give in."

"Well, then, all hope is lost," he lamented. For some minutes Miss
Vernon gave no response, sitting upon the arm of the chair, a perplexed
pucker on her brow and a thoughtful swing to her slippered foot.

These young people had known each other since earliest childhood.
They had played together with the same neighborly toys and they had
grown up together with the same neighborly ideals. Both had whirled in
the social swing until the sensation palled. The most exclusive set in town
regarded them as among its most popular members. It was quite natural
that their wedding should be the most brilliant and fashionable of the year.
Their position in society demanded the sacrifice, and her aunt saw the
urgent need for making it, notwithstanding the opposition of the young
people themselves.

Ridgeway was a couple of years older than his affianced bride, and she
was just short of twenty-three. She, an orphan since early childhood, lived
with her widowed aunt--the social gourmand, to quote Hugh Ridgeway--
and he made his home next door with his sister and her husband. The two
brown stone houses were almost within arm's reach of each other. She had
painted dainty water colors for his rooms and he had thrown thousands of
roses from his windows into her boudoir. It had been a merry courtship--the
courtship of modern cavalier and lady fair. Ridgeway's parents died when

he was in college, and he was left to enlarge or despise a fortune that rated him as a millionaire and the best catch in town--at that time.

He was a member of the Board of Trade, but he was scarcely an operator in the strictest sense of the word. If he won he whistled, if he lost he whistled. It mattered little. Good looking, well dressed, generous to a fault, tainted but moderately with scandal, he was a man whom everybody admired, but who admired few in return--a perfectly natural and proper condition if one but stops to consider.

Miss Vernon was beautiful--of that there was no question. Tall, fair, brown-eyed and full of the life that loves, she ruled the hearts of many and--kept her hand for one. Her short, gay life had been one of luxury and ease. She had known few of its cares; its vicissitudes belonged to the charities she supported with loyal persistency. Her aunt, society mad, was her only mentor, her only guide. A path had been made for her, and she saw no other alternative than to travel it as designed. A careless, buoyant heart, full of love and tenderness and warmth, allowed itself to be tossed by all of the emotions, but always sank back safely into the path of duty and rectitude. It was not of sufficient moment to combat her aunt's stubborn authority; it was so much easier to do her own sweet will without conflict and then smile down on the consequences.

Possibly it is true that she did not love her aunt. If that were the case, she kept it well to herself. She could not have been blamed, however, for disliking the dictator. Hugh Ridgeway was more or less right when he said that no one in town admired the old lady. She was hard, devoid of humor, wrapped up in her own selfishness; shrewd, capable and resourceful. Her brother, on his deathbed, signed the instrument which made this arrogant relative the arbiter of the girl's future for many years to come. She was appointed guardian and trustee until legal age was attained, and as such she was absolute in her power. The large fortune was to be held in trust by this aunt, Mrs. Torrence, and the Hon. Stanley Goodland, until Grace was twenty-three years of age. The income from the investments in bonds, real estate and high-class securities was to be handled by Mrs. Torrence as she saw fit in the effort to better the young woman's mental and social estate. To do her justice, she performed the duties well and honorably, even though her measure of human nature was not full to overflowing. Grace, with a mind and heart of her own, undertook to cultivate human nature from her own point of view after years of tolerance, and she succeeded so well that her aunt was none the wiser.

On one point, however, the paragon was so firm and unassailable that Grace was obliged to confess failure to her lover, after weeks and weeks of splendid argument. Her aunt forced an issue. The marriage of her niece was to be brilliant to the verge of confusion and the ante-nuptial season was to be one which the city should not forget while its promoter lived to enjoy the emoluments. She knew she was making her niece unhappy, but she argued that her niece was too deeply in love to appreciate the value of opportunity. Besides, on her wedding day, Grace Vernon would be twenty-three years of age, mistress of herself, her fortune, and her husband's home. That day would end the reign of Elizabeth Torrence. The arbiter was determined that the reign should end in a blaze of glory.

As for Grace and Hugh, they were to be married. That had been decided upon by destiny years and years ago and ratified after Hugh had reached an age of discretion. He said that twenty-five was the year of discretion, if not of reason.

After the first transports, each began to consider the importance of the union, not only to themselves, but to the world at large. In their reflective moments they realized that the marriage would be the most wonderful event in the whole history of the homes of Vernon and Ridgeway. Never before had a Vernon married a Ridgeway, and--vice versa. Therefore, the whole world would visit upon such a union its undivided attention. That is the view all engaged people take of marriage.

Miss Vernon had employed six weeks of argument in convincing Mr. Ridgeway that a church wedding was imperative, although she admittedly preferred the simpler form, where the minister conducts the ceremony in the presence of two witnesses and a ring. Society demanded the exhibition. Mr. Ridgeway warned her that he could not survive the ordeal and would leave her a widow at the altar.

Their difficulties had at last resolved themselves into that condition which confronts every engaged pair; and they, like others, were preparing to inform the world of their intentions.

"There's no way out of it, Hugh," she finally sighed, "unless we decide to give up the hope of getting married. That would break my heart," she said, with her rarest smile.

"This would be the most delightful period of my life if it were not for that distressing announcement, the two months of purgatory between now and the day of the wedding, and then the--calamity. I know it will be a calamity. I can't get through it alive."

"You poor boy! I wish we could have a quiet little Wedding. It would be so sweet, wouldn't it, dear?" she said plaintively, wistfully.

"But instead we are to have a hippodrome. Bah!" he concluded spitefully. "I wouldn't talk this way, dear, if I didn't know that you feel just as I do about it. But," and here he arose wearily, "this sort of talk isn't helping matters. It's a case of church against choice. To-morrow night we'll tell 'em, and then we'll quit sleeping for two months."

"There's only one way out of it that I can see. We might elope," she said laughingly, standing before him and rubbing the wrinkles from between his eyes.

Gradually his gray eyes fell until they looked into hers of brown. A mutual thought sprang into the eyes of each like a flash of light plainly comprehensive. He seized her hands, still staring into her eyes, and an exultant hope leaped to his lips, bursting forth in these words:

"By George!"

"Oh, we couldn't," she whispered, divining his thought.

"We can! By all that's good and holy, we'll elope!" Hugh's voice was quivering with enthusiasm, his face a picture of relief.

"Honestly, do you--do you think we could?" The girl's eyes were wide with excitement, her cheeks burning.

"Can we? What's to prevent? Will you do it, Grace--will you?" cried he.

"What will everybody say?"

"Let 'em say. What do we care? Won't it be the greatest lark that ever happened? You're the smartest woman in the world for thinking of it."

"But I wasn't in earnest," she protested.

"But you are now--we both are. Listen: We can slip away and get married and nobody will be the wiser and then, when we come back, we can laugh at everybody."

"And get our pictures in the papers."

"Then, by Hokey! we won't come back for five years! How's that? That'll fool 'em, won't it? Say, this is great! Life is worth living after all. You'll go, won't you, Grace?"

"I'd go to the end of the world with you, Hugh, but--"

"Oh, say you'll go! Now, listen to this," he urged, leaping to his feet. "We're going to be married anyway. We love one another. You can't be married until the twenty-third of May. Lots of people elope--even in the best of families. Why shouldn't we? If we stay here, we'll have to face all the sort of thing we don't like--"

"Yes, but it won't take us two months to elope," she protested. "Sh! Don't speak above a whisper. Aunt Elizabeth has wonderful ears."

"By Jove, darling, I believe you're two-thirds willing to try it on," he whispered.

"We must be sensible, Hugh. You see, I can't be married until the twenty-third of May. Well, aunt is determined to announce the engagement to-morrow night. Don't you see we couldn't elope until the twenty-second at best, so we're doomed for two months of it in spite of ourselves. If we get through the two months why should we elope at all? The worst will be over?"

"We can't escape the announcement party, I'll admit, but we can get away from all the rest. My scheme is to elope to a place that will require seven or eight weeks' time to reach. That's a fine way to kill time, don't you see?"

"My goodness!"

"Why not? We can do as we like, can't we? And what a bully lark! I'd be a downright cad to ask you to do this, Grace, if I didn't love you as I do. We can use assumed names and all that!"

"Oh, dear, dear, doesn't it sound lovely?" she cried, her cheeks red with excitement.

"The twenty-third of May isn't so far off after all, and it won't be half so far if we're doing something like this. Will you go?"

"If I only could! Do you really think we--we could?"

"Whoop!" he shouted, as he seized her in his arms and rained kisses upon her face. Then he held her off and looked into her eyes for a moment. Then he gave another whoop, kissed her, released her and did a wild dance about the room. She stood beside the big chair, equally as excited, laughing unrestrainedly at his hilarity. At last he brought up at the other side of the chair.

"But where could--I mean, shall we elope to?" she finally asked.

"Anywhere. Bombay--Australia? Let's make it a stunner, dear--let's do it up right."

"And be married away over there? Oh, Hugh!"

"Certainly. They can marry us over there as well as anywhere. Here, I'll write the names of ten places and we'll draw one from my hat." He sat down before a table and feverishly wrote upon the backs of a number of his calling cards the names of as many cities, his companion looking over his shoulder eagerly. Without ado he tossed the cards into a jardinière in lieu of a hat. "Draw!" he said tragically.

"Wait a minute, Hugh. What have we to elope from? There isn't the faintest objection in the world to our marriage."

"There you go--backing out!"

"No; I'm just as willing as you, but doesn't it seem rather absurd?" Her hand hung over the jardinière irresolutely.

"It will be the greatest wedding tour that mortals ever took. Draw!"

"Well, then, there's the card. Mercy!" she cried, dropping a card on the table. "That's a long distance, Hugh."

He picked up the card and his face paled a little as he read:

"Manila!"

They sat down in the chair, she on the arm as before. After a moment he glanced at her perplexed face, and asked:

"Are you afraid to go, Grace?"

"It isn't that, Hugh. I was just wondering if we could reach Manila by the twenty-third of May. It is unlucky to change the wedding day after it has been once selected," she said softly.

"Grace Vernon, you are an angel. I was afraid you would show the white feather. It's a go, then--Manila! We can start next week and get there in good time."

"Next week? Impossible!" she cried in alarm.

"Nonsense! You can get ready for a trip to New York, making your preparations for a sea voyage secretly. I'll attend to all the details. It will be easy. No one will ever dream of what we are doing until we cable the news home to your aunt."

"Oh, I must tell Aunt Elizabeth!"

"Not much! That's no way to elope. We must do it correctly or not at all. Nobody is to know until we are really married. Can you get ready in a week?"

"If I really must."

"Can't take any more time than that if we want to reach Manila in time for the wedding."

"Oh, Hugh! We can't go to Manila!" she cried, suddenly starting to her feet in distress. "My Uncle Harry lives there. He is my mother's only brother and he's been there since the close of the war. He's in the hemp business. Oh, dear! How provoking!" she concluded almost piteously.

"It's fine!" he exclaimed jubilantly. "We can be married at his home. I'm sure he'll be happy to have us. You can write and tell him we're coming, dear. Lord!" with great relief in his voice, "that simplifies matters immensely. Now we have an excuse for going to Manila. But above all things don't cable to him. Write a nice long letter and mail it just before we start."

She was silent a long while, staring soberly at the blaze in the grate.

"There'll be no bridesmaids and ushers over there, Hugh."

"We don't want 'em."

Silence for a few minutes.

"In a week, did you say?"

"Positively."

"Well, I'll be ready," she said solemnly.

He kissed her tenderly, lovingly, pressed her cold hand and said encouragingly:

"We'll meet in New York next Monday afternoon. Leave everything to me, dear. It will be much pleasanter to go by way of London and it will help to kill a good deal of time."

"Hugh," she said, smiling faintly, "I think we're proving that father was right. I can't possibly arrive at the age of discretion until I am twenty-three and past."

CHAPTER II
THE BEGINNING OF FLIGHT

Mr. Ridgeway paced back and forth outside the iron gates in the Grand Central Station on the afternoon of April 1st, 190--, a smile of anticipation and a frown of impatience alternating in his fresh, young face. Certain lines of care seemed to have disappeared since we saw him last, nearly a week ago, and in their stead beamed the light of a new-found interest in life. Now and then he took from his pocket a telegram; spectators stared amusedly at him as he read and reread:

DETROIT, MICHIGAN, March 81, 190--.

To H.B. Ridge:

Got away safely. Meet me Forty-second Street, New York, to-morrow at three. Feel awfully queer and look a fright. Sympathetic lady, next compartment, just offered condolences for loss of my husband. What are the probabilities of storm? Be sure and find out before we start.

SISTER GRACE.

"Isn't that just like a girl!" he muttered to himself. "Where else would Forty-second Street be but New York! London?"

They had decided to travel as brother and sister and to adopt Ridge as the surname. Hugh had taken passage for Liverpool on the liner *Saint Cloud*, to sail on the second, having first examined the list of passengers to ascertain if there were any among them who might know him or his companion in the adventure. The list was now complete, and he, assured that there was no danger of recognition, felt the greatest weight of all lifted from his mind.

He had also considerably inquired into the state of the weather and learned that it promised well for the voyage. The whole affair was such a glorious lark, such an original enterprise, that he could scarcely restrain himself in his exhilaration from confiding in his chance hotel acquaintances.

Purposely, the night before, he had gone to an hotel where he was unknown, keeping under cover during the day as much as possible.

According to the prearranged plan, they were to go aboard ship that evening, as the sailing hour was early in the morning.

He was waiting for her train. Every now and then his glance would shoot through the throng of people, somewhat apprehensively, as if he feared, instead of hoped, that some one might be there. This searching glance was to determine whether there might be any danger of Chicago or New York acquaintances witnessing the arrival of the person for whom he waited. Once he recognized a friend and dodged quickly behind a knot of people, escaping notice. That is why he audibly muttered:

"Thank Heaven!"

Every nerve was tingling with excitement; an indescribable desire to fly, to shout, to race down the track to meet the train, swept through him. His heart almost stopped beating, and he felt that his face was bloodless. For the twentieth time in the last two hours Ridgeway looked at his watch and frowningly exclaimed:

"Only five after two! Nearly an hour to wait!"

He sat down for a moment, only to arise the next and walk to the board announcing the arrival of trains. Almost immediately one pulled into the station. Perceiving a bystander--one of the sort that always give the impression of being well-informed--he inquired casually where it was from.

"Chicago," was the ready answer.

"Great Scott! Lucky I came early! Grace's idea of time--oh, well, only the small matter of an hour out of the way."

Quickly he sprang forward, taking up a good position to watch. First came a man hurriedly and alone. A bunch of people followed him. Hugh peered unsuccessfully here and there among them. Another bunch; she was not in it, and he began to feel a trifle nervous. Now came the stragglers and he grew bewildered. Finally, the last one--a woman hove in sight. With renewed hope he scanned her approach. It was not Grace! His brain was in a whirl. What could have happened? Where was she? Again he jerked out the telegram.

"Meet me Forty-second Street, New York, at three," he read half-aloud. "Nothing could be plainer," he mused in perplexity. "No train at three; another at--she must be on a later one."

"What time is the next Chicago train due?" he inquired anxiously at the Information Bureau.

"Five-thirty, sir," politely answered the official.

"Five-thirty!" he repeated disgustedly.

Again the telegram was brought out and this time shown.

"On what road did you expect the lady?" was the question put with well-simulated interest that every few minutes was practised on different individuals.

"Road?" Hugh stared blankly at his questioner. "What road?" Then, like a flash, the solution of the problem pierced his brain.

"What an ass I am!" he burst out, and added sheepishly: "West Shore!"

Purposely avoiding the other's face for confirmation of his self-depreciatory exclamation, together with its unmistakable expression of professional tolerance for the imbecilities of mankind, Hugh looked at the time. It was two-thirty. Tearing out of the station, he hailed a cab.

Inside, and moving fast, he winced a little as he thought of his late strictures on girls and their ways. What a shame to have abused Grace, when he himself had told her to take the Wabash as essential to their plan. What a blooming idiot he was! New York in the telegram meant, of course, the New York side of the river. He recovered his equanimity; the world was serene again.

With a sharp pull the cabman brought up at the ferry and Hugh took his stand among those waiting for the boat to disgorge its load of passengers.

At that moment a thought struck him, and acting on it, he called out:

"Hi! porter!"

"Here, sir!"

"Where can I get some note paper?"

"All right, sir!" and in an instant a pad of paper was forthcoming.

Hugh took out his pencil and wrote a brief note. Then, in a low voice, he said:

"Here, porter! I want you to do something for me."

"Yes, sir!"

"I'll make it worth your while, but I won't hare you attending to any one else--understand?"

The porter demonstrated with a nod his perfect comprehension of what was required, and there followed from his employer a minute description of the lady.

"Young, slight, tall, fair, black hat and veil, and--"

"In mourning, sir, undoubtedly?"

"Mourning! No, of course not. Cannot a lady wear black without being in mourning?" Hugh expostulated sharply.

"Certainly, sir; but generally--"

Whatever costume the worldly-wise porter would have approved as *en régle* for a lady, under conditions to his thinking so obviously indiscreet, the description was forestalled by the ingenuous young man, who, dissimilarly apprehensive and oblivious to the innuendo, was heard to grumble:

"What on earth is the matter with people? Everybody seems to delight in painting this most delectable of undertakings in the most funereal colors!" and went on anxiously: "You're sure you won't miss, her?"

With an indulgent smile for the youth and inexperience of his patron, and glancing surreptitiously at the size of the bill in his hand, the attendant calmly announced that there was not the faintest possibility of an error. He took his position a little to the right of and behind Hugh, like an adjutant at dress parade. Through the ferry rushed the weary, impatient travellers. Owing to the place Hugh had taken at one side of the run, Grace, at first, did not perceive him. Anxiety, almost fright, showed in her face; there passed through her a thrill of consternation at the thought that perhaps he had not received her telegram. The tense figure clasped the travelling-bag convulsively, and her brown eyes flashed a look of alarm over the waiting throng. Another moment and their gaze met; a voice ringing with happiness assailed her; her heart throbbed again, and the blood rushed back to her troubled face.

Hugh started forward.

"Hello, old man!" came suddenly from out of the crowd, and two heavy bags plunked down on the floor; two strong hands grabbed Hugh by the shoulders and their owner cried out boisterously: "What in the name of all the gods are you doing here in New York?"

Hugh's heart was in his mouth. His blood froze within him. For, shaking him with the embrace of a playful bear, was his old friend McLane Woods--his chum at Princeton.

Dazed, and not daring to look up, the entangled man made a wild, imploring gesture to the porter The latter caught it, stepped forward and placed the note in the girl's hands.

"In case I am held up, go to the Astor. Will follow," were the words she read quickly. With ready wit and only one stealthy glance at the two men, Grace speedily followed in the wake of the too obsequious porter, who placed her in a cab.

"To the Astor!" was the transferred instruction. The cabman, quick to note the ambiguity in the direction given, prepared, with the subtlety of his kind, for a long drive downtown.

However, the little comedy had not quite escaped attention. There was a note of banter in the strident voice that again addressed Hugh, the speaker accompanying it with a resounding slap on the back.

"Congratulations in order, old man? Come--you're caught--own up! Who is she?" This with a crony-like dig in the ribs. "Runaway match, eh?"

At the other's greeting, Ridgeway promptly assured himself that all was lost, and was about to return the welcome as best he could, when the danger in the final words checked him, compelled a subterfuge.

Assuming a stony glare, an unnatural twist of the mouth, the "old man" turned his bewildered glance upon the speaker, allowing it to resolve itself into a sickening show of reproachfulness, and said in a voice that almost made its owner laugh, it was so villainously artificial:

"You have the best of me, sir!"

An amazed expression came over the face of Mr. Woods. His glowing smile dwindled into an incredulous stare.

"Don't you know me, Hugh?" he finally demanded, half indignantly.

"I do not, sir. My name is not Hugh, by the way. It is evident that you mistake me for some one else," answered Mr. Ridgeway solemnly and gutturally.

"Do you mean to say--oh, come now, old man, don't stand up there and try to make a monkey of me. When did you get in?" cried Woods.

"Pardon me," sharply responded the other, "but I must insist that you are mistaken. I am Dr. James Morton of Baltimore. The resemblance must be remarkable."

Woods glared at Hugh, perfectly dumb with amazement. He passed his hand over his eyes, cleared his throat a time or two, but seemed completely at a loss for words to express himself.

"Are you in earnest?" he stammered. "Are you not Hugh Ridgeway of Princeton, ninety--" but Hugh interrupted him politely.

"Assuredly not. Never was at Princeton in my life. Yale. Will you give me your name and the address of your friend, please? By Jove, I'd like to hunt him up some time!" Hugh was searching in his pockets as if for a pencil and memorandum-book and waiting for his old chum to give him his name.

"Well, of all the--" muttered Woods, looking into the other's face penetratingly. "I never heard of anything like it. My name is McLane Woods, and the man who looks like you is Hugh Ridgeway of Chicago. I--I'll be hanged if it isn't too strange to be true."

"Very strange, indeed," smiled Hugh, striving to maintain the expression he had assumed at the beginning--a very difficult task.

"But this isn't all. At Newburg, I boarded the train, and happening to go through, I saw some one that I could have sworn was a Miss Vernon, whom I met when visiting Ridgeway in Chicago. I started to speak to her; but she gave me such a frigid stare that I sailed by, convinced that I was mistaken. Two such likenesses in one day beats my time. Doesn't seem possible, by George! it doesn't," exclaimed the puzzled New Yorker, his eyes glued to the countenance of the man before him, who, by the way, had almost betrayed himself at the mention of Miss Vernon's name. A thrill of admiration ran through him when Woods announced his reception by the clever girl who was running away with him.

"I'll do my best to meet this Mr. Ridgeway. I am frequently in Chicago," said he. "Glad to have met you, Mr. Woods, anyhow. If you are ever in Baltimore, hunt me up. I am in the E--- Building."

"With pleasure, doctor; how long will you be in New York?"

"I am going away to-morrow."

"Won't you come with me to my club?" began Woods, but Hugh interrupted by beckoning to the omnipresent porter.

"Thanks! Much obliged! Like to, you know, but have an appointment!" And, shaking his hand, "Good-by!"

"Good-by!" gasped Woods reluctantly, as if desiring one word more. But Hugh, with a grin on his face that awakened renewed expectations on the part of the porter, was making, stiff and straight, for the baggage-room. Once, looking back over his shoulder, he saw that Woods was standing stock still; and again, with another smile, he watched his mystified friend slowly depart.

"Now, then, my man, tell me quickly--you gave her the note? What did she do? Where did she go? Out with it--why don't you speak?"

"All right, sir. Everything's all right. The lady has gone to the hotel," replied the man as soon as Hugh gave him a chance to answer.

"Good. Find me another cab, quick. And here," handing him a dollar.

Meanwhile, Grace Vernon, quite sanguine of soon being with Hugh, was approaching the lower part of the city, reasoning, quite logically, that a downtown hotel was selected on account of the probable absence of the ultra-fashionable set. There, their secret would be safe,--and also they would be nearer the steamer.

Arriving at her destination, Grace dismissed the disappointed cabman, and entered the ladies' waiting-room, where she rang for the clerk.

"Is there a Mr. Ridge staying here?" she asked of him with an assurance that, she flattered herself, was admirably assumed.

"No such person with us, madam. Were you expecting him?"

"Why, yes," she replied, a little confused. "He should be here any minute."

And to his inquiry as to whether she would require anything in the meantime, there came a reply in the negative and he departed.

With a sigh of relief at being alone, she crossed over to a desk and busied herself in writing a long letter. This accomplished, she arose, moved over to the window and looked out. The waiting-room faced the main artery of the city, and below her was the endless stream of humanity. Endeavoring to check a slight feeling of uneasiness that was fast coming over her at Hugh's unexpected non-appearance, she tried to concentrate her thoughts on the panorama of the streets. A half hour passed. Then, in spite of herself, nervousness assailed her. What could be keeping him? Had he met with an accident? Or, could she have made a mistake in the name under which he was to register--could he be waiting for her all the time? Back and forth, to and fro the girl paced. Thoroughly alarmed and in spite of a sense of mortification at such an undertaking, she again interviewed the clerk.

"Will it be convenient for me to see the register?" she inquired, forced to conceal her embarrassment.

The clerk obligingly brought the book and eagerly she scanned the list. Unfortunately, for her, there was no mistake. Nothing like Ridgeway, Ridge or Hugh's handwriting greeted her anxious eyes.

A silence that seemed an inconceivably long one to the almost overwrought girl was broken by the clerk asking would she register?

Grace could hardly restrain her agitation. The critical moment had come. Something must be done. But what? Should she register and under what name? Or, should she wait longer; and if not, where should she go? Finally, with a desperate effort, she looked imploringly at him, and with heightened color, gasped:

"No, thank you; I'll wait a little longer for my--my--brother."

It was out. The prevarication had been uttered, and Grace felt as if she had committed a crime and punishment was at hand. Tears of distress came to her eyes; the situation was becoming intolerable.

It was just then that there came a shrill cry:

"Miss Ridge!"

Grace remained immovable. The name she had inquired for a few minutes ago was called without bringing a sign or change of expression to the beautiful face, on which the wondering eyes of the clerk were fixed. He started to speak, but was withheld by her impassibility.

Again the same cry, and this time, the last word was accentuated. A boy entered.

As the clerk, slightly raising his eyebrows, turned toward her, Grace gave a little start; an enlightened glance shot from her eyes; the significance of the call gradually dawned upon her.

"I am Miss Ridge!" came excitedly from her trembling lips, the hot blood crimsoning her cheeks.

"A telephone--"

"For me?" she asked uneasily.

"From Mr. Ridge; wants you to wait," finished the boy.

"Thank you! Oh, thank you!" The girl beamed her relief on the staring bell-boy. And, the message having been delayed, the grateful words were hardly spoken before Hugh, almost distracted, rushed into the room. Regardless of appearances or consequences, the tall young fellow seized her and kissed her in a fashion that would have brought terrible rebuke, under any other circumstance, and which certainly caused the clerk to consider this Mr. Ridge the most demonstrative brother that in a long experience in hotel life he had ever encountered. When Hugh held her at arm's length to give his admiring gaze full scope, he saw tears of joy swimming in her eyes. Her voice quivered as she sighed:

"I should have died in another moment!"

"You are the dearest girl in all the world!" Then he explained to her the cause of the delay. After getting rid of Woods, he had rushed to the Hotel Astor, where he expected to find her waiting for him. All inquiries as to whether any lady answering to her description had been seen there had resulted in failure. He would have been there yet, growing angrier all the while, had not a gentleman who had overheard his troubles suggested that he telephone the Astor House, in the hope that the lady might be waiting there.

At the end of this recital of his vexatious experience Hugh seized her travelling-bag, and together they made their way out of the hotel.

"Oh, Hugh!" cried Grace, hanging back a little. "What did Mr. Woods say to you? What did you say? Do you know he tried to speak with me on the train?"

"Honestly, I don't remember, dear--sister. He's the most muddled man, though, in New York, I'll bet a dollar. And now that I think of it, it wasn't absolutely necessary; but when he guyed me about a runaway match, it paralyzed me, and I had to do something, so I swore that I had never heard of such a person as Ridgeway."

Grace was too astounded to speak.

"Then he told me of meeting you," he continued, "and that settled it. Poor old Woods! What a trump you were, Grace!"

"You wouldn't have thought so if you could have seen me when I first boarded the train. My! I was blue! Fortunately, I did not see him until we were nearly here. Hugh Ridgeway--Ridge, I mean--do you know what I did? It will make you very angry!" she said as they waited for a cab.

"Nothing could make me angry." This was said ten seconds later, when they were inside the cab and a nervous, smiling young woman at his side was squeezing his arm expressively. "Driver!" he called out, "go uptown--anywhere--through the park until I tell you to stop!" and turning to her, added: "We'll have a bit of dinner somewhere and then go aboard. Now, what did you do?"

"Well," she went on, "I actually tossed up a quarter in the compartment to see whether I should go on or turn back."

"You did? Really? Who won?"

"I did," she answered naïvely.

"No; I did. I am beginning to feel too lucky to be awake. And would you have turned back if you had lost? Would you have left me here with all this anticipation to dispose of?" he cried.

"If it came tails, I was to turn back. It came tails."

"What! And you came anyhow?"

"Well, you see, after the first flip I concluded to make it two out of three trials. So I flipped again, Hugh, and it came tails. Then I made it three out of five. That was only fair, wasn't it?"

"Certainly. Seven out of thirteen or eleven out of twenty, just so you won."

"I tossed that coin seventeen times, and the final count was nine for New York and eight for Chicago. The train had started, so I didn't flip again. Wasn't it a narrow majority, dear?"

"If it were not for appearing ridiculous, I would kiss you seventeen times right here. Oh, how about your baggage--luggage, I mean?" he cried.

"The transfer man will take them to the dock. I have ten big ones--new steamer trunks. You'll never know how much trouble I had in getting them packed and out of the house."

"Ten! Great Scott! I have but two!"

"Don't worry, dear. You can pack some of your things in mine--coming home, of course," she said laughingly.

"Great, isn't it?" he chuckled. "Nobody on earth ever did anything like it. But before I forget it, how did you leave your aunt?"

"Poor Aunt Elizabeth! She will be so disappointed. I promised to do a lot of shopping for her. But she's well and can endure the delay, I fancy. To prepare her for the shock, I told her that I might stay East for a couple of weeks, perhaps longer. She does not suspect a thing, but she was awfully cut up about my leaving at this time."

"I'm glad you quieted Aunt Elizabeth, for it would be just like her to send detectives after us." Both laughed as he whispered this to her. As the cab whirled away she said:

"What happy fools we are!"

"Sit back, quick! Cover your face," he suddenly cried.

"What--who is it?" she giggled.

"We just passed a policeman, and he looked rather hard at the windows," he cried, with a broad grin.

"Oh, you ninny!"

"Well, we must elope with fear and trembling or it won't count," he cried. "Is there anything you have to buy before we sail? If there is, we must attend to it now, because we leave at a most outlandish hour in the morning."

Miss Vernon looked alarmed for a moment, the real enormity of the escapade striking her with full force. But she smiled in the next and said that she could make a few necessary purchases in a few minutes if he would direct the cabman. "It's a long way to Manila, you know," she said. "Hugh, I noticed in the paper the other day that this is the season for typhoons, or whatever you call them, in the Indian Ocean. I looked them up in the dictionary. There's a picture of one in action, and they must be dreadful things. One of them could tear our ship to pieces in a minute, I should judge. Wouldn't it be awful--if--if--"

"Pshaw! Typhoons are nothing! It's a simoon that you're thinking about, and they happen only on the desert. In what dictionary did you see that?"

"Webster's, of course."

Mr. Ridgeway did not continue along that line, but mentally resolved to look into Webster's on the sly, and, furthermore, to ask the captain of the *Saint Cloud* to tell him all he knew about typhoons.

"Have him drive to Arnold's, Hugh."

She left him in the carriage in front of the store, promising to be gone not more than five minutes. Ten minutes passed and Hugh resignedly lighted a cigarette, stepping to the sidewalk to smoke. After he had smoked four cigarettes a perceptible frown approached his brow. He looked at the big doorway, then at his watch, then at the imperturbable cabman. Her five minutes had grown to half an hour. His good nature was going to the bad and he was about to follow in her footsteps when suddenly he saw her emerging from the store.

"I had to mail a letter," she explained as they drove off. "Oh, Hugh, I'm so nervous, I know that I will do something silly before we sail."

"A letter?"

"Yes; I mailed one letter to Uncle Harry before I left Chicago, you know, but I forgot something important, so I had to write again to-day."

"What did you forget?"

"I forgot to tell him you were coming out on the same ship and would look after me as if I were your own sister, Hugh."

Strange to say, neither of them smiled as their hands met in a warm, confident clasp.

CHAPTER III
THE FIRST OBSTACLE

A drizzling rain began to fall and an overcast sky, cold and bleak, dropped lower and lower until it covered the dripping park like a sombre mantle. The glass in the hood of the hansom kept out the biting rain, but the drear approach of a wet evening was not to be denied. For nearly three hours Hugh and Grace had been driven through the park and up the Riverside, killing time with a nervous energy that was beginning to tell. The electric lights were coming on; pavements glistened with the glare from the globes; tiny volcanoes leaped up by thousands as the patting, swishing raindrops flounced to the sidewalks.

"Isn't it dismal?" murmured Grace, huddling closer to his side. "I thought the weather man said it was to be nice? It's horrid!"

"I think it's lovely!" said he beamingly. "Just the sort of weather for a mystery like this. It begins like a novel."

"I hope it ends as most of them do, commonplace as they are. Anyhow, it will be fun to dine at Sherry's. If any one that we know should see us, we can say--"

"No, dear; we'll not attempt to explain. In the face of what is to follow, I don't believe an accounting is necessary. This is to be our last dinner in good old America for many a day, dear. We'll have a good one, just for history's sake. What kind of a bird will you have?"

"A lark, I think," she said with a bright smile.

"Oh, one doesn't eat the lark for dinner. He's a breakfast bird, you know. One rises with him. Bedsides, we should try to keep our lark in fine feather instead of subjecting it to the discomforts of a gridiron in some--"

His observations came to an abrupt close as both he and his companion pitched forward violently, barely saving themselves from projection through the glass. The hansom had come to a sudden stop, and outside there was a confused sound of shouting with the crunching of wood and the scraping of wheels. The horse plunged, the cab rocked sharply and then came to a standstill.

"What is it?" gasped Grace, trying to straighten her hat and find her bag at the same time. Hugh managed to raise the glass and peer dazedly forth into the gathering night. A sweep of fine rain blew into their faces. He saw a jumble of high vehicles, a small knot of men on the sidewalk, gesticulating hands on every side, and then came the oaths and sharp commands.

"We've smashed into something!" he said to her.

"Some one is hurt! Confound these reckless drivers! Why can't they watch where--"

"Come down off that!" shouted a voice at the wheel, and he saw a huge policeman brandishing his club at the driver above. "Come down, I say!"

"Aw, the d---- fool backed into me," retorted the driver of Hugh's hansom. His fare noticed that they were at the Sherry corner, and the usual crowd of seven-o'clock cabs was in full evidence.

"That'll do--that'll do," roared the officer. "I saw the whole thing. Ye've cracked his head, you dirty cur."

Two men were holding the horse's head and other policemen were making their way to the side of their fellow-officer. Evidently something serious had happened.

"What's the trouble?" Hugh called out to the officer.

"You'll find out soon enough," answered the policeman. "Don't butt in--don't butt in!"

"Here, here, now!" exclaimed Mr. Ridgeway. "You've no right to talk like that to--"

"Oh, I ain't, eh? Well, we'll see if somebody else has a right. You dudes can't kill people and then get off with talk like that. Not much, my Johnny. You go along, too, an' explain yer hurry to the captain."

"But I've got a lady here--"

"Tush! tush! Don't chew the rag. Stay in there!"

Other officers had dragged the driver from the cab, jostling him roughly to the outer circle of wheels. The man was protesting loudly. Rain had no power to keep a curious crowd from collecting. Hugh, indignant beyond expression, would have leaped to the ground had not a second and superior officer stepped up and raised his hand.

"Don't get down, sir," he said with gentle firmness. "I'm afraid you'll have to go to the station for a few minutes."

"But, confound it, officer--I have nothing to do with this row."

"That may be true, sir. You can explain all that at the desk. We have to get at the bottom of this. This is no place to argue."

A moment later the hansom, with a bent axle, was hobbling its way down the street engineered by bluecoats. Hugh, seeing that it was useless to remonstrate, sank back in the seat and swore audibly.

"Don't worry about it, Hugh," said a soft voice in his ear. "We can explain, can't we?"

"You can't explain anything to asses, Grace," he lamented, "especially if they wear buttons." They lapsed into a mournful, regretful silence. For five full minutes the hansom wobbled painfully along and then pulled up in front of a building which Hugh lugubriously recognized as a police station. "We've got to make the best of it, dear. Did you ever hear of such beastly luck? I'll see if they won't let me go in alone and square things. You won't be afraid to sit out here alone for a few minutes, will you? There's really nothing to be alarmed about. This driver of ours is in trouble, that's all. We're not to blame. A word or two will fix everything. I'll be out in a jiffy."

But the bluecoats would not see it that way. Miss Vernon was compelled to climb down from the seat and march indignantly into the desk sergeant's presence. Hugh at once began to explain and to expostulate against what he called an outrage.

"What had we to do with it? The truth is, I don't know what has happened," he was saying.

"Neither do I," said the bewhiskered sergeant shortly. "Who are you, sir?"

"These people saw the whole thing, sir. They were in the hansom when Bernhardt smashed him, an' this felly had ordered him to get to Sherry's in five minutes if he had to kill some one," explained the officer who had first addressed Hugh in the crowd.

"That's a lie," cried Hugh. "I said if he had to kill the old plug. Who is Bernhardt? What the deuce is it all about?"

"I don't believe the gentleman saw the row," said the polite roundsman. "It happened in the crush there."

"Somebody shall pay for this outrage," exclaimed Ridgeway. "It's beastly to drag a lady and gentleman into a police station like common criminals when they--"

"That will do, sir," commanded the sergeant sharply. "You'll talk when you are asked to, sir."

Turning to the patrolman, he asked, "Has that fellow been taken to the hospital?"

"The ambulance came up just as we left, sir."

"Bernhardt says he didn't hit him. He says the guy fell off his own cab."

"Don't cry, dear," Hugh managed to whisper to Grace as they took the seats designated by a brusque man in blue.

"Never!" she whispered bravely. "It's a lark!"

"Bravo! We'll have that bird yet--at Sherry's." Then he approached the desk with determination in his eye. "Look here, officer, I demand respectful attention. Whatever it was that happened between those cabmen, I had nothing to do with it, and I am absolutely ignorant of the trouble. We have a dinner engagement, and I want you to take our statements, or whatever it is you want, and let us go our way."

"What is your name?" shortly.

"Why--er--that isn't necessary, is it?" floundered Hugh.

"Of course it is. Name, please."

"Will it get into the papers?"

"That's nothin' to me. Will you answer now, or do you want to stay here till mornin'?"

"My name is Smith."

"Place of residence?"

"Brooklyn."

"Who's the lady?"

"My sister."

"Step up here, lady, if you please!"

Hugh felt the floor giving away beneath him. That Grace could not have heard a word of the foregoing examination, he was perfectly aware. Vainly, and with a movement of his lips, he essayed to convey the name she should answer.

"Don't butt in, you!" was the instant warning given by the observant officer, and then--

"Lady, what is *your* name?"

For a moment the question bewildered the girl. With considerable misgiving she discerned that another occasion for prevarication was unavoidable, and something like a sigh escaped her lips; but as suddenly fear gave way to a feeling of elation. How clever Hugh would consider her remembrance of his instructions! What felicity to extricate him from this predicament! Alone, she would save the situation!

Unblushingly, and with a glance at him for instant approval, she stepped forward and pronounced jubilantly the alias agreed upon:

"Ridge--Miss Ridge is my name."

A smothered exclamation of dismay burst from Hugh's lips.

"Eh, what? Miss Ridge, and your brother's name--Smith?" ejaculated the man of authority.

For a brief moment there was a pause of embarrassment; and then with a dazzling, bewitching smile directed at her questioner, she electrified them both:

"Most assuredly. Mr. Smith is my half-brother."

Hugh could have shouted for joy, as he watched the somewhat amused discomfiture of the officer.

"Where do you live?"

"St. Louis," gasped she, with blind confidence in luck.

"Oh, humph! Well, wait a minute," he said, and both were gratified to see a good-natured grin on his face. "Buckley, see if there is a family named Smith in Brooklyn with connection in St. Louis. Sit down, Miss Ridge, please, and don't be worried. This is what we have to do. Your driver slugged another of his kind and he's likely to die of the fall he got. We'll have to use you as witnesses, that's all, an' we must have you where we can put our hands on you in the mornin'. The captain will be here in an hour or two and you can probably manage to give some kind of bond for your appearance. People like you don't like to appear in court, you see, so we've got to make sure of you."

"But we must go to our--our dinner," she wailed so prettily that he coughed to cover his official severity.

"Can't be helped, ma'am. Duty, you know. The captain will soon be here. Would you like to telephone, sir?"

Hugh stared and looked embarrassed. Who was there for him to talk to over the 'phone? And that brought another ghastly thought to mind. Who could he ask to give security for his or her appearance in the morning? He found words to say he would telephone to his friends, a bright idea suddenly coming to the rescue. Grace looked her amazement and alarm as he marched into the telephone booth. Bravely he called up Sherry's and, with the sergeant listening, he sent word to the head waiter to inform Mr. ---- (mentioning the name of a very prominent society leader) that Mr. Smith and Miss Ridge were unavoidably detained and could not join the party until quite late, if at all. He came from the booth very much pleased with himself, and sat down beside Grace to await developments.

"What are we to do?" she whispered.

"Give me time to think, dear. I fooled him that time. Perhaps I can do it again. Great bluff, wasn't it? What do you suppose Mr. ---- will think?"

"But if they should insist upon holding us till morning," she cried, on the verge of tears, trouble looming up like a mountain.

"They won't dare do that. They'll probably send us to a hotel with a plain-clothes man unless we give bond, but that's all. I'll try another bluff and see how it works. There's no use kicking about it. We're not in a position to stir up much of a row, you see, dear."

He tried it when the captain came in unexpectedly a few minutes later, and with the most gratifying results. He obtained consent to go with a plain-clothes man to a nearby restaurant for a "bite to eat." In the meantime he was to send a messenger boy with a note to an influential friend in Brooklyn, requesting him to hurry over and give security for their appearance. If this failed, they were to go to a hotel under guard.

"The only thing that sounds fishy about your story, Mr. Smith, is that you say you are brother and sister," said the captain. "Driving all afternoon in the park with your own sister? Queer."

"She's from Missouri, you know," said Hugh with a fine inspiration. The captain laughed, even though he was not convinced.

"Now, Grace, dear," said Hugh as they waited for the cab to be called, "our adventure is on in dead earnest. We have to give this plain-clothes man the slip and get aboard the *Saint Cloud* before they have time to think. They won't look for us there and we're safe."

"Hugh, I'm frightened half to death," she whispered. "Can we do it? Would it not be wiser to give up the whole plan, Hugh, and--"

"Oh, Grace!" he cried, deep regret in his voice. "What a cad I am to be dragging you into all this sort of thing! Yes, dear. We'll give it up. We'll go back to Chicago. It's too much to ask of you. I'll--"

"No, no, Hugh! Forgive me. I'll be strong and firm. I wouldn't give it up for all the world. I--I was just a bit weak for a second, you know. It does look pretty big and wild, dear,--all that is ahead of us. But, after all, it's like any sea voyage, isn't it? Only we're going to be married when it's over. We Wouldn't think anything of taking a trip to Manila under ordinary circumstances, would we? It's all right, isn't it?" He squeezed her hand cautiously but fervently.

To their disgust the plain-clothes man took the seat opposite them in the brougham, remarking as he did so that he had sense enough to get in out of the rain. They had no opportunity to concoct a plan for escape, and it was necessary for them to go on to the restaurant in Longacre Square. It occurred to Hugh that it would be timely to explain why they were not dressed for dinner. They were on their way to the hotel to dress when the fracas took place. The plain-clothes man was not interested. Evidently the authorities did not apprehend much trouble from the two young people; their guardian performed his duties perfunctorily and considerately. He even disappeared from view after they entered the restaurant.

"We'll have that bird," said Hugh, "before we do anything else. I'm hungry. Haven't eaten since last night, dear. I've been too excited to think of eating--or sleeping."

In a quiet corner of the big café they had their bird and just enough champagne to give them the courage that counts. With their heads close together they planned and plotted until they forgot the rain that pattered against the window panes, and dreariness turned to rosy assurance.

"Just a little nerve, dear," said he as they arose. "Do as I have told you and trust to luck. It can't fail."

The plain-clothes man was just outside the door. Scores of people were hurrying past, umbrellas raised in the face of the drizzle. Down Broadway the glare of lights was broken and left hazy in the fog like rain. The sidewalks in the distance looked like a bobbing field of black mushrooms, shiny and sleek. The air was chill with the wet shadows of a night that hated to surrender to the light of man.

"Where's the cab?" demanded Hugh. "Get it up here quick. I don't want to keep my friend waiting at the station. Come in and have a drink, officer. It's no fun standing around this kind of weather. No job for a decent human being, I'd say. Especially when one's set to watch respectable people and not criminals. This is a rattling good joke on me--and my sister. I need about three good, stiff drinks? We'll go in next door here. Get into the cab, Marian, We won't be inside two minutes."

If the plain-clothes man was willing to take the drink, all well and good, but if he refused--but he did not refuse. He looked carefully about, shivered appropriately, and said he "didn't care if he did." Grace urged them to hurry as she entered the cab and Hugh gave his promise. Scarcely had the two men passed beyond the light screen doors when Grace Vernon coolly stepped from the cab and hurriedly made her way off through the crowd of umbrellas, first telling the driver to wait for her in front of the drug store.

A moment later she boarded a Broadway car, and excited, but intent only on reaching a place where she could safely engage a cab to take her to the dock. And all the time she was hoping and praying, not for herself, but for the important young gentleman who was clicking his righteous glass in a den of iniquity.

CHAPTER IV
READY FOR THE SEA

Ridgeway, his nerves tense and his eyes gleaming, marched his thoroughly chilled companion up to the bar. He manoeuvred so that the plain-clothes man stood with his back toward the door, and he seemed to be in no especial haste to attract the attention of the bartender. As they gave their order for drinks, Hugh saw Grace, in his mind's eye, slipping from the carriage and off into the crowd--and every fibre of his heart was praying for success to attend her flight. He found himself talking glibly, even volubly to the watcher, surprised that he could be doing it with his mind so full of other thoughts.

"Awful night to be out. I'd hate to have a job like yours," he was rattling on, heaving intermittent breaths of relief as he saw the size of the drink the other was pouring out for himself.

"I've been at it for twelve years. I don't mind anything just so it helps to make a comfortable home for the old lady and the kids."

"Ah, the kids," said Hugh, grasping at the subject as if it were the proverbial straw. "How I love kids! How many have you?"

"Four. The oldest is ten."

"They're worth working for, I'll bet. Nothing like children. How many have you?"

"Four," said the officer, looking at him in surprise.

"I'm a little deaf," explained Hugh, recovering himself quickly. "I thought you said ten."

"No; the oldest is ten. Yes; they're worth slaving for. I've hung onto this job all these years just because it might go hard with 'em if I gave it up and tried something else."

Hugh looked into the sober, serious face and a lump flew to his throat. It struck him as probable that this man was to lose his position the next morning. A sort of pity assailed Ridgeway for an instant, but he put it away resolutely.

After all, he had Grace to think of and not the children of the plain-clothes man.

They had a second drink and it fired his brain with a gleeful desire for action. The plain-clothes man shivered as he swallowed the fiery stuff. He looked thin and haggard and ill, a condition which Hugh, in his hatred, had failed to observe until this moment.

"You certainly have a home and some money saved up by this time," he said, trying to suppress the eager gleam in his eyes.

"We've had lots of sickness and it's taken nearly everything. Besides, I've been too d---- honest. It's my own fault that I haven't a big wad put away."

"What is your name?" demanded Hugh suddenly.

"Friend."

"I understand all that. But what is your name?"

"That's it--George Friend--Street Station."

"Oh, I see." Hugh also saw the picture of this poor fellow as he stood before his superior later on with his luckless tale, facing a thirty-days' lay-off at the lowest. "By the way, I want to write a short note." He secured envelope, paper and stamp from the bar and hastily wrote a brief letter. The inscription on the outside of the envelope was "George Friend,--Police Station, New York," and there were three one-hundred-dollar bills inclosed with the note of explanation. "I'll mail it later," he said. "Come on."

They went forth into the rain, Hugh's blood leaping with excitement, the plain-clothes man shivering as if he were congealing. Mr. Ridgeway dashed across the pavement and peered into the cab. Grace was not there, just as he had hoped and expected.

"The lady's in the drug-store below, sir," announced the cabman.

"Wait here" called Hugh to the plain-clothes man. "I'm afraid she's ill. She's gone to the drug-store." He hurried toward the drug-store as the officer began to question the driver. A second later Mr. Ridgeway turned the corner and was off like the wind toward Sixth Avenue. Turning into an alley, he fled southward, chuckling to himself as he splashed through the puddles and mudholes. He heard shouts in the distance and he did not decrease his speed until he neared the street opening below. There he ran into some one and fell. Besmeared and bespattered, he quickly picked himself up; and when, a moment later, he gained the sidewalk, no one would hardly have recognized in the dilapidated-looking creature the dapper Hugh Ridgeway. Police whistles were calling behind him, nearer and nearer, but he walked boldly out into the street and up to Sixth Avenue. His nerves were tingling and his breathing was hard to control after the mad dash through the alley, but he slouched along in the lee of the buildings to escape the downpour, stopping near the corner.

Suddenly he rushed out and hailed a passing cab, climbed inside and gave orders to drive as quickly as possible to the Twenty-third Street Ferry. Then he sat up boldly and stared forth with all the courage that his escape inspired.

"By Jove," he was shouting inwardly, "that poor devil was on my heels. He looked hard as he hustled past, but I stared back just as hard. It took nerve to face him. Hang it all, I'm sorry for him. He wasn't to blame. But this letter will cheer him up. It's for the kids if anything happens to him."

Apparently changing his mind at Herald Square, he instructed the driver to go down Thirty-fifth Street to Eighth Avenue and drop him at the corner. After leaving the cab he ventured into an all-night shop and bought a cheap raincoat, slouch hat and umbrella. Then, like a thief, he stole forth and warily made his way toward the dock. It was bad going and he hailed a second cab. Before climbing into it, he crossed and dropped an envelope into the mailbox.

"There," he muttered, "that helps my conscience. By Jove, this has been a corking start for the adventure. Talk about dime novels!"

He instructed the driver to take him to a point not far from the dock, a precaution which suddenly invested itself. It would be wise to approach the liner by stealth, taking no chances. They were sailing by one of the obscure lines, not for economy's sake, but to avoid possible contact with friends of their own class.

As he rattled off through the night, huddled back in the blackness of the cab, Hugh began to have the first pangs of uneasiness. The distressing fear that all had not gone well with Grace flooded his brain with misgivings and feverish doubts. A clock in a shop window told him it was nearly ten o'clock. He was cursing himself for permitting her to rush off alone in a night like this, into a quarter that reeked with uncertainty and disorder. Vague horrors presented themselves to his distressed mind; calamity stared at him from the mouth of every dark alley; outrage, crime, misfortune, danced in every shadow. As for himself, he was a sorry sight and enough to frighten

Grace into convulsions at one glance. Rain-soaked, muddy, bedraggled, it was not the débonnaire Chicagoan of old who skulked away from the cab at a certain black corner and made his way stealthily, even fearfully, toward the distant dock.

Every sound startled and alarmed him; every pedestrian looked like a pursuer in plain clothes or blue. A couple of policemen eyed him sharply and he trembled in his boots. The sudden, overpowering recollection that he had the passage tickets in his pockets with the reservations and the luggage checks almost sent him flying through the air, so swift was his pace. He lost his way twice, but was set straight by unsuspecting bluecoats.

At last he zigzagged his way through devious channels and into the presence of a company's official, who informed him that Miss Ridge had not gone aboard nor had she presented herself at the dock during the evening. Hugh's jaw dropped and a sick, damp perspiration started on his forehead. Hardly knowing what he did, he went aboard and plied his questions right and left, hoping that she might have come through unobserved. But she was not there, and it was half past ten o'clock.

Out into the drizzle he sallied once more, racked by a hundred doubts and misgivings. Reproaching himself fiercely for a fool, a dolt, he posted himself at the approach to the dock and strained his eyes and ears for the first sight of Grace Vernon. Other people went aboard, but an hour passed before he gave up all hope and distractedly made up his mind to institute a search for the missing girl. He conjectured all manner of mishaps, even to the most dreadful of catastrophes. Runaway accident, robbery, abduction, even murder harassed his imagination until it became unbearable. The only cheerful alternative that he could hope for was that she might not have escaped the authorities after all and was still in custody, crushed and despairing. Reviling himself with a bitterness that was explicit but impotent, he started off resolutely to seek the aid of the police--the last extremity.

A quick little shriek came to his ears, and then the door of a cab that had been standing at the opposite corner flew open.

"Hugh! Hugh!" called a shrill voice. His heart gave a wild leap and then his long legs did the same--repeatedly. As he brought up beside the cab, Grace Vernon tumbled out, sobbing and laughing almost hysterically.

"Good Heavens!" shouted he, regardless of the driver, who grinned scornfully from his private box above, the only witness to this most unconventional comedy of circumstances.

"I've been--been here an hour--in this cab!" she cried plaintively. "Oh, oh, oh! You'll never know how I felt all that time. It seemed a year. Where did you get those awful-looking clothes, and--"

"What--aw--oh, the coat? Great Jehoshaphat! You don't mean to say that--"

"I thought you were a detective!" she sobbed. "Oh, how wretched I've been. Pay the man, dear, and take me--take me any place where there is light. I'm dying from the sight and sound of this awful night."

Mr. Ridgeway lost no time in paying the driver and getting her on board the *Saint Cloud*. She tried to explain as they hurried along, but he told her there was time enough for that.

"We may be watched, after all," he said, looking anxiously in all directions, a habit that had grown upon him to such an extent that he feared it would cling to him through life. "Go to your stateroom, dearest, and I'll send you something hot to drink. Good Heavens, what an eternity it has been! Oh, if you could only know what I've been calling myself!"

"I'm ashamed to admit it, dear, but *I've* been calling you things, too. And I've been so worried about you. How did you get away from that man?"

"Not now, dear. I'll meet you out here in the library in half an hour. I'll see about the luggage."

"You must change your clothes, Hugh. You're frightfully wet. Send my small trunk and bag right up, dear."

Like a thief and murderer, Hugh slunk out and attended to the trunks and bags, watching all the time for the dreaded plain-clothes man and his cohorts, trembling with a nervous fear so unbecoming in a strong man that the baggage master smiled in derision and imagined he was looking upon a "greenie" who was making his first voyage and was afraid of the sea. Offering up a prayer of thankfulness, he bolted into his own stateroom soon afterward and came forth later on in dry clothes and a new frame of mind. He was exuberant, happy once more.

They did not look like brother and sister as they sat on one of the wide sofas and drank the toddy that came from below in charge of a well-feed steward.

"Be careful, dear!" he warned, with returning reason. "They'll think we're bride and groom."

"Oh, dear me," she lamented. "It is almost out of the question to act like brother and sister after all we've been through to-night."

"Now, tell me all about it. How did it all work out for you," he asked eagerly.

"Well, it was all very simple--although I was frightened half to death--until I drove up to the spot where you saw me a little while ago. I thought it would be wise to take a look around before I tried to go aboard. Just as I left the cab a man rushed past me and I flew back into my seat like a bullet. He was a tall, slouchy fellow, with a sly look. All at once it came to me that he was a detective. You know, they're always mysterious looking. So I stayed in the cab trying to think what to do next. I was quite sure you had not yet arrived, for I had come down as quickly as possible. And I wasn't real sure, either, that you had escaped. I didn't know how many drinks it might take, dear."

"Don't let me forget to tell you how sorry I was for Mr. Plain Clothes and what I did afterward for the kids," interposed Hugh.

"The kids?"

"Yes. His."

"Oh, I see. Well, pretty soon that awful man came out and stood at the corner. He was waiting for some one. He was nervous and sleuth-like. He acted so queerly that I was sure of it. He was after you and me. Of course, I nearly fainted. All the time I was afraid you would run right into his arms, so I was watching from both windows to warn you if possible. My plan was to get you into the cab and drive away like mad. Hours passed, it seemed to me, and--"

"I know the rest!" he cried, laughing so loud that the steward looked up reprovingly.

"Is everything ready, Hugh?" she asked anxiously. "The trunks, the tickets,--everything?"

"Yes, dear," he said tenderly, soberly. "We are ready for the sea."

"God be with us," she said wistfully.

CHAPTER V
MR. AND MISS RIDGE SAIL FOR MANILA

London. A thick fog, and the elopers on board the *Tempest Queen*, one of the fastest and most palatial of the liners which ply between England and the Far East, and for ten years under the command of Captain Shadburn, formerly of the British Navy. For the elopement was now an established fact, and Hugh, looking back on their Atlantic voyage, hoped that in this new ship fortune would be more propitious.

Excitement, an exaggerated dread of being followed by detectives, together with seasickness, had been too much for Grace, and all those weary days she had scarcely left her stateroom. Alone in her bunk, ticketed to the other side of the world, running away from nothing but a foolish aversion, the girl had felt her heart grow cold with a nameless dread, a clammy fear that she had undertaken something that she could not accomplish. Almost hourly each day of that unending voyage, Hugh would knock at her door and beg to be allowed to do something to alleviate her sufferings; then a thrill of new tenderness would dart into her soul as she thought of her champion for all time.

And Hugh. Never had time seemed such an eternity. Do what he would, he could not escape the Nemesis-like conviction that he had led the girl he loved into the most unheard-of folly; had carried her to the point where ruin stood on equal footing with success, and joy itself was a menace. Yet during all these days of torment concerning her enfeebled condition and his recklessness, he remembered with sardonic satisfaction that he had left in the safety vault, in Chicago, a full statement of their plans and intentions, with instructions to have the seal broken on March 30th, one year after date of deposit. If anything happened to them, this was to be the means of shedding light on the mystery. And when in New York he had deposited a second statement, with instructions to send it to Chicago on April 1st, one year later. In this he had made known their itinerary as fully as he could give it at the time. And although he cursed himself often for being a fool, there were moments, and especially as they neared the foreign shores, when he rejoiced over this maddest, jolliest of frolics.

The fact that the short rest in London had done wonders for Grace, together with the hurry and bustle incident to sailing, sent Hugh's spirits higher and higher. As the two watched the ship drawn away from the pier and dragged slowly into clearer waters, the knowledge that they were irrevocably consigned to the consummation of their project acted on him like a stimulant. Just before going on board he had asked, half-fearful that she was losing heart, if she still desired to complete the journey. He told her that it was not too late to turn back and that he would agree to any modification of the original plan that she might suggest.

There was not a waver in the clear brown eyes, nor a quiver in her voice as she replied. Instead, there was a flicker indicating injured pride, followed by the sweetest, tenderest smile that he ever had seen on her face.

"Dear old Hugh! Did I not tell you that I would go to the end of the world with you?"

"But we may go to the bottom of the sea," he interposed, seizing her hands, his face lighting up gladly.

"Then I shall go to the bottom of the sea with you. I never have felt the faintest desire to turn back. It has been my greatest happiness to think that some day we shall reach Manila, where our dear adventure may have its second and most delightful epoch. Would I turn back? Would you?" She looked divinely happy as she answered her first triumphant question with the second.

And so they sailed again.

As on their first voyage, their staterooms adjoined. Passage and accommodation had been booked for H.B. Ridge and Miss Ridge, Chicago, U.S.A.

The following morning, Grace was awakened by a rattling at her stateroom door.

"How are you feeling?" called a well-known voice rather anxiously.

"Quite well, thank you. Is it time to get up?"

"I should say so, Sis."

"All right; in ten minutes." As she set her feet upon the floor she observed a tendency on their part to touch twice before settling finally. A momentary dizziness came over her. She closed her eyes quickly and waited a moment before reopening them. Suddenly Hugh's photograph, which was leaning against her hat on the steamer trunk, ducked slowly toward her as if bowing a polite good-morning, and then fell face downward. Miss Vernon rubbed her eyes and stared at the overturned picture for a full minute before resuming her toilet. Then she laughed nervously and made all haste to get on deck. She was one of the few women who dress quickly and yet look well. Attired in a becoming gown, a jaunty cap, checked raincoat and rough brown gloves, she ventured forth expecting to find Hugh waiting for her. At the same time she was thanking her lucky stars that no longer need she fear the authorities.

Slightly dismayed and a little bewildered, she looked to the right and left, trying to remember which stateroom Hugh occupied. The left, she concluded, and forthwith applied her pretty knuckles to the panel; vigorously. The door flew open, almost taking her breath, and a tall, dark man stood before her, but he was not Hugh Ridgeway. He looked askance in a very polite way.

"I beg your pardon," she stammered in confusion. "I have made a mistake. This isn't Mr.--my brother's room, is it? Oh, dear, how absurd of me." She was turning away as she concluded.

"Can I be of service to you?" asked the stranger, stepping forth. He had a very pleasant voice, but she did not remark it at the time.

"No, I thank you," she hastily replied. "His room is on my right, I remember. Sorry if I disturbed you," and she was pounding on the other door. She glanced back at the stranger's door involuntarily and then away instantly. He was staring at her in a most uncalled-for manner.

And Hugh did not answer! She rapped again and--no response. The calm voice of the stranger came to her reddening ears.

"The gentleman who occupies that room just passed me, going on deck. Straight ahead. That's right." He called the last injunction after her swiftly departing form.

"Thank you," came back to him with a breath between the words. Hugh met her at the bottom of the steps. She rushed recklessly toward him and cried,

"Oh, you don't know how glad I am to see you. Where have you been, Hugh Ridgeway--"

"Sh! Ridge without the 'way.' For Heaven's sake, don't forget that. It's every bit as important on this ship as on the other. I've been on deck for a look. Say, are you all right? Are you still glad you're alive?" He was holding her hands and looking into her eyes.

"Of course I am. What a ridiculous question! None but the good die young, and I'm not very good or I wouldn't be running away with you. But come,--take me on deck. Is it raining? Why, your coat is wet. Hurry, Hugh; I want to take a good look," she cried, dragging him up the steps hilariously. A peculiar smile came to his face as he followed her to the deck.

Neither spoke for a full minute, she gazing dumbly at the bleak waste before her, he lovingly at her pretty, bewildered face.

"Where are we, Hugh?" she finally asked, terrified for the moment. "Where is London?"

"You are not afraid, are you, dearest?" he whispered, his strong arm stealing about her. "We are on the bounding main, ticketed for a port thousands of miles away. London is back there," pointing astern.

She placed her hand in his and looked out over the waters. Nothing but rain, leaden sky and rolling waves. What her thoughts were during the silence that followed he learned when she turned to him again, looking imploringly into his eyes.

"Hugh, you will always be good to me?"

"So long as I live, sweetheart," he said, pressing her hand firmly. For some time they stood alone and silent beneath the awning which covered the promenade, the sleety rain pattering dismally over their heads. But few of the passengers were above deck. Several officers were chatting at the end of the deck-house.

"We have not breakfasted yet, Grace, and I'm as hungry as a bear. Isn't it a relief, dear, not to feel the necessity any longer of keeping a sharp lookout for detectives? Those days on the Atlantic, every other man I met I thought was a sleuth-hound bent on capturing the million-dollar reward that has been offered for our capture by Chicago society."

They went below and found the dining saloon almost deserted. Two or three late risers were drinking a last cup of coffee. Then she told him of the mistake she had made, and together they scanned their fellow-passengers in search of the man who occupied the stateroom adjoining hers on the left. He did not appear for luncheon or dinner, and Hugh cheerfully accused her of murdering him.

The next morning, however, he was seated at the table, directly across from Hugh, a trifle pale and far from hungry. He was making a brave effort to conquer the sickness which had seized him. She nudged Hugh and nodded toward the quiet, subdued eater. He looked across and then gave her a questioning glance. She winked affirmatively.

"Poor devil," muttered Hugh. "I suppose he was just beginning to feel sick when you yanked him out, as if you were telling him the boat was on fire."

"Yanked him out? I did nothing but rap on his door. If he were sick, why did he open it and stare at me in such a remarkably healthy fashion?"

"Because you rapped, I suspect. It's no wonder that he stared at a beautiful young lady who had the temerity to visit him before breakfast. Nice-looking fellow, though, I'll say that much for your sake, sister. And what's more, I believe he's an American," said Hugh, surveying the stranger critically.

"I haven't observed his face," she responded curtly.

"How did you happen to recognize him? By his shoes? You naturally looked down when you saw your mistake, of course, but I don't see how you can get a glance of his shoes now, under the table."

"I mean I have not noticed whether his face is handsome, Hugh."

"Better take a look then. He's particularly good-looking with that piece of beefsteak in his check."

Grace glanced slyly at the man across the table, noting his pale cheeks and the dark rings beneath his eyes. Hugh had misrepresented the facts; he was not eating at all. Instead, he was merely toying with his fork, making uncertain circles in the layer of brown, gravy which covered the plate, his cheek resting on the other hand, a faraway look of distress in his eyes. They were directed at the plate, but saw it not.

"Poor fellow," she murmured compassionately; "he's been awfully sick, hasn't he?"

"Oh, I don't know," said Hugh heartlessly. "They don't go to eating in a day's time if they have been very sick."

A bright look flashed into her eyes and they danced with merriment as she whispered something in his ear.

"By George, maybe you're right. He's a detective and chasing us to earth."

The stranger looked at them in a half interested manner when they laughed aloud over the harrowing supposition. They noticed that his eyes were blue and bloodshot, wan and fatigued. He gave Grace a second glance, sharper than the first, and politely resumed his manufacture of circles in the brown gravy and brown study. Miss Vernon flushed slightly.

As they left the table she said to Hugh:

"He remembers me, but he certainly understands it was a mistake, doesn't he?" Hugh looked at her distressed face and laughed.

The weather later that morning was a delightful surprise for all. The sky had resumed its blue and the air was fresh and clear. Notwithstanding the pleasant weather, there was a heavy sea running, the ship rolling uncomfortably for those who were poor sailors. Deck chairs on all sides were occupied by persons who had heroically determined to make the most of the brightness about them.

The elopers found their chairs and joined the long line of spectators. Hugh glanced admiringly at Grace now and then. Her cheeks were warm and glowing, her eyes were bright and flashing with excitement, her whole being seemed charged with animation.

The wan-faced stranger followed them on deck a few minutes later. His eyes were riveted on a chair nearby and his long body moved swiftly toward it. Then came a deep roll, the deck seemed to throw itself in the air, and, with a startled look, he plunged headlong toward Miss Vernon's chair.

His knee struck the chair, but he managed to throw his body to one side. He went driving against the deck-house, sinking in a heap. Miss Vernon gave a little shriek of alarm and pity, and Ridgeway sprang to the side of the fallen man, assisting him to his feet. The stranger's face was drawn with momentary pain and his eyes were dazed.

"Pardon me," he murmured. "I am so very awkward. Have I hurt you?"

"Not in the least," cried she. "But I am afraid you are hurt. See! There is blood on your forehead." She instantly extended her handkerchief, and he accepted it in a bewildered sort of a way, placing it to his forehead, where a tiny stream of blood was showing itself.

"A piece of court plaster will stop the flow," said Hugh critically, and at once produced the article from his capacious pocket-book. Grace immediately appropriated it and asked for his knife.

"You are very good," said the stranger, again pressing the handkerchief to his head. The act revealed to him the fact that he was using her handkerchief for the purpose, soiling it, perhaps. His face flushed deeply and an embarrassed gleam came to his eyes. "Why, I am using your handkerchief. I assure you I did not know what I was doing when I took it from you. Have I ruined it?"

Miss Vernon laughed at his concern and her face brightened considerably. As she looked into his clear blue eyes and his square, firm face she observed for the first time that he was quite a handsome fellow.

"It won't soil it at all," she said.

"But it was thoughtless, even rude of me, to take yours when I had my own. I am so sorry."

"Do you think this will be large enough, Hugh?" she asked, holding up a piece of black court plaster. The stranger laughed.

"If the cut is as big as that I'd better consult a surgeon," he said. "About one-tenth of that, I should say."

"All right," she said cheerfully. "It is your wound."

"But you are the doctor," he protested.

"I dare say it is too big to look well. People might think you were dynamited. Does it pain you?" she asked solicitously. For an instant their eyes looked steadily, unwaveringly, into each other,--one of those odd, involuntary searches which no one can explain and which never happen but once to the same people.

"Not at all," he replied, glancing out over the tumbling waves with a look which proved they were strange to him. Hugh dashed away and soon returned with a glass of brandy, which the stranger swallowed meekly and not very gracefully. Then he sat very still while Grace applied the court-plaster to the little gash at the apex of a rapidly rising lump.

"Thank you," he said. "You are awfully good to a clumsy wretch who might have crushed you. I shall endeavor to repay you both for your kindness." He started to arise from Hugh's chair, but that gentleman pushed him back.

"Keep the chair until you get straightened out a bit. I'll show you how to walk deck in a rough sea. But pardon me, you are an American like ourselves, are you not? I am Hugh Ridge, and this is my sister--Miss Ridge."

"My name is Veath--Henry Veath," the other said as he bowed. "I am so glad to meet my own countrymen among all these foreigners. Again, let me thank you."

"Hardly a good sailor?" observed Hugh.

"As you may readily guess."

"It's pretty rough to-day. Are you going to Gibraltar and Spain?"

"Only as a bird of passage. I am going out for our government. It's a long and roundabout way they've sent me, but poor men must go where opportunity points the way. I assure you this voyage was not designed for my pleasure. However, I enjoyed a couple of days in London."

"An important mission, I should say," ventured Mr. Ridge.

"I'm in the revenue service. It is all new to me, so it doesn't matter much where I begin."

"Where are you to be stationed?" asked Hugh, and something told him what the answer would be before it fell from the other's lips.

"Manila."

CHAPTER VI
HENRY VEATH

Mr. Veath's abrupt announcement that he was bound for Manila was a decided shock to Grace, Hugh escaping because of his intuitive revelation. After the revenue man had gone below to lie down awhile before luncheon the elopers indulged in an animated discussion of affairs under new conditions.

"Well, we can make use of him after we get there, dear," said Hugh philosophically. "He can be a witness and swear to your age when I go for the license." "But, Hugh, he thinks we are brother and sister, and we cannot tell him anything to the contrary. It would be awfully embarrassing to try to explain."

"That's so," mused he. "I doubt whether we could make him believe that brothers and sisters marry in Manila. There's just one thing to do."

"It seems to me there are a great many things to do that we didn't consider when we started," ventured she.

"We must let him believe we are brother and sister until after we are married. Then we'll have the laugh on him. I know it's not very pleasant to explain your own joke, or to tell the other fellow when to laugh, but it seems to be the only way. We can't escape him, you know. He is to be at his post by the twentieth of May."

"After all, I think we ought to be nice to him. We can't put him off the boat and we might just as well be friendly. How would you enjoy travelling to Manila all alone? Just put yourself in his place."

"Maybe he thinks he's lucky to be travelling alone."

"That's very pretty, sir. Would you rather be travelling alone?"

"Not at all. I'm only saying what he may think. The poor devil may be married, you know."

"Oh, do you really think so?" cried she.

"He looks a little subdued."

"That's because he's seasick."

"But, to return to our own troubles--you think, then, we would better adopt Mr. Veath for the voyage and break the news to him impressively after the deed is done?"

"I think so, don't you? It is sure to be embarrassing, any way you put it, isn't it?" she asked, laughing nervously.

"Oh, I don't know," he replied airily. "People of our nerve should not be embarrassed by anything on earth." He arose and assisted her to her feet. Then, slipping his arm through hers, he started for the companionway. "The prospect of being brother and sister for ten thousand miles is rather obnoxious to me," he went on. She looked at him in surprise and then blushed faintly. As they descended the steps, he put his arm around her shoulder. At the bottom he stopped and glanced around apprehensively, something like alarm appearing in his face. His arm slipped from her shoulder to her waist and contracted suddenly.

"What is the matter, Hugh?" she whispered, looking quickly about as if expecting a calamity.

"Is any one in sight?" he demanded anxiously.

"I don't see a soul," she answered.

"Then I'm going to give up the brother act for a moment or two. This is a good, sequestered spot, and I'm going to kiss you." And he did so more than once. "That's the first chance I've had to kiss you since we came aboard. What an outrage it is that brothers cannot be more attentive to their own sisters than to other men's sisters."

"It seems to be customary for brothers to neglect their sisters," she suggested demurely.

"A brother who neglects his sister ought to be horsewhipped," declared he.

"Amen to that. They use the cat-o'-nine-tails on board ship, you must remember," she said, smiling.

Shortly afterward he dropped in to see Veath and was welcomed gladly. He was lying in his berth, and Hugh sent for a bottle of his champagne. Two glasses of the wine put new life into him and something of a sparkle flew to his dull eyes, as if cast there by the bubbling liquor. His tongue loosened a little, Hugh finding him to be a bright, sensible fellow, somewhat ignorant of the ways of the world, but entirely capable of taking care of himself. Moreover, with the renewed vigor displaying itself, he was far better looking than his new acquaintance had thought. His blue eyes, keen and clear, appealed to Hugh's love for straightforwardness; his wide mouth bespoke firmness, good nature, and the full ability to enjoy the humorous side of things. The lines about his clean-cut, beardless face were a trifle deep, and there was a network of those tiny wrinkles which belong to men of forty-five and not to those of twenty-eight.

Evidently his had not been a life of leisure. As he lounged easily upon the edge of the berth, Hugh could not but admire his long, straight figure, the broad shoulders and the pale face with its tense earnestness.

"Manila, you know, is an important post these days," said Veath. "There's a lot of work to be done there in the next few years. I'm from Indiana. Every able-bodied man in our district who voted right and hasn't anything else to do wants a government job. Of course, most of them want to be consul-generals, postmasters, or heads of bureaus, but there are some of us who will take the best thing that is offered. That's why I am going to Manila. Politics, you know, and my uncle's influence with the administration." Ridgeway observed that wine made loquacious a man who was naturally conservative. "Where are you going?" he continued.

"We are going to Manila."

"What!" gasped Veath. "You don't mean it!"

"Certainly. Why not?" and Hugh smiled delightedly over the sensation he had created.

"Why--why, it seems improbable," stammered Veath. "I had looked upon Manila as the most wretched hole in the world, and yet I find you going there, evidently from choice."

"Well, you'll have to change your opinion now," said Hugh.

"I do--forthwith. It cannot be such a bad place or you wouldn't be taking your sister there. May I ask what is your object in going to Manila?"

Hugh turned red in the face and stooped over to flick an imaginary particle of dust from his trousers' leg. There was but one object in their going and he had not dreamed of being asked what it was. He could not be employed forever in brushing away that speck, and yet he could not, to save his life, construct an answer to Veath's question. In the midst of his despair a sudden resolution came, and he looked up, his lips twitching with suppressed laughter.

"We are going as missionaries."

He almost laughed aloud at the expression on Veath's face. It revealed the utmost dismay. There was a moment's silence, and then the man in the berth said slowly:

"Is Miss Ridge a--a missionary also?"

"The very worst kind," replied Hugh cheerily.

"Going out among the natives, I suppose?"

"What natives?"

"Why,--the Igorrotes, or whatever they are, of course."

"Oh, of course--to be sure," cried Hugh hastily. "I am so d--d absent-minded."

Veath stared in amazement.

"You must not think it strange that I swear," said Hugh, mopping his brow. "I am not the missionary, you know."

"Oh," was the other's simple exclamation. Another pause and then, "You don't mean to say that such a beautiful woman is going to waste her life among savages?"

"She's got her head set on it and we think the only way to break her of it is to give her a sample of the work. I am going with her ostensibly to protect, but really to make her life miserable."

"I rather admire her devotion to the church," said Veath, still a trifle dazed.

"She's a great crank on religion," admitted Hugh. Then he could feel himself turn pale. He was passing Grace off as a missionary, and thereby placing her under restrictions that never before had entered into her gay life. Veath would treat her as if she were of fragile glass and it would not be long until the whole boat would be staring at the beautiful girl who was going to the heathen. Remorse struck him and he tried to flounder out of the position.

Grace Vernon

"I should not have said that about her views. You would never take her to be an ardent church-member, and she is particularly averse to being called a missionary. The truth about the matter is that very few people home know about this move of hers and there is no one on ship who even suspects. She would not have had me tell it for the world."

"My dear Mr. Ridge, don't let that trouble you. She shall never know that you have told me and I shall never repeat it. Please rest assured; her wishes in the matter are most certainly to be considered sacred," cried Veath warmly.

"Thanks, old man," said Hugh, very much relieved. "Your hand on that. I am not sorry I told you, for I'm sure you will be careful. She objects to the--the--well, the notoriety of the thing, you know. Hates to be glared at, questioned, and all that sort of thing."

"She is very sensible in that respect. I have but little use for the people who parade their godliness."

"That's just the way she looks at it. She would be uncomfortable all the way over if she thought that a single person knew of her intentions. Funny girl that way."

"If I were you, I don't believe I'd tell any one else," said Veath hesitatingly.

"That's all right, Veath. Depend upon me, I'll not breathe it to another soul. It shall not go a bit farther. Grace wants to go about the good work as quietly as possible. Still, I am bound to make her forget the heathen and return to America another woman altogether." Mr. Veath, of course, did not understand the strange smile that flitted over his companion's face as he uttered the last remark. "I'm glad I met you, Veath; we'll get along famously, I'm sure. There's no reason why we shouldn't make the voyage a jolly one. I think we'd better get ready for luncheon," said Hugh, looking at his watch.

Hugh took his departure, and fifteen minutes later was seated at one of the tables in the dining-room with Grace beside him. He had told her of the missionary story and was trying to smile before her display of genuine annoyance.

"But I don't want him to treat me as if I were a missionary," she pouted. "What fun can a missionary have?"

"Oho, you want to have fun with him, eh? That's the way the wind blows, is it? I'll just tell Mr. Veath that you pray night and day, and that you don't like to be disturbed. What do you suppose he'd be if he interrupted a woman's prayers?" demanded he, glaring at her half jealously.

"He'd be a heathen and I should have to enlighten him," she answered sweetly.

Just then Mr. Veath entered the saloon and took a seat beside her. She looked surprised, as did Mr. Ridgeway. They looked to the far end of the table and saw that Veath's original chair was occupied by another man.

"I traded seats with that fellow," murmured Veath, a trifle red about the ears. Miss Vernon's face assumed a stony expression for an instant, but the gleam of pure frankness in his eyes dispelled her momentary disapproval. "You don't mind, do you?" he asked hastily.

"Not at all, Mr. Veath," she said, forgetting that a moment before she had considered him presumptuous. "On the contrary, I think it is so much nicer to have you on this side of the table. We can talk without having everybody in the room hear us."

"I have just heard that we are bound for the same destination and we can certainly speculate among ourselves as to the outcome of our individual and collective pilgrimages. We can talk about shipwrecks, pirates, simoons, cholera, sea serpents--"

"And the heathen," said Hugh maliciously, but not looking up from his plate.

"Ahem!" coughed loyal Mr. Veath.

"Are there any heathen over there?" asked Miss Vernon very innocently but also very maliciously. She smiled at Hugh, who leaned far back in his chair and winked solemnly at the bewildered Veath. That gentleman, manlike, interpreted Hugh's wink as the means of conveying the information that the tactful young lady asked the question merely to throw him off the scent. So he answered very politely but very carefully.

"I hear there are more missionaries than heathen."

"Indeed? Don't you think that the women who go out as missionaries among those vile creatures are perfect idiots, Mr. Veath?"

"Well,--ahem, ah," stammered Veath, "I can't say that I do. I think, if you will permit me to disagree with you, that they are the noblest women in the world."

"Excellent sentiment, Veath," said the merry Ridgeway, "and quite worthy of endorsement by this misguided sister of mine. She despises the heathen, you know."

"Oh, I am sure she does not despise them," cried Veath.

"But I do--I think they ought to be burned alive!"

A dead silence, during which the two men were unnecessarily intent upon the contents of their plates, followed this explosion. Miss Vernon demurely smiled to herself, and finally kicked Hugh's foot. He laughed aloud suddenly and insanely and then choked. Veath grew very red in the face, perhaps through restraint. The conversation from that moment was strained until the close of the meal, and they did not meet at all during dinner.

"Perhaps we have offended him," said Grace as they strolled along the deck that evening.

"It's probable that he thinks we are blamed fools and does not care to waste his time on us."

"Then why did he change his seat?"

"Evidently did not want us to be staring him out of countenance all the time. I notice, sister, that he took the seat next to yours and not to mine," remarked he insinuatingly.

"Which proves that *he* is no fool, brother," she retorted.

CHAPTER VII
GLUM DAYS FOR MR. RIDGE

Gibraltar. And the ship stopping only long enough to receive the mail and take on passengers; then off again.

During the voyage in the Bay of Biscay, Veath had done all in his power to relieve Hugh of the boredom which is supposed to fall upon the man who has a sister clinging to him. At first Hugh rather enjoyed the situation, but as Veath's amiable sacrifice became more intense, he grew correspondingly uncomfortable. It was not precisely what he had bargained for. There was nothing in Veath's manner which could have been objectionable to the most exacting of brothers.

When he was trespassing Hugh hated him, but when they were together, with Grace absent, he could not but admire the sunny-faced, frank, stalwart Indianian. When Hugh's heart was sorest, a slap on the back from Veath, a cheery word and an unspoken pledge of friendship brought shame to take the place of resentment.

She was troubled, as well as he, by the turn of affairs; her distress managed to keep her awake of nights, especially when she began to realize there was no escape from consequences. That usually pleasant word "brother" became unbearable to her; she began to despise it. To him, the word "sister" was the foundation for unpublishable impressions.

Poor Veath knew nothing of all this and continued to "show Miss Ridge a good time." On the second night out of Gibraltar, he and Grace were strolling the deck. He was happy, she in deep despair. Down at the other end of the deck-house, leaning over the rail, smoking viciously, was Hugh, alone, angry, sulky. It was a beautiful night, cool and crisp, calm and soft. A rich full moon threw its glorious shimmer across the waves, flashing a million silvery blades along the watery pavement that seemed to lead to the end of the world. Scores of passengers were walking the deck, and all were happy, save two.

For two days Hugh had found but little chance to speak with Grace. She had plotted and calculated and so had he, but Veath gallantly upset the plans.

"This can't go on any longer, or I'll go back," vowed Hugh as he glared with gloomy eyes at the innocent path of silver.

"Your brother is not very sociable of late, is he, Miss Ridge?" asked Veath, as they turned once more up the deck toward the disconsolate relative. "There are a great many pretty young women on board, but he seems to ignore them completely. I haven't seen him speak to a woman in two days."

"Perhaps he is in love," she murmured half sedately. Poor, lonely Hugh! How she longed to steal up from behind and throw her arms about his neck. Even though both fell overboard, it would be a pleasure, it seemed to her.

"We ought to go over and jolly him up a bit," suggested Veath, innocently magnanimous. She hated him at that moment.

"He is probably enjoying himself better than if we were with him," she said rather coldly.

"Lovers usually like moonshine," he said.

"I did not say he was in love; 'perhaps' was the word, I think," said Grace.

"I believe one of the rules of love is that a brother never confides in his sister. At any rate, she is sure to be among the last."

"I think Hugh would tell *me* of his love affairs," she answered, a merry sparkle coming into her eyes. "He thinks a great deal of my opinions."

"And I suppose you tell him of your love affairs," he said jestingly. She blushed furiously.

"He has a whole book full of my confidences," she finally said, seeking safety in exaggeration.

"Quite an interesting volume. How does it end? With an elopement?"

"Elopement! What do you--oh, ah, I--ha, ha! Wouldn't that be a jolly way to end it?" She laughed hysterically, recovering quickly from the effects of the startling, though careless question. For a few moments her heart throbbed violently.

Hugh came swinging toward them, his cigar tilted upward at an unusual angle because of the savage position of the lower jaw. His hands were jammed into his pockets and his cap was drawn well down over his eyes. He was passing without a word, ignoring them more completely than if they had been total strangers. He would, at least, have glanced at strangers.

"Hello, Mr. Ridge, going below?" called Veath.

"I'm going wherever the ship goes," came the sullen reply.

"Hope *she's* not going below," laughed the disturber.

"It's my only hope," was the bitter retort from the companionway.

"He's certainly in love, Miss Ridge. Men don't have the blues like that unless there's a woman in the case. I think you'd better talk to your brother. Tell him she'll be true, and if she isn't, convince him that there are just as good fish in the sea. Poor fellow, I suppose he thinks she's the only woman on earth," commented Mr. Veath, with mock solemnity.

"She may be as much at sea as he," she said,--and very truthfully.

"Well, if love dies, there is a consolation in knowing that the sea casts up its dead," was his sage, though ill-timed remark.

Grace slept but little that night, and went early to breakfast in the hope that she might see Hugh alone. But he came in late, haggard and pale, living evidence of a sleepless night. Veath was with him and her heart sank. During the meal the good-natured Indianian did most of the talking, being driven at last, by the strange reticence of his companions, to the narration of a series of personal experiences. Struggle as he would, he could not bring a mirthful laugh from the girl beside him, nor from the sour visaged man beyond. They laughed, of course, but it was the laugh of politeness.

"I wonder if she is in love, too," shot through his mind, and a thrill of regret grew out of the possibility. Once his eye caught her in the act of pressing Hugh's hand as it was being withdrawn from sight. With a knowing smile he bent close to her and whispered: "That's right, cheer him up!" Grace admitted afterward that nothing had ever made her quite so furious as that friendly expression.

But jealousy is jealousy. It will not down. The next three days were miserable ones for Hugh. The green-eyed monster again cast the cloak of moroseness over him--swathed him in the inevitable wet blanket, as it were. During the first two days Veath had performed a hundred little acts of gallantry which fall to the lot of a lover but hardly to that of a brother--a score of things that would not have been observed by the latter, but which were inwardly cursed by the lover. Hugh began to have the unreasonable fear that she cared more for Veath's society than she did for his. He was in ugly humor at lunch time and sent a rather peremptory message to Grace's room, telling her that he was hungry and asking her to get ready at once.

The steward brought back word that she was not in her room. She had been out since ten o'clock.

Without a word Ridgeway bolted to Veath's room and knocked at the door. There was no response. The steward, quite a distance down the passageway, heard the American gentleman swear distinctly and impressively.

He ate his luncheon alone,--disconsolate, furious, miserable. Afterward he sought recreation and finally went to his room, where he tried to read. Even that was impossible.

Some time later he heard her voice, then Veath's.

"I wonder if Hugh is in his room?" she was asking.

"He probably thinks we've taken a boat and eloped Shall I rap and see?" came in Veath's free voice.

"Please--and we'll tell him where we have been."

"You will like thunder!" hissed Hugh to himself, glaring at the door as if he could demolish it.

Then came a vigorous pounding on the panel; but he made no move to respond. Again the knocking and a smile, not of mirth, overspread his face.

"Knock! Confound you! You can't get in!" he growled softly but triumphantly. Veath tried the knob, but the door was locked.

"He's not in, Miss Ridge. I'll see if I can find him. Good-by--see you at luncheon."

Then came Grace's voice, sweet and untroubled: "Tell him we'll go over the ship another time with *him*."

"Over the ship," growled Hugh almost loud enough to be heard. "So they're going to square it by taking brother with them another time--eh? Well, not if I know it! I'll show her what's what!" A minute later he rapped at Miss Vernon's stateroom. She was removing her hat before the mirror, and turning quickly as the irate Hugh entered, she cried:

"Hello, Hugh! Where have you been, dear?"

"Dear! Don't call me dear," he rasped.

"Why, Hugh, dear,--Mr. Veath looked everywhere for you this morning. I said I would not go unless he could find you. You would have enjoyed it so much."

"And you really wanted me?" he asked guiltily.

"Of course, I did--we both did. Won't you ever understand that I love you--and you alone?"

"I guess I'll never understand love at all," he mused.

"Now where were you all morning?" she demanded.

"He didn't look in the right place, that's all."

"Where was the right place?"

"It happened to be in the wrong place," he said. He had been playing a social game of bridge in the room of one of the passengers. At this moment Veath was heard at the door. Hugh heartily called out to him, bidding him to enter.

"Why, here you are! Been looking everywhere for you, old man. Sorry you were not along this morning," said the newcomer, shaking Ridgeway's hand.

"I didn't care to see the ship," said Hugh hastily.

"Why, how funny!" cried Grace. "How did you know we had been over the ship?"

"Instinct," he managed to gulp in the confusion.

Veath started for the dining-room, followed by Grace and Hugh, the latter refraining from mentioning that he had already lunched--insufficiently though it had been; but with the return of reason had come back his appetite and gradually he felt the old happiness sifting into his heart.

CHAPTER VIII
THE BEAUTIFUL STRANGER

They were now well along in the Mediterranean. The air was cool and crisp, yet there were dozens of people on deck watching the sunset and the sailors who were trimming the ship. There were passengers on board for China, Japan, India and Australia. A half hundred soldiers, returning to the East, after a long furlough at home, made the ship lively. They were under loose discipline and were inclined to be hilarious. A number were forward now, singing the battle songs of the British and the weird ones of the natives. Quite a crowd had collected to listen, including Ridgeway and Veath, who were strolling along the deck, arm in arm, enjoying an after-dinner smoke, and had paused in their walk near the group, enjoying the robust, devil-may-care tones of the gallant subalterns.

Miss Vernon was in her stateroom trying to jot down in a newly opened diary the events of the past ten days. She was up to ears in the work, and was almost overcome by its enthusiasm. It was to be a surprise for Hugh at some distant day, when she could have it printed and bound for him alone. There was to be but one copy printed, positively, and it was to belong to Hugh. Her lover as he strode the deck was unconscious of the task unto which she had bent her energy. He knew nothing of the unheard-of intricacies in punctuation, spelling and phraseology. She was forced at one time to write Med and a dash, declaring, in chagrin, that she would add the remainder of the word when she could get to a place where a dictionary might tell her whether it was spelled Mediterranean or Mediteranian.

Suddenly, Hugh pressed Veath's arm a little closer.

"Look over there near the rail. There's the prettiest girl I've ever seen!"

"Where?"

"Can't point, because she's looking this way. Girl with a dark green coat, leaning on an old gentleman's arm--"

"I see," interrupted Veath. "By George! she's pretty!"

"No name for it! Have you in your life ever seen anything so beautiful?" cried Ridgeway. He stared at her so intently that she averted her face.

"Wonder who she can be? The old man must be her father. Strange we haven't seen them before. I'm sure that she hasn't been on deck."

"You seem interested--do you want a flirtation?"

"Oh, Grace wouldn't stand for that--not for a minute."

"I don't believe she would object if you carried it on skilfully," smiled the other.

"It wouldn't be right, no matter how harmless. I couldn't think of being so confoundedly brutal."

"Sisters don't usually take such things to heart."

Hugh came to himself with a start and for a moment or two could find no word of response, so deeply engrossed was he in the effort to remember whether he had said anything that might have betrayed his secret.

"Oh," he laughed awkwardly, "you don't understand me. Grace is so--well, so--conscientious, that if she thought I was--er--trifling, you know, with a girl, she'd--she'd have a fit. Funniest girl you ever saw about those things--perfect paragon."

"Is it possible? Are you not a little strong on that point, old man? I'm afraid you don't know your sister any better than other men know theirs."

"What's that?" demanded Hugh, suddenly alert and forgetful of the stranger.

"The last person on earth that a man gets acquainted with, I've heard, is his sister," said Veath calmly. "Go ahead and have a good time, old fellow; your sister isn't so exacting as you think--take my word for it."

It was fully five minutes before Hugh could extract himself from the slough of speculation into which those thoughtless words had driven him. What did Veath know about her ideas on such matters? Where did he learn so much? The other spoke to him twice and received no answer. Finally he shook his arm and said:

"Must be love at first sight, Ridge. Are you spellbound?" Hugh merely glared at him and he continued imperturbably: "She's pretty beyond a doubt. I'll have to find out who she is."

"That's right, Veath; find out," cried Hugh, bright in an instant. "Make her have a good time. Poor thing, she'll find it pretty dull if she hangs to her father all the time."

"He isn't a very amusing-looking old chap, is he? If that man hasn't the gout and half a dozen other troubles I'll jump overboard."

The couple arousing the interest of the young men stood near the forward end of the deck-house. The young woman's face was beaming with an inspiration awakened by the singers. Her companion, tall, gray and unimpressionable, listened as if through coercion and not for pleasure. His lean face, red with apoplectic hues, grim with the wrinkles of three score years or more, showed clear signs of annoyance. The thin gray moustache was impatiently gnawed, first on one side and then on the other. Then the military streak of gray that bristled forth as an imperial was pushed upward and between the lips by bony fingers. He was a picture of dutiful rebellion, Immaculately dressed was he, and distinguished from the soles of his pointed shoes to the beak of his natty cap. A light colored newmarket of the most fashionable cut was buttoned closely about his thin figure.

The young woman was not tall, nor was she short; she was of that indefinite height known as medium. Her long green coat fitted her snugly and perfectly; a cap of the same material was perched jauntily upon her dark hair. The frolicking wind had torn several strands from beneath the cap, and despite the efforts of her gloved fingers, they whipped and fluttered in tantalizing confusion. In the dimming afternoon the Americans could see that she was exquisitely beautiful. They could see the big dark eyes, almost timid in the hiding places beyond the heavy fringing lashes. Her dark hair threw the rich face into clear relief,--fresh, bright, eager. The men were not close enough to observe with minuteness its features, but its brilliancy was sufficient to excite even marvelling admiration. It was one of those faces at which one could look for ever and still feel there was a charm about it he had not caught.

"I've never seen such a face before," again murmured Ridgeway.

"Tastes differ," said Veath. "Now, if you'll pardon me, I think Miss Ridge is the more beautiful. She is taller and has better style. Besides, I like fair women. What say?" The question was prompted by the muttered oath that came from Hugh.

"Nothing at all," he almost snarled. "Say, Veath, don't always be talking to me about my sister," he finally jerked out, barely able to confine himself to this moderately sensible abjuration while his brain was seething with other and stronger expressions.

"I beg your pardon, Ridge; I did not know that I talked very much about her." There was a brief silence and then he continued: "Have a fresh cigar, old man." Hugh took the cigar ungraciously, ashamed of his petulance.

By this time the early shades of night had begun to settle and the figures along the deck were growing faint in the shadows. Here and there sailors began to light the deck lamps; many of the passengers went below to avoid the coming chill. In her stateroom Grace was just writing: "For over a week we have been sailing under British colors, we good Americans, Hugh and I,--and I may add, Mr. Veath."

Another turn down the promenade and back brought Ridgeway and Veath face to face with the old gentleman and the young lady, who were on the point of starting below. The Americans paused to let them pass, lifting their caps. The old gentleman, now eager and apparently more interested in life and its accompaniments, touched the vizor of his cap in response, and the young lady smiled faintly as she drew her skirts aside and passed before him.

"Did you ever see a smile like that?" cried Hugh, as the couple disappeared from view.

"Thousands," answered his companion. "They're common as women themselves. Any woman has a pretty smile when she wants it."

"You haven't a grain of sentiment, confound you."

"They don't teach sentiment on the farm, and there's where I began this unappreciative existence of mine. But I am able to think a lot sometimes."

"That's about all a fellow has to do on a farm, isn't it?"

"That and die, I believe."

"And get married?"

"Naturally, in order to think more. A man has to think for two after he's married, you see."

"Quite sarcastic that. You don't think much of women, I fancy."

"Not in the plural."

Captain Shadburn was nearing them on the way from the chart-house, and the young men accosted him, Veath inquiring:

"Captain, who is the tall old gentleman you were talking to forward awhile ago?"

"That is Lord Huntingford, going over to straighten out some complications for the Crown. He is a diplomat of the first water."

"Where are these complications, may I ask?"

"Oh, in China, I think. He is hurrying across as fast as possible. He leaves the ship at Hong Kong, and nobody knows just what his mission is; that's between him and the prime minister, of course. But, good-evening, gentlemen. I have a game of cribbage after dinner with his Lordship." The captain hurried below.

"A real live lord," said Veath. "The first I've seen."

"China," Hugh repeated. "I hope we may get to know them."

CHAPTER IX
MR. RIDGEWAY'S AMAZEMENT

At dinner Hugh was strangely exuberant, jesting gaily and exchanging rare witticisms with Veath, who also appeared immensely satisfied. As they left the saloon he said:

"Let's take a turn on deck, Grace."

"Won't you include me?" asked Veath.

"Certainly," answered Grace promptly.

"Be delighted," echoed Hugh, swallowing as if it were an effort.

"I must get a wrap," said Grace. "I won't delay you more than five minutes."

"I'll get my overcoat and some cigars," added Hugh.

"And I'll write a short letter to post at Malta," said Veath, and they separated.

A short while later, a steward passed Hugh's stateroom, and he called to him to step to the next door and tell Miss Ridge that he was ready.

"Miss Ridge just went up with her gentleman--" the man responded; but Hugh interrupted, slamming the door. For several minutes he stood glaring at the upper corner of his berth; then he said something strong. Every vestige of his exuberance disappeared, his brow clouded and his heart seemed to swell painfully within its narrow confines.

As he was about to ascend the steps of the companionway, he heard the swish of skirts and then a sharp scream. In an instant he was half way up, his arms extended. Lord Huntingford's daughter plunged into them, and he literally carried her to the foot. She was pale and trembling and he was flushed. He had looked up in time to see her falling forward, vainly striving to reach the hand rail.

"Are you hurt?" he asked anxiously. The young lady sat down upon the second step before answering, a delightful pink stealing over her face.

"I--I don't believe I am," she said. "My heel caught on a step and I fell. It was so clumsy of me. I might have been badly hurt if you had not caught me as you did."

"These steps are so uncertain," he said, scowling at them. "Somebody'll get hurt here some day. But, really, are you quite sure you are, not hurt? Didn't you twist your--your--"

"Ankle? Not in the least. See! I can stand on both of them. I am not hurt at all. Let me thank you," she said, smiling into his eyes as she moved away.

"May I assist you?" he asked eagerly.

"Oh, no; I thank you, Mr. Veath. I would not have my preserver perform the office of a crutch. I am not hurt in the least. Good-afternoon."

Hugh, disconcerted and piqued by her confusion of names, answered her wondrous smile with one that reflected bewildered admiration, and finally managed to send after her:

"I wouldn't have lost the opportunity for the world."

That evening he was sitting out on deck in contemplative silence enjoying his after-dinner smoke. Farther down were Grace and Veath. Suddenly turning in their direction, Hugh perceived that they were not there; nor were they anywhere in sight. He was pondering over their whereabouts, his eyes still on the vacant chairs, when a voice tender and musical assailed his ears--a voice which he had heard but once before.

"Good-evening, Mr. Veath."

He wheeled about and found himself staring at the smiling face of the young lady who had fallen into his arms but a few hours before.

"Good-evening," he stammered, amazed by her unexpected greeting. "Have--have you fully recovered from your fall?"

"I was quite over it in a moment or two. I wanted to ask you if you were hurt by the force with which I fell against you." She stood with one hand upon the rail, quite close to him, the moonlight playing upon her upturned face. He never had seen a more perfect picture of airy grace and beauty in his life.

"Why mention an impossibility? You could not have hurt me in a fall ten times as great."

His tall figure straightened and his eyes gleamed chivalrously. The young woman's dark, mysterious eyes swept over him for a second, resting at last upon those which looked admiringly into them from above. She made a movement as if to pass on, gravely smiling a farewell.

"I beg your pardon," he said hastily. "You called me Mr. Veath a moment ago. It may be of no consequence to you, yet I should like to tell you that my name is Ridge--Hugh Ridge."

"It is my place to beg forgiveness. But I understood your name was Veath, and that you were--were"--here she smiled tantalizingly--"in love with the beautiful American, Miss Ridge."

"The dev--dick--I mean, the mischief you did! Well, of all the fool conclusions I've ever heard, that is the worst. In love with my sister! Ho, ho!" He laughed rather too boisterously.

"But there is a Mr. Veath on board, is there not?--a friend?"

"A Mr. Henry Veath going into the American Revenue Service at Manila."

"How stupid of me! However, I am positive that I was told it was Mr. Veath who was in love with Miss Ridge."

"But he isn't," hastily cried Hugh, turning hot and cold by turns. "He's just a friend. She--she is to marry another chap." Here he gulped painfully. "But please don't breathe it to a soul. She'd hate me forever. Can I trust you?" To himself, he was saying: "I am making a devil of a mess of this elopement."

"This is a very large world, Mr. Ridge, and this voyage is a mere trifle in time. When we leave the ship we may be parting forever, so her secret would be safe, even though I shrieked it all over the East. You will return to America before long, I presume?"

"I'm sure I don't know. We may stay a year or no."

"Then the wedding is not a thing of the immediate future?"

"Oh, yes--that is, I mean, certainly not."

"Pardon me for asking so many questions. It is very rude of me." She said it so penitently that Hugh, unable to find words, could only wave his hands in deprecation. "Isn't it a perfect evening?" she went on, turning to the sea. The light breeze blew the straying raven hair away from her temples, leaving the face clearly chiselled out of the night's inkiness. Hugh's heart thumped strangely as he noted her evident intention to remain on deck. She turned to him swiftly and he averted his eyes, but not quickly enough to prevent her seeing that he had been scrutinizing her intently. What she may have intended to say was never uttered. Instead, she observed, a trifle coldly:

"I must bid you good-night, Mr. Ridge."

"Pray, not yet," he cried; "I was just about to ask if we might not sit in these chairs here for a little while. It is early and it is so charming to-night." He looked into her eyes again and found that she was gazing searchingly into his. A light smile broke into life and she seemed to be satisfied with the momentary analysis of the man before her.

"It does seem silly to stay below on a night like this. Shall we sit here?" She indicated two vacant chairs well forward. The young lady scorned a steamer rug, so he sat beside her, conscious that, despite her charming presence, he was beginning to feel the air keenly. But he could not admit it to this slight Englishwoman.

For half an hour or more they sat there, finding conversation easy, strangely interesting to two persons who had nothing whatsoever in common. He was charmed, delighted with this vivacious girl. And yet something mournful seemed to shade the brilliant face now and then. It did not come and go, moreover, for the frank, open beauty was always the same; it was revealed to him only at intervals. Perhaps he saw it in her dark, tender eyes--he could not tell. He saw Henry Veath pacing the deck, smoking and--alone. Hugh's heart swelled gladly and he spoke quite cheerily to Veath as that gentleman sauntered past.

"Now, that is Mr. Veath, isn't it?" demanded his fair companion.

"Yes; do you think we should be mistaken for each other?"

"Oh, dear, no, now that I know you apart. You are utterly unlike, except in height. How broad he is! Hasn't he a wonderful back?" she cried, admiring the tall, straight figure of the walker.

"He got that on the farm."

"It is worth a farm to have shoulders like his, I should say. You must introduce Mr. Veath to me."

Hugh looked at the moon very thoughtfully for a few moments and then, as if remembering, said that he would be happy to do so, and was sure that Veath would be even happier.

At this moment the tall, lank form of Lord Huntingford approached. He was peering intently at the people in the chairs as he passed them, plainly searching for some one.

"There is Lord Huntingford looking for you," said Hugh, rising. He saw a trace of annoyance in her face as she also arose. "I overheard him telling the captain that Lady Huntingford--your mother--plays a miserable game of crib."

She started and turned sharply upon him.

"My mother, Mr. Ridge?" she said slowly.

"Yes; your father was guying Captain Shadburn about his game, you know."

The look of wonder in her eyes increased; she passed her hand across her brow and then through her hair in evident perplexity, all the while staring at his face. There was a tinge of suspicion in her voice when she spoke.

"Mr. Ridge, don't you know?"

"Know what?"

"You surely know that I am not Lord Huntingford's--"

"You don't mean to say that you are not his daughter," gasped Hugh, dubious as to her meaning.

"I am Lady Huntingford."

"His wife?"

"His wife."

Hugh, too dumbfounded to speak, could do no more than doff his cap as she took the arm of the gray lord and softly said to him:

"Good-night, Mr. Ridge."

CHAPTER X
A SHARP ENCOUNTER

The *Tempest Queen* carried a merry cargo. The young officers, the Americans and rich pleasure seekers from other lands--young and old-- made up a happy company. Of all on board, but one was despised and loathed by his fellow-travellers--Lord Huntingford. Not so much for his manner toward them as for his harsh, bitter attitude toward his young wife.

He reprimanded and criticised her openly, very much as he would have spoken to a child, and always undeservedly. She endured patiently, to all appearances, and her cloud of humiliation was swept away by the knowledge that her new friends saw the injustice of his attacks. She did not pose before them as a martyr; but they could see the subdued and angry pride and the checked rebellion, for the mask of submission was thin, even though it was dutiful.

The two young women, unlike as two women could be, became fast friends. The Englishwoman was refinement, sweetness, even royalty itself; the American, proud, equally refined, aggressive and possessed of a wit, shrewdness and spontaneity of humor that often amazed the less subtle of the two. Tinges of jealousy sometimes shot into Grace's heart when she saw Hugh talking to the new friend, but they disappeared with the recollection of her Ladyship's pure, gentle nobility of character. It is seen rarely by one woman in another.

And Veath? The stalwart, fresh-hearted, lean-faced Indianian was happier than he had dreamed he could be when he drearily went aboard a ship at New York with the shadow of exile upon him. He had won the friendship of all. The brain of the Westerner was as big as his heart, and it had been filled with the things which make men valuable to the world. Men called him the "real American," and women conveyed a world of meaning in the simple, earnest expression--"I like Mr. Veath."

Veath was now unmistakably in love with Grace Vernon. The fact was borne in upon him more and more positively as the sunny days and beautiful nights drew them nearer to the journey's end. Occasionally he lapsed into strange fits of dejection. These came when he stopped to ponder over certain prospects, hopes and the stores of life. At times he cursed the fate which had cast him into the world, big and strong, yet apparently helpless. It had not been his ambition to begin life in the capacity which now presented itself. His hopes had been limitless. Poverty had made his mind a treasure; but poverty had also kept it buried. He saw before him the long fight for opportunity, position, honor; but he was not the sort to quail. The victory would be glorious when he thought what it might bring to him from Grace Ridge--she who was going to be a missionary. A long, hard fight, indeed, from revenue officer to minister plenipotentiary, but it was ambition's war.

And Hugh? As the days went by, his jealousy of Veath became almost intolerable. He dared not speak to Grace about it, for something told him she was not to be censured. Even in his blind rage he remembered that she was good and true, and was daring all for his sake. In calmer moments he could not blame Veath, who believed the young lady to be sister, and not sweetheart.

In view of his misery, Mr. Ridgeway was growing thin, morose, and subject to long fits of despondency which Grace alone could comprehend. Both were dissatisfied with the trip. That they could not be together constantly, as they had expected, caused them hours of misery. They were praying for the twenty-third of May to come, praying with all their hearts. Beside whom did Hugh walk during the deck strolls and at Port Said? With his sister? No, indeed; that would have been unnatural. Who was Grace's natural companion? Henry Veath or any one of a dozen attractive young officers. How could it have been otherwise?

She was popular and in constant demand. There were not many young women aboard and certainly but two or three attractive ones. From morning till far in the night she was besieged by men--always men. They ignored Hugh with all the indifference that falls to the lot of a brother. Time after time they actually pounced upon the couple and dragged her away without so much as "By your leave." They danced with her, sang with her, walked with her and openly tried to make love to her, all before the blazing eyes of one Hugh Ridgeway. On more than one occasion he had gone without his dinner because some presumptuous officer unceremoniously usurped his seat at table, grinning amiably when Hugh appeared.

The sweet, dear little moments of privacy that Hugh and Grace obtained, however, were morsels of joy which were now becoming more precious than the fondest dreams of the wedded state to come. They coveted these moments with a greediness that was almost sinful.

On many nights Grace would whisper to Hugh at the dinner table and would creep quietly on deck, meal half finished, where he would join her like a thief. Then they would hide from interruption as long as possible.

One night they enjoyed themselves more unrestrainedly than ever before in their lives. They were walking self-consciously and almost guiltily near the forward end of the deck-house when they saw Veath approaching far behind. Their speed accelerated, and for half an hour they walked like pedestrians in a racing match, always keeping some distance ahead of poor Veath, who finally, like the sly fox, sat down and waited for them to hurry around and come upon him unexpectedly. He, of course, never knew that they were trying to avoid him, nor could he imagine why brother and sister were so flushed, happy and excited when he at last had the pleasure of joining them in their walk. And, strange to say, although they had been wildly happy in this little love chase, they felt that they had mistreated a very good fellow and were saying as much to each other when they almost bumped into him.

Womanly perception told Grace that Veath's regard for her was beginning to assume a form quite beyond that of ordinary friendship. She intuitively felt that he was beginning to love her. Perhaps he was already in love, and was releasing those helpless little signs which a woman understands, and which a man thinks he conceals impenetrably. The *Queen* was leaving Port Said and she was leaning on the rail beside the big Indianian.

"Why are you going out to be a missionary?" he suddenly asked. Then he flushed painfully, remembering when too late that he had sworn to Hugh that he would not speak to her of the matter. "I beg your pardon," he hurried on; "I promised--that is, I should not have asked you that question. I forgot, hang my stupidity."

"Mr. Veath, I am not going out to be a missionary. Nothing was ever farther from my mind," she said, rather excitedly.

"Not going to be a--why, Hugh said you were. There I go, giving him away again."

"Hugh was jesting. I a missionary! How could you have believed him?"

"Are you in earnest?" he cried.

Nedra | 79

"Of course I am in earnest," she said, trying to look straight in those bright eyes, but failing dismally. Something in his glance dazzled her. It was then that she knew the truth as well as if his mind were an open book.

"Why are you going to the Philippines?" he persisted.

She gave him a quick, frightened glance and as hastily looked away. The red of confusion rushed to her cheeks, her brow, her neck. What answer could she give?

"We are--are just taking the trip for pleasure," she stammered. "Hugh and I took a sudden notion to go to Manila and--and--well, we are going, that's all."

"You don't mean to say you are making this as a pleasure trip?" he asked, staring at her with a different light in his eyes.

"A mere whim, you know," she hurried on. "Look at those Arabs over there."

"But a pleasure trip of this kind must be awfully expensive, isn't it?" he insisted.

She hesitated for an instant and then said boldly: "You see, Mr. Veath, Hugh and I are very rich. It may not sound well for me to say it, but we have much more money than we know how to spend. The cost of this voyage is a mere trifle. Please do not think that I am boasting. It is the miserable truth." His face was very pale when she dared to look up at it again, and his gaze was far off at sea.

"And so you are very rich," he mused aloud. "I thought you were quite poor, because missionaries are seldom overburdened with riches, according to tradition, or the gospel, or something like that. This is a pleasure trip!" The bitterness of his tone could not be hidden.

"I am sorry if you have had an idol shattered," she said.

"Something has been shattered," he said, smiling. "I don't know very much about idols," he added. "How long do you expect to remain in Manila?"

"But a very short time," she said simply.

"And I shall have to stay there for years, I suppose," he returned slowly. His eyes came to hers for a second and then went back to the stretch of water like a flash. That brief glance troubled her greatly. Her heart trembled with pity for the man beside her, even though speculation wrought the emotion.

In her stateroom that night she lay, dry-eyed and wakeful, her inward cry being: "It is a crime to have wounded this innocent man. Why must he be made to suffer?"

She could not tell Hugh of her discovery, for she knew that he would be unreasonable, perhaps do or say something which would make the wound more painful. During the days that followed Veath was as pleasant, as genial, as gallant as before; none but Grace observed the faint change in his manner. She was sure she could distinguish a change, yet at times, when he was gayest, she thrilled with the hope that her belief was the outgrowth of a conceit which she was beginning for the first time to know she possessed. Then came the belief again and the belief was stronger than the doubt. She could not be mistaken.

In the meantime an unexpected complication forced itself upon Hugh Ridgeway. Perforce he had been thrown more or less constantly into the society of that charming creature, Lady Huntingford. Not that the young rakes in uniform were content to pass her by, but because she plainly preferred the young American. It had not occurred to Mr. Ridgeway that his Lordship might be expected, with reasonable propriety, to unmask a jealous streak in addition to other disagreeable traits. The British subalterns probably knew the temper of the old diplomat's mind, which, in a degree, explains their readiness to forgo the pleasure of a mild flirtation with her Ladyship. Hugh, feeling like a despised pariah, naturally turned to her in his banishment. She was his friend, his one beacon of light in the dark sea of unhappiness.

Others noticed it; but Hugh was blind to the scowl which never left the face of Lord Huntingford in these days. The old nobleman knew full well that his wife loathed and detested him--just as the whole ship knew it; his pride rankled and writhed with the fear that she was finding more than friendship to enjoy in her daily intercourse with the good-looking Mr. Ridge. Gradually it became noticeable that he was watching her every act with spiteful eyes, and more than one observer winked softly at his neighbor, and shook his head with a meaning unmistakable.

The clash came one night in the Red Sea, just before the ship reached Aden. Hugh, reviling himself and the whole world, had been compelled to stand by and see Lieutenant Gilmore, a dashing Irishman, drag the unwilling Miss Ridge off for a waltz. Her protestations had been of no avail; Gilmore was abominable enough to say that she had no right to stow herself away with a stupid old brother when there were so many "real nice chaps on board." And this in Hugh's presence, too! And he could not resent it! Alone and miserable the pariah sent his unspoken, bitter lamentation to the stars as he stood in savage loneliness far aft, listening to the strains of waltz music.

"'Pon my soul! Of all the assinine idiots, bar none, the enlightened inspirer of this glorious voyage certainly ranks supreme! And I didn't have brains enough to foresee that this would surely happen! Brains? Faugh! Chump!"

Hugh might have apostrophized himself in this fashion until dawn had not a harsh, rasping voice from out of the semi-darkness broken in on his doleful revery.

"Pardon me, sir, do you play cribbage?"

Hugh turned half about and faced the speaker. He could hardly believe his ears, his eyes. Was it possible that the haughty Lord Huntingford had fixed upon him as the next lamb to be fleeced? Ugly stories concerning the government emissary's continuous winnings, disastrous losses of the young subalterns inveigled into gambling through fear of his official displeasure, were not unknown to Hugh. A civil declination was on his lips; but keenly searching the shrivelled face leering into his own, Hugh saw written there something that compelled consideration, challenged a refusal. Promptly and in affirmative speech he reversed his intention.

Slowly the left hand of Lord Huntingford produced from behind his back an exquisitely carved ebony cribbage-board; and assuming the position of host, indicated with exaggerated courtesy and a wave of his free hand the way to the smoking-room.

Hugh, following him along the deck, was hastily reviewing the voyage; and failing to recall any previous occasion wherein the nobleman had addressed him his sense of perplexity increased. Was there some hidden purpose, some crafty machination lurking behind the elaborated manner with which the invitation was delivered? On the other hand, perhaps, his imagination was playing him a trick, and this selection of an adversary was merely accidental.

And yet, had he but known, it was his own absorbing jealousy of Veath that precluded the recognition of a like sentiment directed against him, even surpassing in intensity its owner's lust for gain at play.

The smoking-room was empty, which, to the younger man, appeared as rather extraordinary, and served to augment his supposition that such a condition was presupposed. This, in turn, was dimissed, for he remembered that the usual occupants were either dancing or looking on.

Taking the initiative, as if such a course was incumbent, Lord Huntingford placed his cribbage-board on a table and drew up chairs for both; with equal politeness the proffered seat was accepted, Hugh registering inwardly a determination to force high stakes, and, if possible, recoup the losses of the young officers. Not for an instant did he doubt his ability to detect the slightest irregularities in the count of his discredited opponent.

"Sovereign a point?"

"Done! Five, if you like!"

This answer from the young American caused an avaricious glint to leap into the other's eyes. Plainly, two master passions fought for supremacy: an inordinate greed for money and a choleric determination to prohibit any further attentions to his wife. The struggle was brief, for the vehemence of his enmity, triumphant, the hope of immediate emolument was sacrificed, and the rooking of the young man postponed to some future occasion. Then, subtly concealing his purpose, he nodded an ambiguous acceptance.

Cards were ordered. A steward fetched them and awaited further commands.

Lord Huntingford strangely distrait, it seemed to Hugh, considering the amount at stake, shuffled the pack and offered them for the cut. This conventional operation performed and his Lordship successful, he dealt the hands, at the same time giving the steward a sharp order to leave. The man's reception of his dismissal was so insolent that it attracted Hugh's attention. Looking up, to his surprise, he recognized his room steward.

"With whom have I the pleasure of playing?" came suddenly from Lord Huntingford.

"Ridgeway, Hugh--"

Quick as the thought in the mind preceding it, inevitably connected, the name escaped unwittingly from his lips; for with the discovery of the steward's identity there flashed like a bolt from the blue an appalling recollection! Exposed to view on the table in his stateroom were valuable documents addressed to him by his banker, which he had forgotten to replace in his dispatch-box!

"Eh? What's that? What name?" The interrogation, icily formal, told nothing; but upon its answer hinged limitless consequences.

Hugh was in a dilemma. Should he correct himself, or rely on the slip passing unobserved? The peculiar expression on the steward's face returned to him; and he wondered if the knowledge of his adopting an incognito had been elicited from the garrulous servant, and the Englishman about to take advantage of it? Reddening with anger as much against himself as against the cynical old aristocrat, who was cornering him cavalierly, he decided to brave exposure:

"Ridge! H.B. Ridge is my name, Lord Huntingford!"

There was a reckless disregard of possibilities in the eyes that fastened themselves on the face of the nobleman for a clue, some enlightenment as to the impression produced; but all in vain. The shrewd, small eyes answered the scrutiny impassively, and without as much as the flicker of an eyelid. Taking one of the little ivory pegs, he stuck it in the starting hole at the end of the cribbage-board. Unconsciously, while waiting for the mental move which would determine his future address, Hugh following the other's lead, picked up one and pegged. Then to his infinite relief Lord Huntingford apparently allowed the correction, accepted the alias.

"Ridge!" he pronounced with malicious uncertainty. "Ridge! I am acquainted with the English Ridges;" and the sneer in the voice increased. "Do I understand you to pretend that you are one of that distinguished family?"

Hugh clenched his lips and his blood boiled at the treatment.

"I am an American, Lord Huntingford," spoken easily, his pride showing only by a perceptible lift of the head; "and my ancestors were not Tories in the Revolution. Relationship, if any, would be--er--distant. I claim none."

"A trifle strained," admitted his Lordship, laughing disagreeably.

At that moment the band could be heard in the distance playing the strains of a waltz; also the voices of the couples who were promenading and passing the open door. To Hugh's amazement, Lord Huntingford, obviously heedless of his peculiar action, recommended shuffling the stack of cards, though the dealt hands remained untouched on the table. Instinctively,

Hugh was convinced that no play was intended. There was something on the mind of the wily old diplomat far more momentous than a mere game of cards; yet no chance had been given to him to penetrate into the other's motives.

It was not long forthcoming.

Suddenly, clear as a bell, Hugh distinguished the laughter of Lady Huntingford, and involuntarily he smiled. This seemed to enrage his Lordship. Hatred and menace shone from his eyes as he glanced at the man opposite him. With an oath he rose, walked to the door and closed it. Then ruthlessly laying aside the last vestige of his assumed courtliness, he picked up his stick from the table, leaned far over, shook it in Hugh's face, and became an irascible, shouting old man.

"Look here, young man--Ridge--Ridgeway--or whatever your blasted name--do you think I'll allow you to carry on an affair with my wife--my wife, sir?" he vociferated. "Henceforth, I forbid you to speak to her! Do you hear me?"

It was debatable whether Hugh was more astonished at the mention of Lady Huntingford's name in connection with his own, or at the stick in dangerously close proximity to his countenance. It was some time before he could find words; but his face from red went white.

"And if I decline?"

There was that in the low tone that should have warned the aggressor from further insult; but forgetting that the swaggering domination he had been accustomed to exercising over his own countrymen, officially his inferiors, would not for a moment be tolerated by one of another nationality, he again broke out.

"You bounder! Yankee upstart! I'll thrash you, and then have the captain put you on shore at the first port--you infernal impostor!"

In an instant Hugh was over the table. He tore the stick from Lord Huntingford's hand and clutched his throat, forcing him down on the seat cushions. With the exception of the younger man's hard breathing and some gasps from the other, the struggle was noiseless. Not until Lord Huntingford was growing black in the face did Hugh come to his senses. Then releasing one hand from the throat, he pinned him with the other and a knee.

"You old scoundrel!" Hugh began, jerking out the scathing words; "if it were not for your old age and your wife I'd drag you on deck and make you apologize on your knees before them all. I'll spare you that degradation; but if I ever hear of you mentioning the name Ridegway--I've my own reasons for concealing it, and they don't concern you--I'll make some charges in regard to your card playing that will bar you from every club in the world, and, unlike your poor dupes, I am in a position to substantiate them without fear of consequences."

Lord Huntingford grudgingly mumbled a throttled promise, and Hugh allowed him to regain his feet. At that instant Veath, with Grace and Lady Huntingford, standing behind him, opened the door of the smoking-room.

"Here, Veath!" called out Hugh to the astonished Indianian. "I want you to bear witness that Lord Huntingford has promised to keep absolutely quiet about a little altercation of ours, and--"

The quick gesture of caution from Veath came too late. Lady Huntingford with astonished eyes was gazing into the room at them. Hugh promptly went over to her.

"You must pardon me, Lady Huntingford; I am sorry to cause you any pain or annoyance. In a dispute over the cards with your husband I forgot myself for a moment. Pray forgive me."

Ridgeway quietly strode away with Grace and Veath. Lady Huntingford directed a look of unutterable contempt at her husband, turned on her heel and left him to slink away as quickly as possible, like a cur that has felt the whip.

CHAPTER XI
DISCOVERED

Lord Huntingford could not forgive the man who had put his aristocratic nose out of joint in such an effective manner. He was, however, as polite as nature would permit him to be to Miss Ridge and Mr. Veath. As for Hugh, that young gentleman thought it the wiser plan, when unavoidably relating a mild description of last night's encounter, to abstain from acquainting Grace with Lord Huntingford's discovery of his name--whether accidental or otherwise. Quite rightly he surmised that it would unnecessarily distress her, and he preferred not to cross the bridge until he came to it.

It was the evening following the conflict. As night approached, the sun fell behind the shores of the Red Sea, the stars twinkled out through the blackness above, and yet they had not caught a glimpse of her Ladyship. At dinner, he and Grace had agreed that she had either renounced them entirely, or had been compelled to avoid him in particular. Veath was less concerned. He was thinking of another woman.

Hugh and Grace again stole away for a few moments of seclusion on deck. They found chairs and sat down, neither very talkative.

"Oh, Hugh, just think where we are," she murmured at last. "Thousands of miles from home, and no one the wiser save ourselves. Chicago is on the other side of the world."

"Are you sorry you came, dear?"

"I am glad. But isn't it awful to consider how far we are from everybody we know? We might just as well be dead, Hugh." She was very solemn and wide-eyed.

"I am afraid you are losing heart," he said disconsolately.

"Why, Hugh Ridgeway--Ridge, I mean,--how can I afford to lose heart now? Don't ever say that to me again."

"Yes; we are a long way from home, dear," mused he after a while.

"How far are we from Manila?" she asked suddenly.

"A million miles, judging by the way time goes. We'll be there in twenty days, the captain says."

"What do you suppose Mr. Veath will say when he hears of our marriage?" This question was propounded after a longer interval of silence than usual.

"Why should we care what Mr. Veath says? If he doesn't approve, let him go to--" but Hugh checked his fiery speech as abruptly as he began it.

"He will be awfully shocked to learn how we have deceived him," she went on, as if he had not spoken.

"Well, do you care?" demanded Hugh.

"Yes, I care," she cried. "I shall be very sorry if he loses the good opinion he may have formed. He is the kind of a man who would not understand such an affair as this."

"But, then, we are not obliged to tell him. We can get married and leave Manila at once without ever seeing him again. After that we will be Mr. and Mrs. Ridgeway, and he could never find the people known as Hugh Ridge and sister."

"That would be a shameless way to treat him. He has been so true, so good, Hugh," she cried reproachfully. For quite a while their eyes lingered upon the dark water without seeing it, their thoughts centred upon the fast approaching end of their relationship with Henry Veath.

"I wish he could be told," murmured she, her voice far away.

"I couldn't do it to save my soul. What would he say?" There was an awed anxiety in his voice.

"I don't care what other people say, but I do care what he says. He seems so honest, so far above tricks of this kind."

"What's one man's opinion, anyhow, especially when he's to be buried in Manila for years?"

"Oh, Hugh! How lonely he will be in that strange place. And how dreadful it will be in us to sneak away from him like cowards, just as if we cared nothing for him at all. He doesn't deserve that, does he?"

"No, he doesn't, that's a fact. We can't treat him like a dog."

"I wish he could be told," sighed she pensively.

"When?"

"You might try to tell him at any time," she said, a perceptible strain in her voice.

"I'll tell you what I'll do," said he, taking her hand in his. "I will tell him the day before we reach Manila."

"I'm afraid it will be too late," she cried, all a-flutter.

"Too late? Why?"

"I mean," she went on confusedly, "he might think we had waited too long." She was thinking of Veath's wistful eyes.

"Hello! Here you are," cried a strong voice, and Veath loomed up through the shadows. Hugh released her hand and dropped back in the chair from which he had half risen to kiss her. "You hide away like a pair of silly lovers. There's nothing prosaic about this brother and sister. Do you know, I have often marvelled over one thing in connection with you. You don't look any more like brother and sister than the sea looks like dry land."

The pair caught breath sharply and Hugh almost snorted aloud. Grace could do nothing but look up to where she saw the red fluctuating glow of a cigar tip in the darkness. It made her think of a little moon which could breathe like herself.

"It all goes to show how deceptive appearances can be," went on Veath easily. "Don't you want to walk, Miss Ridge? I'm sure you need exercise."

"I promised Hugh I would drive away his blues, Mr. Veath. Thank you, but I believe I'll sit here for a while and then go below," she said, a trifle disconnectedly.

"We'll take Hugh along," said Veath obligingly. "Come along, both of you."

"Excuse me, Henry, but I don't feel like walking," said Hugh, a tinge of sullenness in his manner.

"Lazy, eh? Well, I'll bring Miss Ridge back in half an hour. You wouldn't have me wander about this dismal old boat alone, would you? Smoke a cigar, Hugh, and I'll take care of your sister while you count the stars." He offered Hugh a cigar.

Hugh rose suddenly and started away.

"Hugh!" called she, "come and walk with us." He could distinguish the loving entreaty, the trouble in her tones, but he was unreasonable.

"Never mind me," he sang out with an assumption of cheerfulness. Grace flushed hotly, her heart swelling with injured pride. Without another word she rose and walked away with Veath. Indignation burned within her soul until she went to sleep, hours afterward.

Ridgeway stamped the full length of the promenade before he came to an understanding with himself. On reaching that understanding, he whirled and walked back to where he had left them, expecting to find Veath occupying the chair he had vacated. Of course they were not to be found, so he threw himself on one of the chairs, more miserable than he had been since they started on their voyage. The lady in the chair to his left stirred nervously and then a soft laugh came from her lips.

"Are you sleepy, Mr. Ridge?" she asked. Hugh turned quickly and looked into the face of Lady Huntingford.

"Not at all," he replied. "But how strange it seems that you should always appear like the fairy queen when I am most in need of a bracer. Oh, I beg your pardon," he went on, rising in some perturbation. "I forgot that there is a--a barrier between us. War has been declared, I fear."

"I am ready to make friendly overtures," she said gaily. "Isn't there some such thing as a treaty which requires a strong power to protect its weaker ally in time of stress?"

"You mean that we may still be friends in spite of all that happened last night?" he cried. She nodded her head and smiled, and he shook her hand as only an impulsive American would.

"But Lord Huntingford? What will he say?" he asked.

"His Lordship's authority can be carried to a certain limit and no farther," she said, and her eyes flashed. "He knows when to curse and abuse; but he also knows when that attitude might operate against him. He is not in a position to push me to the wall."

"What do you mean?"

"I mean he knows enough not to drive me to the point where I would turn and fight." Hugh never had seen her so entrancing as she was in that dim light, her face the picture of proud defiance.

"I wonder not a little that you have not asked for a divorce long before this."

"You are not a woman or you would not ask that."

"Lots of women ask for divorces."

"It should be the last resort with any woman. But let us talk of something else. Where is your sister? I have not seen her to-day."

This question was particularly ill-timed, for it restored the forgotten bitterness to the position from which it had been temporarily driven by the interruption.

"I don't know," he answered.

"I thought I heard her talking to you here a few moments ago--in fact, I saw you."

"Where were you?"

"I passed within a dozen feet of you. Neither of you saw me, I am sure. You would not have cut me intentionally, would you?"

"I should say not. You walked past here?"

"Yes, you were tying her shoe-string."

"What!" exclaimed he, starting to his feet, "tying Grace's shoe-string?" The first thought that rushed to his mind was that Veath had knelt to plead his love to Grace Vernon.

"Lady Huntingford, let us walk," he exclaimed. It was a fierce, impatient command instead of a polite invitation. The pretty young woman calmly lay back in her chair and laughed. "If you won't come, then please excuse me. I must go."

"Why are you so eager to walk, Mr. Ridgeway?" she asked.

"Because I want--what was that you called me?" he gasped, his heart almost turning upside down.

"Ridgeway. That's your name, isn't it?"

"What do you mean?"

"Oh, a great many things," she said with a serious face.

Hugh was visibly annoyed. There was to be more trouble from the nobleman; evidently he did not intend to keep his promise.

"In the first place," she continued, "I must acknowledge that I forced from my husband an account of last night's affair; he also told me your name. But, believe me, it will go no further. I cannot thank you enough, Mr. Ridgeway," the color stealing into her cheeks.

Ridgeway bowed.

"In the next place," she went on playfully, "you are very jealous of Mr. Veath. Tut, tut, yes you are," with a gesture of protest. "He thinks Miss Ridge is your sister, and she is not your sister. And lastly, nobody on board knows these facts but the very bright woman who is talking to you at this moment."

"But you are mistaken, madam," with a last attempt at assumption of dignity.

"Would I say this to you if I were not positive? You think you are very clever; I'll admit that you are. Your secrets came to me through an accident. Do not think that I have pried into your affairs. They really forced themselves upon me."

"Tell me what you know, for Heaven's sake," cried the dismayed Ridgeway.

"I was in your sister's room earlier in the day. Her trunk was open and I saw a portfolio with Vernon in silver lettering; and I was more mystified than ever when I observed that the initials on her trunk were 'G.V.' All day yesterday I tried to solve the problem, taking into consideration the utter absence of family resemblance between you, and I was almost sick with curiosity. To-day I was convinced that her name is not Ridge. She inadvertently signed her name to the purser's slip in my presence, and she did not sign the--yours. She scratched it out quickly and asked him to make out another one. Now, what is this mystery?" She bent her gaze upon his face and he could not meet it.

"Do you want to know the reason why I did not see you yesterday?" she continued.

"Yes," he murmured, mopping his brow.

"Because I was so distressed that I feared I could not face either of you, knowing what I do."

"What do you mean?"

"I know you are running away." Not a word was spoken for a full minute. He could scarcely breathe. "You do not deny it?" she questioned gently. "Please do not fear me."

"I do not fear you," he half whispered, sinking his chin in his hands. Another long silence.

"There are some circumstances and conditions under which a woman should not be condemned for running away," she said in a strained, faraway voice. "Has--has she children?"

"Good Heaven!" cried Hugh, leaping to his feet, horror-struck.

CHAPTER XII
THE HARLEQUIN'S ERRAND

Lady Huntingford, alarmed by his manner, arose and steadied herself against the deck-house. His exclamation rang in her ears, filling them with its horror. At length he roughly grasped her arm, thrusting his face close to hers, fairly grated out the words:

"You think she is a wife?"

"I feared so."

"She is not! Do you hear me? She is not!" he cried so fiercely that there was no room for doubt. "She is the purest, dearest girl in the world, and she has done all this for me. For God's sake, do not expose us." He dropped back in the chair. "It's not for my sake that I ask it, but for hers," he went on quickly.

"I'm sure I have wronged her and I have wronged you. Will you believe me?"

He did not answer at once. His turbulent brain was endeavoring to find words with which to convince her of the innocence of the escapade. Looking up into her eyes, he was struck by their tender staunchness. Like a flash came to him the decision to tell her the true story, from beginning to end.

"Lady Huntingford, I will tell you everything there is to tell. It is not a long tale, and you may say it is a very foolish one. I am sure, however, that it will interest you."

"You shall not tell me a word if you do so in order to appease my curiosity," she began earnestly.

"I think it is best that you should know," he interrupted. "One favor first. You will earn my eternal gratitude if you do not allow Grace to feel that you have discovered our secret."

"You have my promise. I have kept many secrets, Mr. Ridge." He drew his chair quite close to hers. Then he told her the full story of the adventure, from first to last. She scarcely breathed, so deeply was her interest centred in this little history of an impulse. He spoke hurriedly, excitedly. Not once did she take her eyes from his earnest face, almost indistinguishable in the darkness; nor could he remove his from hers.

"And here we are approaching Aden, your Ladyship," he concluded. Her big dark eyes had held him enthralled, inspiring him to paint in glorious colors every detail of the remarkable journey. As he drew to a close, her hand fell involuntarily on his knee. A tremor dashed through his veins, and his heart throbbed fiercely.

"How glorious it must be to love like that," she almost whispered. There was a catch in her voice, as she uttered that soft, dreamy sentence, almost a sigh. She turned her face away suddenly and then arose, crying in tones so low and despairing that he could hardly believe they came from the usually merry lips: "Oh, how I envy her this life and love! How wonderful it all is!"

"It has its drawbacks," he lamented. "As a brother I am a nonentity, Lady Huntingford; it's not altogether relishable, you know. It's a sort of pantomime, for me, by Jove. I'm the fool, and this seems to be the fool's errand."

"If you will play a part in the pantomime, Mr. Ridge, let an Englishwoman suggest that you be the harlequin. How I loved the harlequin in the Drury Lane pantomimes at Christmas time! He was always the ideal lover to me, for there was no trick, no prank this bespangled hero could not play to success. He always went incognito, for he wore his narrow mask of black. He performed the most marvellous things for his Columbine,--and was she not a worthy sweetheart? No, no, Mr. Ridge:--not the fool, I pray. Please be the harlequin," she cried in rare good humor.

"As you like it," he said, reflecting her spirits. "I am the harlequin and this is, perforce, the harlequin's errand." They were silent for a long time, then he said soberly:

"It was such a foolish thing to do, after all." She looked up at him for a moment, the bitterness fading from her hungry eyes, a smile struggling feebly into power. Then came the radiance of enthusiasm.

"Foolish!" she exclaimed, with eyes sparkling and breast heaving. "It was magnificent! What a brave girl she is! Oh, how clever you both are and how much you will enjoy the memory of this wonderful trip. It will always be fresh and novel to you--you will never forget one moment of its raptures.

How I wish I could have done something like this. If I dared, I would kiss that brave, lucky girl a thousand times."

"But you must not let her suspect," cautioned he.

"It would ruin everything for her if she even dreamed that you had told me, and I would not mar her happiness for the world. Really, Mr. Ridge, I am so excited over your exploit that I can scarcely contain myself. It seems so improbable, so immense, yet so simple that I can hardly understand it at all. Why is it other people have not found this way to revolutionize life? Running around the world to get married without the faintest excuse save an impulse--a whim. How good, how glorious! It is better than a novel!"

"I hope it is better than some novels."

"It is better than any, because it is true."

"I am afraid you are trying to lionize me," he jested.

"You have faced a British lion," she said slowly.

"My only regret is that he is old and clawless."

"We are retracing our steps over dangerous ground," she said with a catch in her breath.

"You would have me to believe that I am a brave man, so I am determined to court the danger of your displeasure. How did you happen to marry this old and clawless lion?"

She did not exhibit the faintest sign of surprise or discomfiture, certainly not of anger. Instead, she looked frankly into his eyes and answered: "That is what I thought you would ask me. I shall not refuse to answer. I married because I wanted to do so."

"What!" exclaimed he incredulously. "I had hoped--er--I mean, feared that you had been--ah--sort of forced into it, you know."

"Since my marriage I have discovered, however, that there is no fool like the ambitious fool," she went on as if he had not spoken. "Do you understand what I mean?"

"That you married for position?"

"That I married simply to become Lady Huntingford."

"And you did not love him at all?" There was something like disgust, horror in Hugh's voice.

"Love him?" she exclaimed scornfully, and he knew as much as if she had spoken volumes. Then her face became rigid and cold. For the first time he saw the hard light of self-mastery in her eyes. "I made my choice; I shall abide by it to the end as steadfastfully as if I were the real rock which you may think me to be. There is nothing for me to tell--nothing more that I will tell to you. Are you not sorry that you know such a woman as I? Have you not been picking me to pieces and casting me with your opinions to the four winds?"

"I am truly sorry for you," was all that he could say.

"You mean that you despise me," she cried bitterly. "Men usually think that of such women as I. They do not give us a hearing with the heart, only with the cruel, calculating brain. Think of it, Mr. Ridge, I have never known what it means to love. I have been loved; but in all my life there has been no awakening of a passion like that which sends Grace Vernon around the world to give herself to you. I know that love exists for other people. I have seen it--have almost felt it in them when they are near me. And yet it is all so impossible to me."

"You are young--very young," he said. "Love may come to you--some day."

"It will be envy--not love, I fear. I threw away every hope for love two years ago--when I was transformed from the ambitious Miss Beresford to Lady Huntingford, now thoroughly satiated. It was a bad bargain and it has wounded more hearts than one. I am not sorry to have told you this. It gives relief to--to something I cannot define. You despise me, I am sure--"

"No, no! How can you say that? You are paying the penalty for your--of your--"

"Say it! Crime."

"For your mistake, Lady Huntingford. We all make mistakes. Some of us pay for them more bitterly than others, and none of us is a judge of human nature except from his own point of view. I am afraid you don't feel the true sympathy I mean to convey. Words are faulty with me to-night. It shall be my pleasure to forget what you have confessed to me. It is as if I never had heard."

"Some men would presume greatly upon what I have told to you. You are too good, I know, to be anything but a true friend," she said.

"I think I understand you," he said, a flush rising to his temples. After all, she was a divine creature. "You shall always find me the true friend you think I am."

"Thank you." They were silent for a long time, gazing out over the sombre plain of water in melancholy review of their own emotions. At last she murmured softly, wistfully, "I feel like an outcast. My life seems destined to know none of the joys that other women have in their power to love and to be loved." The flush again crept into his cheek.

"You have not met the right man, Lady Huntingford," he said.

"Perhaps that is true," she agreed, smiling faintly.

"The world is large and there is but one man in it to whom you can give your heart," he said.

"Why should any man desire possession of a worthless bit of ice?" she asked, her eyes sparkling again.

"The satisfaction of seeing it melt," he responded.

She thought long over this reply.

CHAPTER XIII
THE CONFESSION OF VEATH

"Hugh, have you observed anything strange in Mr. Veath lately?"

The interrogation came suddenly from Grace, the next morning, on deck. They had been discussing the plans for a certain day in May, and all the time there was evidence of trouble in her eyes. At last she had broached a subject that had been on her mind for days.

"Can't say that I have." The answer was somewhat brusque.

"I am convinced of one thing," she said hurriedly, coming direct to the point. "He is in love with me."

"The scoundrel!" gasped Hugh, stopping short and turning very white. "How dare he do such--"

"Now, don't be absurd, dear. I can't see what he finds in me to love, but he has a perfect right to the emotion, you know. He doesn't know, dear."

"Where is he? I'll, take the emotion out of him in short order. Ah, ha! Don't look frightened! I understand. You love him. I see it all. It's as--"

"Stop! You have no right to say that," she exclaimed, her eyes flashing dangerously. His heart smote him at once and he sued humbly for pardon. He listened to her views concerning the hapless Indianian, and it was not long before he was heart and head in sympathy with Veath.

"Poor fellow! When I told him last night that I was to be married within a year he actually trembled from head to foot. I never was so miserable over a thing in my life," she said dismally. "Really, Hugh, I can't bear to think of him finding out how we have played with him."

"Shall I tell him all about it?" asked he in troubled tones.

"Then I should not be able to look him in the face. Dear me, elopements have their drawbacks, haven't they?"

Other passengers joined them, Veath and Lady Huntingford among them. In the group were Captain Shadburn, Mr. and Mrs. Evarts, Mr. Higsworth and his daughter Rosella, Lieutenant Hamilton--a dashing young fellow who was an old and particularly good friend of Lady Huntingford. Hugh noted, with strange satisfaction, that Hamilton seemed unusually devoted to Miss Higsworth. In a most casual manner he took his stand at the rail beside her Ladyship, who had coaxed Captain Shadburn to tell them his story of the great typhoon.

Presently, a chance came to address her.

"Grace tells me that your name is an odd one, for a girl--woman, I mean--Tennyson. Were you named for the poet?"

"Yes. My father knew him well. Odd, isn't it? My friends call me Lady Tennys. By the way, you have not told Grace what I told you last night on deck, have you?" she asked.

"I should say not. Does she suspect that you know her secret and mine?" he asked in return.

"She does not dream that I know. Ah, I believe I am beginning to learn what love is. I worship your sweetheart, Hugh Ridgeway."

"If you could love as she loves me, Lady Huntingford, you might know what love really is."

"What a strange thing it must be that you and she can know it and I cannot," she mused, looking wistfully at the land afar off.

At Aden everybody went ashore while the ship coaled at Steamer Point, on the western side of the rock, three miles from the town proper. Multitudes of Jewish ostrich-feather merchants and Somali boys gave the travellers amusement at the landing and in the coast part of the town. The Americans began to breathe what Hugh called a genuinely oriental atmosphere.

They were far from Aden when night came down and with it the most gorgeous sunset imaginable. Everybody was on deck. The sky was aflame, the waters blazed and all the world seemed about to be swept up in the wondrous conflagration. Late in the afternoon a bank of clouds had grown up from the western line, and as the sun dropped behind them they glowed with the intensity of fiercely fanned coals of huge dimensions. At last the fiery hues faded away, the giant holocaust of the skies drew to an end, and the soft afterglow spread across the dome, covering it with a tranquil beauty more sublime than words can paint.

Grace looked eagerly among the impressed spectators for Henry Veath. Somehow she longed for him to see all this beauty that had given her so much pleasure. He was not there and she was conscious of a guilty depression. She was sitting with Hugh and Lady Huntingford when, long afterward, Veath approached.

"I'd like a word with you, Hugh," he said after the greetings, "when the ladies have gone below."

"It is getting late and I am really very tired," said Grace. It was quite dark, or they could have seen that her face was pale and full of concern. She knew instinctively what it was that Veath wanted to say to Hugh. Then she did something she had never done before in the presence of another. She walked quickly to Hugh's side, bent over and kissed his lips, almost as he gasped in astonishment.

"Good-night, dear," she said, quite audibly, and was gone with Lady Huntingford. The astounded lover was some time in recovering from the surprise inspired by her unexpected act. It was the first time she had ever been sisterly in that fashion before the eyes of others.

"I hope I have said nothing to offend them," said Veath miserably. "Was I too abrupt?"

"Not in the least. They've seen enough for one night anyhow, and I guess they were only waiting for an excuse to go below," replied Hugh. To himself he said, "I wonder what the dickens Grace did that for? And why was Lady Huntingford so willing to leave?"

Veath sat nervously wriggling his thumbs, plainly ill at ease. His jaw was set, however, and there was a look in his eyes which signified a determination to brave it out.

"You know me pretty well by this time, Hugh," he said. Hugh awoke from his abstraction and displayed immediate interest. "You know that I am straightforward and honest, if nothing else. There is also in my make-up a pride which you may never have observed or suspected, and it is of this that I want to speak before attempting to say something which will depend altogether upon the way you receive the introduction."

"Go ahead, Henry. You're serious to-night, and I can see that something heavy is upon your mind."

"It is a very serious matter, I can assure you. Well, as you perhaps know from my remarks or allusions on previous occasions, I am a poor devil. I have nothing on earth but the salary I can earn, and you can guess what that will amount to in Manila. My father educated me as best he could, and I worked my way through college after he had given me to understand that he was unable to send me there himself. When I was graduated, I accepted a position with a big firm in its engineering service. Within a year I was notified that I could have a five months' lay-off, as they call it. At the end of that period, if matters improved, I was to have my place back. Out of my wages I saved a couple of hundred dollars, but it dwindled as I drifted through weeks of idleness. There was nothing for me to do, try as I would to find a place. It was a hard pill to swallow, after four years of the kind of work I had done in college, but I had to throw every plan to the winds and go to the Philippines. My uncle, who is rich, sent me money enough to prepare for the voyage, and here I am, sneaking off to the jungles, disgusted, discouraged and disappointed. To-night I sit before you with less than one hundred dollars as the sum total of my earthly possessions."

"By George, Veath, just let me know how much you need--" broke in Hugh warmly, but the other silenced him, smiling sadly.

"I'm greatly obliged to you, but I don't believe it is money that I want now--at least, not borrowed money. When you told me that your sister was to become a missionary, I inferred that you were not burdened with worldly goods, and I felt at home with you both--more so than I should, I believe--"

"Oh, the devil!"

"But a few days ago your sister told me that she is not to be a missionary and that she is rich enough to make this trip to the Orient for mere pleasure--oh, well, you know better than I how rich you both are." His voice was low and unsteady. "I don't know why you should have told me that she--she was to be a missionary."

"It was--I did it for a little joke on her, honestly I did," mumbled Hugh.

"And it was a serious one for me. Before I knew of her real position she seemed more approachable to me, more as if I could claim her friendship on the grounds of mutual sympathy. I was deceived into believing our lots not vastly unequal, and I have suffered more than I can tell you by the disparity which I now know exists."

"But what difference can it make whether we are rich or poor? We can still be friends," said Hugh eagerly.

"It was when I believed your sister to be a missionary that I learned to love her better than all else in this world. Now do you understand?"

"Great Scott!" gasped his listener, starting from his chair. Now he realised that she had not been mistaken in her fears. "Does she know this?" he managed to ask.

"No, and I dare not tell her--I cannot. I had to tell some one, and to whom should I confess it if not to the brother of the woman I love? It is no disgrace, no dishonor to her. You cannot blame me for being honest with you. Some day after you have gone back to America you can tell her that I love her and always will. She has intimated to me that she is to marry another man, so what chance is there for a poor wretch like me? I don't see how I have endured the awakening from the dreams I have had. I even went so far as to imagine a little home in Manila, after I had won her from the mission field and after I had laid by the savings of a year or two. I had planned to fairly starve myself that I might save enough to make a home for her and--and--" but he could say no more. Hugh heard the sob and turned sick at heart. To what a pass their elopement had come!

Above all things, how could he comfort the unfortunate man? There was no word of encouragement, no word of hope to be given. The deepest pity he had ever felt went out to Henry Veath; the greatest remorse he had ever known stung his soul. Should he tell Veath the truth? Could he do it?

"Do you see my position?" asked Veath steadily, after a long silence. "I could never hope to provide for her as she has been accustomed to living, and I have too much pride to allow my wife to live other than the way in which I would have to live."

"She may not love you," said Hugh, suddenly hopeful.

"But I could win her love. I'm sure I could, Hugh. Even though she is pledged to another man, I could love her so powerfully that a new love would be inspired in her for me. You don't know how I love her. Hugh, you are not angry with me for having told you this?"

"Angry? Great Heavens, no! I'm heartbroken over it," cried Hugh. There were traces of tears in his eyes.

"You know how hopeless it is for me," went on Veath, "and I hope you will remember that I have been honest and plain with you. Before we part in Manila I may tell her, but that is all. I believe I should like to have her know that I love her. She can't think badly of me for it, I'm sure."

Hugh did not answer. He arose and silently grasped the hand of the other, who also had conic to his feet.

"I would to God that I could call you brother," said he.

"Don't say it! It is too wild an improbability," cried Veath.

"Yes; it is more than that: it is an impossibility."

"If in the end I should conclude to tell Miss Ridge of my feelings, will you tell me now that I may do so with your permission?"

"But there is no hope," cried Hugh miserably.

"I do not ask for hope. I shall not ask her to love me or to be my wife. I may want to tell her that I love her, that's all. You can have no objection to that, Hugh."

"I have no objection," murmured Ridgeway, a chill striking deep into his heart.

CHAPTER XIV
ONE LOVE AGAINST ANOTHER

Ridgeway passed another sleepless night. Had not Veath said he could win her love, even though it were pledged to another? The thought gave birth to a fear that he was not perfectly sure of her love, and that it might turn to Henry Veath, after all. In the early morning hours, between snatches of sleep, he decided to ask Lady Huntingford's advice, after explaining to her the dilemma in full. He would also tell Grace of Veath's declaration, putting her on guard. Breakfast time found the sea heavy and the ship rolling considerably, but at least three people gave slight notice to the weather. Hugh was sober and morose; Veath was preoccupied and unnatural; Grace was restless and uneasy. Lady Huntingford, who came in while they were eating, observed this condition almost immediately, and smiled knowingly, yet sadly. Later Hugh Ridgeway drew her to a secluded corner and exploded his bomb. Her cool little head readily devised a plan which met his approval, and he hurried off to warn Grace before it was too late. Lady Huntingford advised him to tell Veath nothing of the elopement, allowing him to believe as he had all along, but suggested a radical change in their future plans. It was her advice that they go on to Japan and be married.

At first Grace demurred to this plan, which he necessarily proposed as his own, holding that it would be absolutely cruel to desert Veath at the last minute. Finally she agreed to the compromise and kissed him with tears in her eyes.

Days passed and the strain grew more tense than ever. The *Tempest Queen* was nearing the Archipelago, after the stops at Penang and Singapore. At Hong Kong the Manila-bound passengers were to be transferred to one of the small China Sea steamers. The weather had been rough and ugly for many days. Lady Huntingford had not left her stateroom in two days. Grace was with her a greater portion of the time, ministering to her wants gently and untiringly. Ridgeway and Veath, anxious and troubled, wandered aimlessly about the ship, smoking cigar after cigar, praying for a cessation of the ugly weather. Finally, all passengers were peremptorily forbidden the deck. The skilled sailors were in constant danger of being washed overboard.

Captain Shadburn admitted that they were being driven from their course by the fury of the typhoon. Secretly he feared that the *Queen* might rush upon a reef at night.

Dinner on the second violent evening was a sombre affair. Lady Huntingford, pale, sweet and wan, made her appearance with Grace, occupying Veath's seat, that gentleman moving to the next chair, its original occupant being confined to his berth. Lord Huntingford, austere and imperturbable, entered some time before his wife and purposely ignored her when she came in.

As the party arose from the table, a heavy lurch of the boat threw Grace headlong into Veath's arms. By a superhuman effort he managed to keep his feet. He smiled down at her; but there was something so insistent in the smile that it troubled her.

"It's an ill wind that blows no good," said Veath softly.

"What blows well for one may blow ill for another," she responded a little coldly, though she did not refuse the proffered arm; and they staggered toward the doorway.

As they passed into the main saloon he suddenly asked her if she would let him speak to her of a matter that long had been on his mind. She did not look him in the face, but she knew it was white and determined. The time had come when he was to tell her that he loved her. He begged for a moment's time and gained her unspoken permission. They sank to a couch near the stairway, Grace giving a last helpless, hopeless glance at Hugh as he and his companion passed from the apartment.

"I can see by the manner in which you act that you know what I want to say to you. It is also plain to me that you would rather not hear me," he said, after a moment.

"Please do not say it," she entreated, and he saw the little hope that he had been nourishing dashed away.

"I did not dream until a few moments ago that you had discerned my love for you, Miss Ridge, but I am not sorry that I have been so transparent. How you have guessed my secret I cannot imagine. I tried to keep it from you," he said, as if he had wounded her. "Perhaps your brother told you."

She was on the point of telling him that Hugh was not her brother, but something checked the impulse and she could only answer by shaking her head.

"You told me that you expect to marry another man, but that has not kept me from telling you that I love you, nor will it prevent me from trying to win your love. Pride, if nothing else, has kept my lips sealed, for what right have I to ask any woman to share my lot? In sheer humiliation I must tell you that my life looks like a failure to me. I have a hard struggle ahead of me. You may say that I am young and strong, but I cannot, for my soul, see anything bright ahead." His voice trembled and she glanced up at his face. He was looking at the diamond that sparkled on her left hand.

"You have no right to say that life is a failure; you have no right to lie down on your arms and give, up the fight. That is the act of a coward. After all, it is not the way to win a woman's love."

"You don't mean--is it possible that you could--" he began.

"No, no! You must not hope. I love another as dearly as you love me. But I will not have you say that you cannot succeed in life. I know you are strong, and I know you are determined. There is nothing impossible to you," she said hurriedly, seeking feverishly to draw him from his purpose. "When first we met you were cheerful and hopeful, strong and full of life. Then some one came into your life and you saw a black cloud of despair arise. It came up easily and you can drive it away just as easily. It is not of your nature to give up, I know. You can win fame and fortune and the love of some one much worthier than I."

"If I live to be a thousand I shall love none as I love you," he said simply. "If you loved me I could win against all the world. Your wealth is a natural barrier between poor love and rich pride, both true possessions of mine. But for the latter the former would win. Can you understand?" he asked almost vehemently.

"I--I--no, I do not understand you," she said panic-stricken. His eyes were flashing again in the same old way and his voice, low pitched, had a gallant ring.

"I mean I'd win your love and I'd make you my wife."

"Mr. Veath! How can you--how dare you--" she began, arising indignantly, yet a trifle carried away by his impetuous manner. Her heart was thumping tumultuously and she dared not look into his eyes.

"Dare!" he cried. "You urge me to fight it out and die in the trenches, as it were, and now you ask me why I dare tell you what I'd do under certain conditions. I merely tell you what I could and would do if I could change the conditions."

"You are a trifle over-confident, Mr. Veath," she said coldly. "Good-night."

"Don't be angry, please," he cried in humility. "You have spoken to me in a way that has awakened a new spirit--the spirit that men call 'do or die.' To-night the storm rages and we are all in danger. I feel that in an hour like this and in a place like this I am worth more than I have ever been or could be in any other position. The fierceness of the night and the sting of your advice combine to give life and nerve to my weak heart. I am not the man who begged you a moment ago to listen to the weakness of a despairing lover; it is another man, another Henry Veath who talks to you now. From this instant I shall begin the battle against old conditions and you shall be the spoils of battle. Grace, look at me! I am going to show you what real determination means. I want you and I'll win you." His tall figure straightened, his blue eyes gleamed and flashed with the fire of enthusiasm. The timid, fearful Veath was gone, and in his stead stood the valiant, aggressive, inspired contestant.

The rolling of the ship sent her staggering toward him, and he caught her by the arms. Steadying himself against the staircase, he cried in her bewildered ear:

"I love you better than all else in the world. You are a part of my life, all of my joy. Do you think I can give you up now that I have found the courage to begin the struggle? I'll win my way and I'll win your love. Nothing but death can stop me now. Come! Don't look as though you hate me for it."

"I do not hate you," she said humbly, almost glaring into his bright eyes, unable to turn from the love which governed them so completely. "But you must not talk like this. I cannot listen to you. Mr. Veath, there is no possible hope."

"The hope to win and the will to win are two different propositions, and it is the latter under which I am enlisted. To me it is worth fighting for to the end of time."

"Oh, you must not say these things to me," she cried fiercely, trying to escape from his eyes.

"I shall not say another word to you after to-night until I am sure I have won the victory. Then I shall ask you to be my wife. To-morrow I'll tell your brother I am bound to win. He must know my honest intentions."

"My brother!" she gasped. Her knees grew weak and a faintness assailed her heart, almost to overpowering. "You--you must not--shall not say a word to Hugh. I forbid you--I--"

"Why are you so agitated? Why am I not to speak to him? He is fair-minded, and I know he likes me."

"You don't know what it would mean to me. There is something you do not know. No, no! You shall not speak to Hugh." It was her turn to command, and he wavered.

"Your will is the law which I obey. He shall not know--not now, at least," he said. "There are to be but two factions in the struggle, then, your love against mine."

"You forget the--the other man," she said, sudden tears springing to her eyes.

"I think only of one woman," he said softly, lovingly.

She leaned wearily against the staircase, her hands clasping the railing. There was a piteous, hopeless entreaty in the dimming eyes as she turned them to his and tried to speak calmly.

"I have something to say to you--to-morrow. Let us say good-night."

"Nothing you can say will alter my love. When the storm to-night is at its worst remember that I will give my life for your sake."

She did not answer, but her hand clasped his arm impulsively. In the doorway they met Hamilton and Gregory, just from the captain, their faces white and fear-stricken. Hugh and Lady Huntingford were hurrying toward them.

CHAPTER XV
THE WRECK OF THE "TEMPEST QUEEN"

"What's wrong?" asked Veath, alarmed by the agitation of the two soldiers.

"Captain Shadburn estimates that we are two hundred miles out of our course, away to the south. It's impossible to get our bearings without the sun, and the Lord only knows where we're running to," said Hamilton, holding to the door casing.

Hugh and Lady Huntingford had joined the others by this time and were listening with blanched faces to the men in uniform.

"It's as black as ink outside," said little Lieutenant Gregory, shivering in a manner most unbecoming in a soldier. "As long as they can keep the boat out of the trough we'll ride the waves safely, but the deuced danger lies in the reefs and little islands. We may be dashing into one of them at this minute."

"You're a cheerful hero," cried Hugh indignantly. "What's the use of imagining a thing like that? It's time enough to think about it when we strike the reef; and, besides, it can't help us any to cry. We can't leave the ship for a walk back to dry land. We're here to see the thing to the end, no matter where it is, and I don't believe in howling before we're hurt."

"That's right," agreed Veath. "Possibly we're out of the course. That happens in every storm that comes up at sea."

"But there are hundreds of reefs here that are not even on the chart," cried Gregory.

"Well, there have been thousands of ships to escape them all, I fancy," said Ridgeway boldly. The two women were speechless.

"And there have been thousands of storms, too," added Veath, a sort of wild exultation ringing in his voice, plain to Grace if not to the others.

"Do not try to deceive us, gentlemen," wavered Lady Tennys. "We can be a great deal braver if we know the real situation. I know you are making light of this dreadful storm out of consideration for Miss Ridge and myself, but don't you think it would be better if we were told the worst? Women are not always the greater cowards."

"Yes, Hugh, we should know the worst," said Grace firmly. "The ship is rolling frightfully, and Lieutenant Hamilton has said enough to assure us that Captain Shadburn is alarmed, even apprehensive."

"Perhaps I am too much of an optimist, but I stick to my statement that while we are in some danger--any fool can see that--we are by no means lost," said Hugh, looking at Gregory when he used the word fool.

"As long as the engine and steering apparatus hold together the crew of the ship can pull her through," said Veath. "I have the utmost confidence in the boat and the men."

"But all the men on the ocean cannot keep her from striking an unseen rock, nor could any ship withstand such a shock," argued the young Englishwoman bravely.

"That's right, Lady Tennys," quickly cried Hamilton. "I don't say the ship will get the worst of a straight fight against the sea, but we won't stand the ghost of a chance if we strike a reef."

"The best thing we all can do is to find some place where there is not quite so much danger of having our brains dashed out against these walls. It's getting so that I can't keep my feet much longer. This is no time to be taking chances of a broken leg, or an arm or a neck, perhaps. We'll need them all if we have to swim to Hong Kong."

Despite his attempted jocularity, Ridgeway was sorely troubled. Common sense told him that they were now in a most perilous position. The dead reckoning of the captain and his chartmaster, while able to determine with a certain degree of accuracy the locality in which the ship was beating, could not possibly account for the exact position of those little islands. He began to think of the life preservers. A feeble smile came to the ladies when he spoke of swimming to Hong Kong, but the men, Veath included, looked serious.

"I think it would be wise if we make every preparation to leave the ship, awful as the prospect may seem. My judgment is that we should take time by the forelock. It will be too late after the crash comes." Veath said this solemnly, and a deeper sense of realization came to all of them. Strange to say, it inspired energy and calmness rather than weakness and panic.

"The life preservers, you mean?" almost whispered Grace. A fearful lurch of the boat caused the whole party to cling desperately to the supports. Before he could answer a ship's officer came scudding down below.

"Captain Shadburn says that every one is to prepare for the worst. The propeller's smashed and we can't live in this sea. Be quick!" cried the pale-faced sailor, hurrying onward. In an inconceivably short space of time the passages and saloons were crowded with rushing passengers. Pandemonium prevailed. Women were shrieking, men yelling and praying. Cooler heads were utterly powerless to subdue the crazy disorder. Ridgeway and Veath hurried the two women to their staterooms, plunging along, almost falling with the savage rolling of the boat.

"For God's sake, hurry!" called Hamilton from afar. "We are turning into the trough."

How our friends got into the cumbersome preservers and prepared themselves for the end they could never have told. Everything seemed a blank, the whole world whirled, all the noises in the universe rolled in their ears. Then they were stumbling, rolling, tearing toward the upper deck, hardly knowing whither they went or how they progressed. Before, behind, beside them were yelling, maddened men and women, rushing upward ruthlessly into the very waves of the ocean, all to be lost.

On the steps Hugh and Grace, who were together in advance of Veath and Lady Tennys, encountered the latter's husband. Pie had fallen, and was grovelling, cursing, screaming, praying on the steps. Hugh pulled him to his feet. With a mad yell he fled onward and upward. At the top he was checked by the sailors, who were vainly trying to keep the people back. He struggled past them and on toward the open deck. An officer caught him and held him firmly until Hugh, Veath, and the two trembling women came up.

"Get back, all of you!" yelled Shadburn. "You can't come out here. Every sailor on deck has been washed overboard!"

"Don't let us sink! Don't let us sink! For God's sake!" shrieked Lord Huntingford. Then he saw his wife. "Save me, Tennys; we are lost! We are lost!"

A great wave swept over the deck, washing all of them back into the companionway, half drowned.

"Is there any hope, Mr. Frayne?" yelled Hugh to the second officer, holding himself and his half-dead sweetheart against the leaping of the boat.

"One chance in a million! Stay back there and we'll try the boats. God knows they can't live in this sea, but they're the only hope. We'll turn clear over with the next big wave. Stay back!" he yelled. "We are trying to get the boats ready. Stay back!"

Hugh and Grace from where they clung could see the great black mountains of water rushing upon them, each wave a most terrifying spectacle. Then again the whole dark, seething ocean seemed to be below them and they were flying to the clouds. The breath of relief died instantly, for again the helpless ship sank into the trough and the foaming mountains towered about her. Grace hid her eyes and screamed with terror. Those huge murderous waves already had swept many from the ship. A score of sailors and as many courageous soldiers were in the churn of the merciless waters.

Crash! A horrid grating sound, splintering! Then the instantaneous shock, the awful, stunning force of a frightful blow and a shipful of human beings were flung violently in all directions, many never to rise again. The *Tempest Queen* had struck! The last chance was gone!

"My God!" groaned the captain. "It's all over!" Then he roared: "All hands! All hands! Stations! To the boats! Stand back there! Women first!"

Ridgeway, dimly realizing that the end had come, staggered to his feet and instinctively reached for the body of the woman who lay before him. He did not know that she was conscious, nor did he know whether the ship was afloat or sinking. A gigantic wave swept over her, tons of water pouring in upon them. Blankly he dragged her to the opening which led to the watery deck, clinging to a railing with all his might. He was gasping for breath, his life almost crushed out of his body. It required all his strength to drag the limp form safely away from the passage, through which now poured their crazed companions, rushing headlong into the sea.

"In the name of God what shall we do?" he heard a hoarse voice shout in his ear. It was Veath, also burdened with the helpless form of a woman.

"It is death here and death there. I am going to trust to the life preservers," gasped Ridgeway, as another wave struck. The constant crackling and crashing told him that the *Tempest Queen* was being ground to pieces on the rock and that she had but a few minutes to live.

"Wait, Hugh, we may get off in a boat," cried the other, but he was not heard. Hugh was in the sea!

Just as Veath began his anguished remonstrance the ship gave a tremendous lurch, an overpowering wave hurled itself upon the frail shell and Hugh Ridgeway's frenzied grasp on the rail was broken. When he saw that he was going, he threw both arms about the girl he had brought to this awful fate, and, murmuring a prayer, whirled away with the waters over the battered deck-house and into the black depths.

They shot downward into the sea and then came to the hideous surface, more dead than alive. His one thought was that nobody in the world would ever know what had become of Hugh Ridgeway and Grace Vernon.

CHAPTER XVI
THE NIGHT AND THE MORNING

Gasping for breath, blinded, terrified beyond all imagination, crying to God from his heart, Hugh gave up all hope. Fathoms of water beneath them, turbulent and gleeful in the furious dance of destruction; mountains of water above them, roaring, swishing, growling out the horrid symphony of death! High on the crest of the wave they soared, down into the chasm they fell, only to shoot upward again, whirling like feathers in the air.

Something bumped violently against Ridgeway's side, and, with the instinct of a drowning man, he grasped for the object as it rushed away. A huge section of the bowsprit was in his grasp and a cry of hope arose in his soul. With this respite came the feeling, strong and enduring, that he was not to die. That ever-existing spirit of confidence, baffled in one moment, flashes back into the hearts of all men when the faintest sign of hope appears, even though death has already begun to close his hand upon them. Nature grasps for the weakest straw and clings to life with an assurance that is sublime. The hope that comes just before the end is the strongest hope of all.

"For God's sake, be brave, darling! Cling tight and be careful when you breathe," he managed to cry in her ear. There was no answer, but he felt that she had heard.

The night was so black that he could not see the spar to which he clung. At no time could he see more than the fitful gleam of dark water as some mysterious glimmer was produced by the weird machinery of the air. He could hear the roar of the mighty waves, could feel the uplifting power and the dash downward from seemingly improbable heights, but he could not see the cauldron in which they were dancing.

It was fortunate that he could not, for a single glimpse of that sea in all its fury would have terrified him beyond control. In sheer despair he would have given up the infinitesimal claim he had for salvation and welcomed death from the smothering tons, now so bravely battled against.

The girl to whom he clung and whose rigid clasp was still about his neck had not spoken, and scarcely breathed since the plunge into the sea. At times he felt utterly alone in the darkness, so death-like was her silence. But for an occasional spasmodic indication of fear as they and their spar shot downward from some unusual elevation, he might have believed that he was drifting with a corpse.

Rolling, tossing, dragging through the billows, clinging to the friendly spar, Hugh Ridegway sped onward, his body stiff and sensationless, his brain fogged and his heart dead with that of the girl to whom he clung so desperately. At last the monstrous waves began to show their outlines to his blinding eyes. The blackness of the dome above became tinged with a discernible shade of ever-increasing brightness. A thrill shot through his fagging soul as he realized that the long night was ending and day was dawning. The sun was coming forth to show him his grave.

Slowly the brightness grew, and with it grew the most dreadful aspect that ever fell upon the eye of man--the mighty sea in all its fury. Suddenly, as he poised on the summit of a huge wave, something ahead struck him as strange. A great mass seemed to rise from the ocean far away, dim, indistinct, but still plain to the eye. With the next upward sweep he strained his eyes in the waning darkness and again saw the vast black, threatening, uneven mass.

An uncanny terror enveloped him. What could the strange thing be that appeared to be rushing toward him? As far as the eye could see on either side stretched the misty shape. The sky grew brighter, a faint glow became apparent ahead, spreading into a splendor whose perfection was soon streaked with bars of red and yellow, racing higher and higher into the dome above. His dull brain observed with wonder that the brightness grew, not out of the sea, but beyond the great object ahead, and he was more mystified than ever. The tiny, fiery beams seemed to spring from the dark, ugly, menacing cloud, or whatever it might be. Finally he realized that it was the sun coming into the heavens from the east, and--his heart roared within him as he began to grasp the truth--the great black mass was land!

"Oh, God! It is land--land!" he tried to shriek. "Grace! Grace! Lookup! See! The land!"

The arms about his neck tightened sharply and a low moan came to his ears. Slowly and painfully he turned his head to look at the face that had been so near in all those awful hours of the night, unseen. His heart seemed to stop beating with that moan, for it bore the announcement that the dear one was still alive.

It was still too dark to distinguish her features plainly. The face was wet and slimy with the salt water; her hair was matted over the forehead and wrapped in ugly strips about the once pretty face, now ghastly with the signs of suffering, fear and--yes, death, he thought, as he strove to see one familiar feature.

Into his eyes came a quizzical stare that slowly changed to an intense look of bewilderment. Gradually they grew wider with horror.

The death-like face was not that of the girl he loved!

While he gazed numbly, almost insanely, upon the closed eyelids, they slowly opened and a pair of wild, dark eyes gazed despairingly into his, expressive of timidity more than fear. The trembling lips parted, but the effort to speak ended in a moan. Again the eyes closed and her arms slipped from his neck.

Every vestige of strength left him with this startling discovery and, had his arm been anything but rigid with paralysis, she might have drifted off with the billows, a fate which her voluntary action invited.

A great wave rushed them violently forward and the next moment Ridgeway, faint, bewildered, and unable to grasp the full force of the remarkable ending to that night in the water, found himself, still grasping his limp burden and the broken spar, washed far upon the sands. A second wave swept them higher, and he realized, as he lay gasping on the edge of the waters, that the vast ocean was behind him and the beautiful woman he had rescued by mistake.

CHAPTER XVII
WAS THE SEA KIND?

He lost consciousness in the attempt to drag himself and his companion farther up the beach. His arms and legs refused to move in response to his efforts, and the last he remembered was that his body was stiff and he was absolutely powerless. When he again opened his eyes he was lying on a grassy sward with spreading green branches above him. For some minutes he lay perfectly still, dimly sensible that he was alive, but utterly unable to fix his whereabouts. Through his brain there still roared the awful waves; in his eyes there still lingered the vision of the sea as it was when dawn first developed the picture.

Fearing that he could not lift his head, he rose to his trembling elbow. His wide eyes swept the view before him. There was the sea not two hundred yards down the slope, rushing and booming upon the stretch of sand which reached within fifty feet of his grassy bed. Behind him grew a forest of queer, tropical trees, the like of which he never had seen before. His jacket had been rolled up as a pillow for his head; his shoes and stockings were off, his shirt bosom unbuttoned. Two soggy life preservers lay near by.

At last he caught sight of a woman, alone, forlorn, the picture of despondency. Far down the beach to his right there rose a rugged, stony formation, extending into the sea and rising several hundred feet in the air. At the base of this rocky promontory a multitude of great boulders lay scattered, some quite large and jagged, others insignificant in size.

Upon one of the smaller stones, well up the slope, sat the figure of the woman he had drugged from the sea and whom he had hated with his last conscious breath. Her head was lying against the sheer wall that ran up alongside, and he could tell that she was staring out toward the sea, which roared against the rocks so close by that the spray must have reached her feet. The distance to this rock was fully three hundred yards. There was a fascination about her loneliness that held him immovable for a long time. Finally he struggled to a sitting posture, faint and dizzy. At the same moment she slowly turned her head and looked in his direction. Half rising, she made a movement as if to come toward him, first peering intently. Then she sank back upon the rock and sent her gaze out to the sea again.

With all the haste he could command he scrambled eagerly toward the rocks, carrying the crumpled jacket in his hand. Not once did she take her eyes from the breakers. Tired and faint, he at last came to the edge of the rocky pile. Here his strength failed him and he sank trembling with exhaustion upon the first friendly stone, still a hundred feet from where she sat. In his bitter rage against her he strove to shout, but the effort was little more than a hoarse whisper. Lying there impotently, he studied her attitude as the minutes crept by, and there came at last into his heart a touch of pity that swelled with the sight of her.

Pain-racked but determined, he again started toward the elevation, crawling over and around the boulders that intervened. He was within five feet of her before he spoke, and then not until he had studied her face for some moments, steadying himself against a large rock. She was more beautiful than ever with her black hair awry and matted, brushed away from the pure white face and fastened recklessly with the shell combs she had worn on board the *Tempest Queen*. Her blue eyes looked mournfully from beneath their long lashes. The slender white hands lay listlessly in the lap of the once white dress, now water-stained, wrinkled and shapeless. In spite of all that dreadful buffeting by the wind and water she was still the beautiful creation of nature he had found so charming in a realm where nature seldom presents herself.

"Lady Tennys," he called hoarsely. "You do not know how I thank God you are alive."

She turned slowly, as if she had known all along of his tortuous approach. Her voice was low and thrilling.

**"'LADY TENNYS, ... YOU DO NOT KNOW HOW
I THANK GOD YOU ARE ALIVE'"**

"I prayed for hours, it seemed, after we were dashed upon this shore, that you might live and that I might die. The knowledge that you saved me through mistake, that you were battling so long and so bravely all through the night for the one you cherished more than all in the world, made me pray from the first that I could be dead before you discovered the horrid error. You picked me up when the crash came and I was too terrified to even think of crying aloud in protest. Then we were in that awful, awful water. It was not until hours afterward that I felt we might escape find that I should have to face your grief." He reached up and clasped her hand.

"Don't--don't talk like that now," he groaned. "I hated you this morning, but--God, it is a relief to have you here to share all this with me. God threw us into the sea and He has saved us. I would to God I could have gone down with--with her, but--but--" and he broke down, his head falling upon his outstretched arms at her feet. A deep sob from Lady Tennys caused him to lift his haggard eyes to hers. "It would have been so much better than to live without her," he cried.

"Why did you not let me go when you found who I was?" she cried almost fiercely. "I wanted to drown, I was hungry to go to the bottom, to be washed away to the end of the ocean, anywhere but here with you when you thought you were saving her. You had forgotten that I existed until that awful moment in the breakers. I heard her cry out to you as we went overboard. All through the night I heard that cry of 'Hugh! Hugh!' It was worse than the worst of deaths!"

At the mention of Grace's piteous cry, even though heard in imagination, Hugh sank limply to the rock, his mouth falling open and his eyes bulging forth in agony. Every drop of blood in his veins seemed frozen with the realization that he had deserted her in that hour when she had most needed him, that he had left her to go down to death without being by her side, that she had cried out to him for help,--had reached out to him in agony. Crazed by a sudden impulse, he sprang to his feet and glared out over the tumbling waves,--ever moving mountains that reached as far as the eye could see. She arose also, trembling and alarmed.

"Where is she? Where is she?" he cried fiercely. "My God! Look at that water! Grace, Grace! My darling, how could I have left you alone to die in that hell of water! Let me come to you now, dearest. I will save you. I will come! Hugh is coming, dearest! Look! She must be out there somewhere. I can reach her if I try. I must go!"

Insane with despair, he leaped to his feet and would have dashed down the steep into the death-dealing breakers had not his companion, with a sharp cry, clutched his arm. He turned fiercely, ready to strike her in his frenzy. His glaring eyes met hers, sweet, wide, and imploring, and their influence told at once upon him. A rush of quiet almost benumbed him, so immediate was the reaction from violence to submission.

"You must not do that!" she cried in horror.

"Let me save her, for God's sake. I cannot leave her to the sea."

"Be calm!" she wailed. "Hours ago I would have leaped into the sea myself, but the thought came to me that she may not be lost after all. There is something for you to live for."

"There is nothing. She is lost," he cried.

"As I stood here, I wondered if she might not have been saved as miraculously as we. Wonder grew into hope and hope took the shape of possibility. Hugh, she may be alive and as safe as we!"

His eyes brightened like a flash; his breath came quickly; he tried to speak, but could not for the joy of hope.

"The hope that she may have been saved and may yet be given back to you kept me from ending the life that did not belong to me, but to her. Hugh Ridgeway, I have spent a thousand years on these rocks, trying to find courage to live. But for me she would be standing here with you. You would have saved her had I not been in the way last night," she whispered. He could see that she suffered, but he was again blind to everything but his own great despair.

"Yes," he cried savagely, "but for you I would have saved her. Oh, I could curse you--curse you!" She shrank back with a low moan, covering her eyes with her hands.

"Don't say that!" she murmured piteously. "I would to God I could have gone down with the ship." His eyes softened and a wave of remorse swept over him.

"Forgive me," he groaned, "I am mad or I could not have said that to you. I did not mean it." He placed his hand on hers, clasping the fingers firmly. "Forget that I spoke so cruelly. I devoutly thank God that your life was spared. We both loved the one who was left behind."

She glanced down at his face doubtingly, unbelievingly, at first. Then a gleam of joy flooded her tired eyes, illumined her face. Sinking down beside him, she placed her head upon his shoulder and wept softly. He did not move from his position on the rock below. His heart was full of tenderness for the living and grief for the dead. His eyes stared out over the sea wistfully.

"I cannot look at that water!" he suddenly shrieked, drawing back in abject terror. "It is horrible! Horrible!"

He left her side and dashed madly away, strength having come with sudden abhorrence. She looked after him in alarm, her eyes wide with the fear that he was bereft of reason. Down the rocks and up the beach he fled, disappearing among the strangely shaped trees and underbrush that marked the outskirts of the jungle. Again she leaned back against the rock and looked at the unfriendly billows beyond, a feeling that she sat deserted forever on that barren shore plunging her soul into the very lowest pits of wretchedness.

Hours afterward he crept painfully from the cool, lonely jungle into the bright glare of the beach,--calmer, more rational, cursing no more. A shudder swept over him, a chill penetrated to the marrow of his bones as he looked again upon the sea. His eyes sought the rocks upon which he had left her; his heart was full of an eagerness to comfort her and be comforted in return.

She still sat upon the rock and he hurried toward her. As on his first approach, she did not move. When he drew quite close, he discovered that she was lying limply back against the supporting boulder. The fear that she was dead and that he was left alone almost struck him to the ground. He reached her side, pale and panting, and then breathed a prayer of rejoicing.

Lady Tennys, her dark lashes resting tranquilly upon her cheek, was lying easily against the staunch old rock, fast asleep.

CHAPTER XVIII
THE WONDERFUL LAND

He did not arouse her at once, but sat below her, looking at her sweet, tired face, peaceful in the slumber that had been so long in coming, wondering what her dreams could be. Far down the shore, near the tree under which he had found himself and to whose shelter she had dragged him,--something told him vaguely,--was the spar that had ridden the waves with them the night before. Long, white and gleaming it lay in the waning sunlight. The sight of it filled him with an enthusiasm he never had known before. His heart swelled with homage to the strong, sturdy piece of timber. It was like a living object to him now, a friend to whom he felt like talking, to whom he could turn for proof positive of an unparalleled experience on the deep.

His eyes grew sad and gloomy as he turned toward the setting king of day. In his imagination, the *Tempest Queen*, with all on board, went down precisely at the point chosen by the sun for his disappearance.

Night coming! Where were they? Upon an unknown shore, Heaven alone knowing how far from habitation, from all shelter save the tree-tops, from all means of sustenance. Night coming! Behind them the mysterious jungle, before them the devil-brewed ocean.

A chilly perspiration broke out over him; a fear even worse than that of the night before attacked him. How far were they from human habitation? What manner of people dwelt in this land? As these thoughts tumbled about in his brain, suddenly came the implacable desire for water. It seemed days since he had tasted it. Like a flash, nature began its demands, and he was almost overcome by the prospect of night on the rocks with no possible hope to find the food and water now so necessary.

Lady Tennys slept on, untouched by the calamities that beset him, her breast rising full and regularly. As he looked upon her lovely face the spirit of chivalry returned. She had thought of him in his unconsciousness and she had been brave and true. Bound by a new determination to find food and water for her and to provide other shelter than the draughty crannies among the rocks, he painfully started up the slope toward the edge of the forest. Soon he stood upon the broad, smooth plateau, looking into the green, sunless depths.

Behind him lay the beach and the fringe of the jungle; to seaward rose the rocky point full two hundred feet higher than the spot on which he stood, panting for breath; to his right, descending gradually, ran the lofty hill to a place, not more than a quarter of a mile away, where it merged into the forest. The ridge on which he stood was not more than one hundred feet wide, a flat, narrow, sloping table. Filled with curiosity, he strode to the opposite side and found himself upon the edge of a sharp decline, almost perpendicular in its fall to the valley below, which was apparently lower than the beach from which he had come.

As far as the eye could reach inland there was a mass of bright green trees, luxuriant and beautiful. Below him was water, a natural harbor of tiny dimensions, running back from the sea which lay off to the far right as he faced the head of this peculiar elevation. Plain to his eye was the contour of this great rock. It resembled the letter L. Along the sea line it stretched high and ugly for nearly a mile, a solid wall, he imagined, some three hundred feet above the water, narrow at the top, like a great backbone. The little cove below him was perhaps a mile across. The opposite shore was low and verdure-clad. The rocky eminence that formed the wall on two sides was the only high ground to be seen for miles around.

Down the slope he sped, dusky shadows beginning to tell of the coming night. His feet finally touched upon the grass-covered soil; he was off the barren rock and at the edge of the dismal forest. Without a quiver he hurried under the great leaves and among the trees. The ground sloped gently downward to the now invisible harbor. He turned in that direction. Monkeys chattered in the trees and strange birds hurtled through the dense growth. His foot struck against a queer green object and an instant later he gave a shout of joy. It was a cocoanut, green and smooth.

Food! In an instant he realized that he had found something that could appease the cravings of hunger for the time being, at least. He searched eagerly, feverishly in the matted grass, and soon had a dozen great nuts piled at the edge of the wood. Then he renewed his search for the water that must keep life in their famished bodies.

The lapping of waves grew louder as he pushed his way through the trees, and a moment later he narrowly escaped plunging into the waters of the shimmering little bay. The coast was semicircular in shape, rising high and black to his left, running low and green to his right. Not one hundred feet to the left were the first signs of the rocky promontory, small, jagged boulders standing like a picket line before the grout mass beyond. Along the rocky side of the wall, sonic distance away, he saw an overhanging shelf of dark gray stone, protruding over the natural floor beneath. An inky darkness back of the projection impressed him with the idea that a cave lay beyond.

At his feet trickled a little stream of clear, sparkling water, coming from the crevasse above, the headquarters of a spring. He fell upon his knees and plunged his hot face into the cool water, swallowing great gulps.

When he arose to his feet everything looked brighter, fairer, happier. The scene, gorgeous a few moments before, was now more than that to his revived senses. A desire to shout jubilantly came over him. With an exultation that he could scarcely control he dashed on up the sand-strewn ledge toward the awning-like rock.

He found that a roomy cave ran back into the hill a dozen feet or more. Its floor was covered with fine white sand, thrown up from the beach during the wind storms, and it was a most perfect shelter,--this hole fifty feet above the placid waters.

Darkness was coming, so he ran back to the little rivulet. In a broken cocoanut shell he secured some fresh water and began his journey to the other side of the ridge. The sun was down to the level of the sea when he came from the rocks and within sight of the spot where he had left his fair companion.

She was not there!

A great trembling fear assailed him and he sank back with a groan of despair. Then he heard his name called faintly and piteously.

"Here I am!" he cried. "Where are you?" A glad cry arose from below, and he saw her coming rapidly from the small boulders near the water, some distance to the left. He hurried to meet her.

"Oh, I thought you had left me to die up there," she gasped as they drew near to each other. "Mr. Ridgeway--Hugh, I am so glad you have come."

"You were asleep when I came back an hour ago. See? I have found water. Drink!" With one hand he reached down and took hers, eagerly upstretched, drawing her to the rock on which he stood. She gulped the contents of the shell with the haste of one half famished.

"How good!" she cried, with eyes sparkling as she took the empty shell from her moist lips. "I was so thirsty that I tried to drink that bitter stuff down there. How horrible it must be to die of thirst. Can we find food, Hugh? Is there nothing to eat? I am so hungry, so hungry." The sparkle faded from her eyes and a look of pain filled them.

"I have found cocoanuts on the other side of the hill. We can make them serve until I have a chance to look farther. Come. We must hurry, or the night will make it impossible for us to cross this hill and find the cave."

"Cave?"

"A wonderful shelter for the night. Can you walk that far? It will not be difficult after we reach the top of this little mountain."

Together they began the tortuous ascent, following as closely as possible the course he had taken. They were scarcely able to stand when they at last reached the top. Neither saw the beauty in the view, so eager were they to find rest and nourishment. As they passed painfully down the slope, he told her of the monkeys, the nuts, the cave, the rivulet, and the splendor of the scene, cheering her lagging spirits with what animation he could assume. A few chattering monkeys welcomed them to the woodland, and she was momentarily aroused to interest in her surroundings, uttering little cries of delight. They came to the pile of nuts, and he took up several in his free arm. The cave was reached at last and both sank exhausted to the white sand. It was now so dark that the stars were gathering above them and objects were indistinct to the vision.

"Thank God!" he exclaimed, lying flat on his back, his arms outstretched.

"I am so tired," she murmured, her head drooping against the wall as she seated herself near the opening. After many minutes he began the task of opening the cocoanuts.

"To-morrow I shall go hunting for something more substantial than these nuts. There must be fruit, berries and vegetables of some kind in the forest," said he.

"How are we to get away from here, Hugh?" she asked. "Where are we? This may be an uninhabited island, and we may have to stay here all of our lives." There was an awe in her voice, and he could imagine that the prospect brought horror to her face. By this time it was almost pitch dark.

"Have I not found food, water and shelter within an hour's time? Can good fortune end with this? Let us sleep peacefully to-night and hope for the best with to-morrow's developments."

"Sleep? Where are we to sleep?"

"In this cave and upon the sand. There is no other place. It is safe, Lady Tennys, and you are to have my coat as a pillow for that tired little head of yours." With this he arose and threw off his coat despite her protests, rolling it into a compact little bundle. Placing this improvised pillow on the sand near the rear of the cave, he said:

"There is your bed, my Lady. It is the very best in the hotel."

"You are so good to me, Hugh,--much better than I thought you could be after--after--"

"Please don't say what you started to say," he interrupted, his voice breaking suddenly. He stood with his shoulder against one of the outer corners of the cave, she sitting quietly behind him. At last he went on, as if the thought came slowly, "Lady Huntingford, forgive my selfishness. I have been bewailing my own misfortune in a most unmanly way, while you have borne your loss bravely, thinking only to comfort me. Forgive me."

"My loss?" she asked in wonder.

"Lord Huntingford," he said gently.

"Oh!" she exclaimed, starting sharply. "Lord--Lord Huntingford! Oh, Hugh, I had forgotten--I had not thought--," but she did not complete the bewildered speech. He could have believed that she did not breathe during the next few moments as she stood there, straight and rigid, clasping his arm convulsively. Then she turned away and walked quickly to the bed on the sand, lying down without a word. He could distinguish nothing of her person save certain outlines in the darkness, and although he listened intently, he heard no sob, no sigh.

Soon his eyes grew heavy and he felt the overpowering force of sleep upon him. Removing his waistcoat, he went to the other side of the cave and prepared to stretch himself out for rest. He paused and listened for a sound from her. None came, so in some trepidation he stepped nearer. Soft, regular breathing, deep and full, told him that she was asleep. In considerable wonder he went back to his hard bed. Out of the confusion of thoughts and impressions that followed her surprising admission, came at last the dim, sleepy understanding of the situation.

She had not thought of Lord Huntingford until he mentioned the old nobleman's name.

With the last faint whirl of wakefulness came the suggestion of roaming wild beasts, creeping up to attack them in the night, but sleep greedily swallowed the half-formed fear.

CHAPTER XIX
THE FIRST DAY IN THE WILDS

The sun was up hours before Ridgeway stretched his stiff arms, blinked his sleepy eyes and peered wonderingly about his strange apartment. Another and more rapid glance failed to reveal Lady Tennys. His jacket was still there, and a round depression showed that her head had rested upon it all night. The packed sand denoted the once present body of the sleeper.

"Good-morning," came a sweet, clear voice from somewhere.

"Hello! Where are you?" he called, greatly relieved.

"In the kitchen, of course, getting breakfast for you. The kitchen is down at the spring, you know. Come down."

He hurried down the path, and found her standing beside the bounding little stream. Her wavy black hair was no longer matted and wild, for, with the water in the cove as a mirror and her big hair comb as the necessary toilet article, she had "done it up" in quite a presentable fashion. Her face was bright and pure in its freshness, her hands were white and immaculately clean; her eyes sparkled with a deeper, clearer blue than ever. She wore an air of resolute confidence in herself.

"I have been up for two hours or more. See how nice and clean I am. Go down there and wash your hands and face and I will comb your hair." She produced an improvised clothes broom, a stout leafy branch from a cocoanut-tree, and swished the sand from his clothing as he turned about for her obediently.

"These clothes of mine are full of sand and scum from the sea, but before the day is over I intend to give them a good scrubbing and drying. Then I'll feel like a new man. But wait! This may be Sunday, not Monday. Can't wash on Sunday, can I? Let's see, the wreck was on Thursday night, yesterday was Friday and--"

"And to-day is Saturday naturally. We must have clean clothes for Sunday. Our parlor, kitchen, and laundry are in the same room, it would seem. Here's a pile of cocoanuts I collected while you slept, and there are some plums or fruit of some kind. They grow back there in the wood a short distance. I saw some gorgeous birds out there, and they were eating the fruit, so it must be wholesome. And those dear, saucy little monkeys! I could watch them for hours."

"Did you run across any boa constrictors or anacondas?" asked he serenely.

"Good Heavens! I never thought of snakes. There may be dreadful serpents in that forest, Hugh." Her eyes were full of alarm.

"I merely asked your Ladyship in order to keep the cook in her kitchen," laughed he.

"An afternoon out is not a luxury in this land, even for the most cooped up of cooks. Snakes! Ugh!" Hugh thought she shuddered very prettily.

"Breakfast will be cold if I don't hurry," he observed. He made his way around the rocky bend to the point where the rivulet emptied into the cove. When he returned to the shady spot he was put to work opening cocoanuts and pouring the milk into the shells of others. She had cleaned the flat surface of a large rock which stood well out from the lower edge of the cliff, and signified her intention to use it as a dining table. He became enthusiastic and, by the exertion of all the strength he could muster, succeeded in rolling two boulders down the incline, placing them in position as stools beside the queer table. Then they stood off and laughed at the remarkable set of furniture.

"I wonder what time it is?" she said as they began to eat. He pulled his forgotten repeater from his watch pocket and opened it with considerable apprehension. It was not running, nor did it appear as if it would ever be of service again.

"How are we ever to know the time of day?" she cried.

"I'll try to fix it. It is only water-clogged. My little compass on the charm is all right and it will give us our bearings, north and south, so that I can get the time by the sun. I'll drive a little stake out there on the level, and when the shadow is precisely north and south, then it is noon. It's all very simple, Lady Tennyson."

"I'm only the cook, Hugh. Won't you please call me Tennys?"

"Thank you; it's such a waste of time to say Lady Tennyson. Shall I order dinner, cook?"

"We'll have a ten-course dinner, sir, of cocoanuts and plums, sir, if you please, sir."

"Breakfast warmed over, I see," he murmured, gazing resignedly toward the trees. Later on he managed to get some life into his watch and eventually it gave promise of faithful work. He set the hands at twelve o'clock. It was broiling hot by this time, and he was thoughtful enough to construct a poke-bonnet for her, utilizing a huge palm leaf. Proudly he placed the green protector upon her black hair. Then, looking into her smiling eyes, he tied the grass cord under her up-tilted chin.

"Perfect!" she cried, with genuine pleasure. "You must make another for yourself." Whether he took it as a command or as a request matters not. Suffice it to say, he soon produced another palm-leaf hat, and she tied it under his chin a great deal more deftly than he had performed the same service for her, consequently with a speed that disappointed him.

He decided to make a short tour of the wood during the afternoon. At first he argued it would be wise to walk far down the coast, in the hope of finding a village of some description along the water front. Then he decided that a trip to the north, through the wood, would be better, as the lower coast could be surveyed from the summit of the great rock.

"You are not afraid to stay here alone for a couple of hours, are you, Tennys?" he asked, discerning solicitude in her face.

"I am not afraid for myself, but for you. You must be very careful, Hugh, and come back to me safely. What can I do? What shall I do if you never come back?" she cried.

"Nothing can happen to me--nothing in the world. See, it's nearly one o'clock now. I'll be back by five. And I'll be careful, so do not be troubled. We must find the way out of this wilderness. Be brave and I'll soon be with you again."

He was soon in the depths of the forest, skirting the little bay toward the north. She stood beside their stone festal board, watching him through uneasy eyes till he disappeared completely from view. A sense of loneliness so overpowering that it almost crushed her fell upon this frail, tender woman as she stood there on the edge of the South Sea jungle, the boundless sea at her back. The luxuries and joys of a life to which she had been accustomed came up in a great flash before her memory's eye, almost maddening in their seductiveness. She glanced at the dress she wore, and a faint, weary smile came to her eyes and lips. Instead of the white, perfect yachting costume, she saw the wretched, shrunken, stained, shapeless garment that to her eyes would have looked appalling on the frame of a mendicant. Her costly shoes, once small and exquisitely moulded to her aristocratic feet, were now soiled and ugly.

From the palace to the jungle! From the wealth of fashion to the poverty of nature! From the scores of titled admirers to the single brave American who shared life with her on the bleak rock, mourning for a love that might never be restored by the unkind depths. A vision of yesterday and to-day! Turning to the sea, she breathed a prayer for the salvation of Grace Vernon, her eyes dimming as she thought of the blithe, cheery girl who had become so dear to her, and who was all the world to Hugh Ridgeway.

Her thoughts went then to Lord Huntingford, her husband. There was scant regret in her heart over the fate of the old nobleman. She was not cruel enough to rejoice, but there was a certain feeling of relief which she could not quell, try as she would, in the belief that he had gone down to death and a younger, nobler man spared. The last she saw of her husband was when he broke past the officers and plunged out upon the deck, leaving her to her fate. That he had been instantly swept overboard she had no doubt. All she could remember of her thoughts at that thrilling moment was the brief, womanly cry for mercy to his soul. After that came the lurch which prostrated her, and then Ridgeway's cry, "Be brave, dearest!"

Bitter tears streamed down her cheeks as she thought of the strong-hearted Veath and the forsaken American girl--and all of the others in that merry company. It was not in such anguish as this that she summed up her individual loss.

Ridgeway was soon in the thick of the jungle. For two or three hours he plunged through beautiful glades, over swelling knolls, across tiny streams, but always through a waste of nature that, to all appearance, had never been touched by a human being save himself.

At last he dropped wearily upon a grassy mound and resigned himself to the conviction that they had been swept upon an absolutely unexplored, perhaps undiscovered, portion of the globe. It did not occur to his discouraged mind that he had covered less than five miles of what might be a comparatively small piece of uninhabited land and that somewhere not far distant lay the civilization for which he sought. His despairing mind magnified the horrors of their position to such an extent that he actually wondered how long it would be before death broke down their feeble resistance. Arising despondently, he turned his steps in the direction of the little cave.

It was not long before he reached a small sandy stretch about five hundred yards from the spot where he had left Lady Tennys. Little waves licked the short strip of sand lazily, seeming to invite him down to meet them on their approach from the big sea whose tidings of woe they bore. High, dark and ominous loomed the great rock on the south. He could not see the cave or the rivulet on account of obstructing trees and a curve in the shore, so he walked down to the very edge of the water, expecting to obtain a view from that point.

A startling discovery flashed upon him as he strode upon the beach. There, in the white, soft sand were plainly revealed the footprints of a bare human foot. He rubbed his eyes and gazed again. Before him were a number of small footprints, running to and from the water. In a dazed, wondering way he sought to follow them, eventually finding where a single line of tracks led directly toward a clump of trees to his left. At the edge of this he found a confusion of bewildering barefoot moulds, mixed with others unquestionably made by a shoe on the foot of a civilized person. Hurrying through the trees, fearful that savages had attacked Lady Tennys at this place, he was suddenly confronted by a spectacle that made him gasp. Down at the water's edge, over near the place where he had left her, he saw white garments spread upon the rocks. She was nowhere to be seen. Like a flash the truth came to him, and he looked at his watch in consternation. It was but three-thirty o'clock. He had told her he would be away until five or after.

Turning about, he dashed back into the depths of the wood. It was after five when he again approached the rendezvous, carrying a quantity of plums and other fruits and a number of gaudy feathers that he had found. Away back in the wood he began to shout to her, long before he was in sight of the hill. She answered cheerily, venturing into the wood to meet him. Her clothes were white, clean, even shapely.

CHAPTER XX
THE SIGN OF DISTRESS

The next morning before she was awake he arose and made a tour of the beach in quest of shell fish, took a plunge in the cool waters of the bay, and again inspected the little footprints in the sand. He smiled as he placed his own foot, a number nine, beside the dainty imprint. On his way back to the cave he killed a huge turtle, the meat of which he promised should keep them alive for several days, if nothing better could be found. As he turned the bend he saw her standing on the ledge at the mouth of the cave, the wind blowing her hair and skirts freely. He called to her, and she turned her face eagerly in his direction. They met among the trees some distance from the spring.

"Where have you been?" she cried, her cheeks glowing.

"Hunting wild beasts," he replied valiantly.

"Pooh! Wild flowers, you mean. I thought perhaps you had gone off to join the monkeys for an old-time frolic in the trees."

"You won't be so frivolous when I tell you of the narrow escape I have had. See that trusty club? See the blood on it?" They were standing close to each other as he held up the blood-spattered stick.

"Oh, Hugh," she gasped, "is it blood?"

"Life's blood," he answered laconically.

"Not yours, Hugh? You are not hurt?" she cried.

"This is the beast's blood, Tennys. I am not so much as scratched, but it was a frightful encounter," he went on, with well-assumed gravity.

"Tell me about it. Where was it? What was it? Tell me everything," she begged. He took her arm and together they proceeded toward their wild home.

"After breakfast I'll take you around the bend and prove to you my valor."

"But I cannot wait and, besides, you have proved your valor. Do tell me where the blood came from."

"That awful thing plunged from the underbrush upon me so suddenly that I was almost paralyzed," he said soberly. "I didn't have much time to think, and I don't know what I should have done if it had not been for this excellent club, which I had cut for a rather inglorious purpose. With one of the very best strokes a golfer ever made I cracked his skull."

"His skull!"

"Likewise his neck. Then I cut his throat."

"Oh, Hugh!" breathlessly.

"And I'm going back after breakfast to carve him up into roasts, steaks and soups enough to last us for a month."

"Oh, it must have been something gigantic. Was it a rhinoceros?" she cried ecstatically.

"Rhinoceros soup!" he exclaimed in disgust. She was properly contrite. "I'll tell you what I killed, if you'll promise to endure the shock--and not tell any one else." He placed his lips close to her little ear and whispered in awe-struck tones, "A turtle!"

"A turtle! Why, a baby could kill a turtle. You are no longer a hero. Enough to last a month! Hugh Ridgeway, are you delirious?" she exclaimed in fine scorn.

"Wait till you see him. He weighs a ton," he said proudly.

After their breakfast of nuts, fruit and water they started for the little beach, Lady Tennys vastly excited. Her exclamations on seeing the sea monster amused Hugh beyond measure.

"I never dreamed a turtle could be so immense," she cried. "This one must be a thousand years old."

"If he is, we'll have tough steaks," observed he grimly. Later on he carved several fine steaks from the turtle and cleaned the upper shell carefully, wisely concluding to retain it for the usefulness it was sure to afford sooner or later. "There is one thing to be done," said he, when they sat down to rest. "I must climb up that mountain and plant a white flag to show that we are here if a ship should pass. I'll do that as soon as I have rested, provided I can find anything white that is large enough to be seen from a distance."

She looked far out over the harbor for a minute, a tinge of red running to her ears.

"A handkerchief would be too small, wouldn't it?" she asked.

"I'm afraid so," he answered glumly.

Soon afterward she left him and went to the cave, bidding him to await her return. When she came back she carried in her hand a broad piece of white cloth, which she laid before him on the grass. There was a look of modest reluctance in her eyes when he glanced quickly up at them. A cherished underskirt, ripped ruthlessly from waistband to ruffle, making one broad white flag of the finest texture, was her offering.

"Use that, Hugh." She could not resist smiling as she pointed to it.

"It will be the very thing," he said, arising and taking the garment from the ground somewhat carefully.

"It won't hurt you," she said, laughing frankly; whereupon he waved it rudely above his head and pointed to the pinnacle of the rock.

"With this I shall scale the rock and skirt the bay!"

Within ten minutes he was on his way up the incline, carrying his stout stick in his hand, another heavier and stronger one being bound to his back with the white signal attached. She accompanied him to the point where the ascent became difficult and full of danger.

"Be careful, Hugh," she said; "it looks so dangerous. If you find there is any possibility of falling, don't attempt to go to the top. You are so daring, you Americans, that you do not recognize peril at all Promise me, or I shall not allow you to go on."

He looked down into her serious upturned eyes and promised. Then he resumed the ascent, with a queer flutter of adulation in his heart.

From time to time he paused to rest. In each instance he looked below, waving his hand encouragingly to the anxious one who watched him so closely. On, over fierce crags, around grim towers, along steep walls, higher and higher he crawled. Twice he slipped and fell back several feet. When he glanced down, cold perspiration standing on his forehead, he saw her bending with averted face, her hands pressed to her eyes as if she expected his body to come crashing to her feet. With recovered energy he shouted to her, and the quick, glad glance upward was enough to make the remainder of the ascent glorious to him. At last, his hands and knees bleeding, he crawled upon the small, flat top of the mountain, five hundred feet above the breakers, three hundred feet above the woman he had left behind.

The sea wind whistled in his ears as he arose to his feet. His knees trembled and he grew momentarily dizzy as he looked out over the vast, blue plain before him. Fear seized upon him; there came a wild desire to plant his flag and hurry from the death-like summit. Sitting down, he nervously unfastened the pole and flag, looking about as he did so for a place to plant the beacon. For one moment his heart sank only to bound with joy in the next. Almost at his elbow ran a crevasse in the rock, deep and narrow. It was but an instant's work to jam the pole into this crevasse, and the white flag was fluttering to the breeze. He was certain it would be days before the winds could whip it to shreds.

A feeling of helplessness and dismay came over him as he gave thought to the descent. In his eagerness to begin the hazardous attempt, he almost forgot the chief object of his climb to the top--the survey of the surrounding country. As far as he could see there stretched the carpet of forest land, the streak of beach and the expanse of water. In the view there was not one atom of proof that humanity existed within a radius of many miles. Growing calmer, he scanned the wonderful scene closely, intently, hoping to discover the faintest trace of aught save vegetable life, all without reward. He was about to begin the descent when a faint cry came to him from far below. Clinging to the edge of the topmost rock, he looked downward.

Lady Tennys was pointing excitedly toward the little bay on his left. A single glance in that direction filled him with amazement, then consternation. Recklessly he entered upon the descent. Obstacles that had seemed impassable as he thought of them on the summit were passed safely and hurriedly.

How he reached her side so quickly, he could not have explained if he tried, but in less than five minutes he stood with her, clasping her hand and looking anxiously toward the sands on which the great back of the turtle lay upward to the sun.

CHAPTER XXI
GODS FROM THE SEA

Drawn up to the beach were three long canoes, near which were nearly a score of brown-skinned, almost wholly naked savages, with spears, shields and war clubs. They were excitedly inspecting the footprints in the sand. Hugh and Lady Tennys looked down upon this startling picture in speechless concern.

"Where did they come from?" whispered he.

"I did not see them until they were beaching the boats," replied his white-faced companion. "Do you think they have seen us?"

"Hardly, but they will begin a search at once. See, they are now starting to follow those tracks. By Heaven, they'll find us, and what chance have we against them? Good Lord, this pocket knife is worse than nothing. We must hide,--and quickly, too."

"Where can we go, Hugh? Where can we go?" she cried, panic-stricken.

"We must climb up among the crags and lie down. They can't see us there, and they certainly can't track us over that stone plateau. Quick! We have no time to lose."

He fairly pushed her ahead of him, up to the row, of sharp, jutting stones. In an instant they were completely obscured from view.

"I'd rather leap off this rock into the sea than be captured by those horrible things," she half sobbed. "Hugh, do you think they would eat us?"

"The Lord knows. I can see them down there holding a consultation. Move over here and you can see the whole valley. Don't be afraid; they can't see us." She moved over timidly. Crouching side by side they watched the operations below. The visitors, evidently mystified by the footprints, were huddled together, gesticulating wildly. They ran hither and thither like so many ants, minutely examining the mysterious tracks. After a long time Hugh gave vent to an exclamation.

"By George! I know what's the matter. They can't understand the prints of our shoes. Our naked footprints are clear enough to them, but I'll bet my soul they've never seen an impression made by a shoe. They are your and my footprints, you know, with and without shoes."

"Mine? Why, Hugh Ridgeway, I--never--oh, I never thought!" she exclaimed, deeply embarrassed after her first expression of wonder and incredulity. Then she leaned forward and strained her eyes as if expecting to see the slender little bottoms of her feet in the tell-tale sand. At that moment the brown band divided into squads, a half dozen coming toward the mountain, the others remaining with the boats.

"They are after us, Tennys. I have no weapon but this club, but I will use it as long as I can stand. I'll protect you to the last. If they kill me, the only thing left for you to do is to crawl to the ledge over there and jump off. We must not be taken."

She felt a strange sense of confidence and security in the broad back of the man beside her. His jaw was set. His cheeks pale, his eyes burning with the intensity that thrilled his whole being. The strong white hand clutched the club fiercely. He was no longer the light-hearted, inconsequent youth she had known on board the ship.

The brown figures came into sight again, flitting here and there, pausing in wonder beside the stone table, inspecting the cracked nuts critically, and closely examining the ground on all sides. At last four or five of them sped up the ledge to the cave.

"They have found our hotel," said Hugh grimly. She gulped and could do no more than nod.

A tall fellow with a long spear and a huge shield, stripped to the loins, about which was a white cloth, ventured up the slope. Suddenly he halted and called his companions to his side. He had found a footprint in a bit of sand on the rocky surface. Without more ado the squad scattered and began the ascent, each man eyeing the ground eagerly. Occasionally those nearest the centre would pause and point to a track. "The good Lord help us!" murmured Ridgeway.

Both were fascinated by the approach of the savages. It was not until they were within a hundred feet of them that Hugh bethought himself and drew her back, entirely out of sight. At least, he thought she could not be seen, but he was mistaken. A portion of her white dress protruded, and a triumphant yell announced the fact that it had met the eyes of a searcher. Wondering what had caused the sudden yell, Hugh peered around the corner of the rock, and to his dismay found the whole band staring at their hiding place.

"They have seen us," he cried. "Remember, Tennys, what I told you. It's probably a case of fight on my part. Let 'em come, spears and all!" He stood erect, his eyes flashing with excitement and eagerness. Taking a few steps to one side, he stood in full view of the searchers, glaring down upon them defiantly, his club in his rigid right hand. He expected a shower of spears. To his utter amazement, however, the fierce-looking warriors, open mouthed and apparently terror-stricken, slunk backward, huddling together, all the time staring at him with bulging eyes. His first thought was that they were surprised to find him so bold, but the next act on their part caused him to gasp with wonder.

With one accord the entire band cast weapons aside and fell face downward, beating their heads against the rock, just as he had seen Arabians and Nubians perform in saluting some mighty potentate. The brown backs remained in that position for a full minute before he could call his trembling companion to his side.

"'Hey, there!' he yelled. 'How are you?'"

"What does it mean?" whispered she at last. "Are they dead?"

"They are really there, then? By George, I thought I was dreaming. Tennys, they are actually doing us homage."

"Then they are harmless," she cried joyously.

"I believe I could go down and cut off their ears without hearing a protest."

"But you won't, will you?"

"It would be barbarous, totally uncalled for, I'm sure. I can't understand their warlike appearance, though. Those fellows look as if they were out for blood."

"Perhaps they are at war with some other tribe and not with the white people. My hus--Lord Huntingford says they fight among themselves incessantly."

"That's it. It is a band of foragers, no doubt. But what are we going to do about it?" Hugh was nonplussed. The brown backs and bobbing heads still stretched before them in almost comical humbleness.

"It may be a trick."

"It stands us in hand to remain where we are until we know what they intend to do next."

"I hope they'll get up and go away."

"I guess I'll yell down and ask them what they want."

"I wouldn't, Hugh," she entreated. "If we leave them alone, they may go away presently." He looked at her and laughed, for he was growing less uneasy with each passing moment.

"Hey, there!" he yelled. "How are you?"

Slowly the head-bobbing ceased and dark faces were lifted toward the elevation. For the first time the newcomers saw the beautiful face of Lady Tennyson. They struggled to their feet, the tall chief stepping forward with outstretched arms. Then in some wild gibberish he began to speak, half to the white witnesses, half to the sky and sun.

"What the dickens is he talking about?" murmured the mystified American. "Perhaps he's asking us to surrender."

"He is either appealing to the sun or praying to the sky," said his companion.

"I have it!" cried Hugh. "He thinks we are angels." Despite the gravity of the moment she giggled delightedly.

"Then we may as well sit down and await developments," she said a moment later, as they observed the whole band go face downward on the sand again--all save the chief. The white people seated themselves on the ledge and watched the impassioned jabberer. Presently the prostrate figures arose and in mute submission spread forth their arms and bent their heads, standing like bronze statues in the glaring sunlight, all to the increased astonishment of those who had expected to become victims of their torture.

"This beats all I ever knew," exclaimed Ridgeway. "It begins to look as though they are either friendly or afraid of us. What shall we do?"

"I will follow you, Hugh, if you think it best to go down to them. I do not believe they will harm us."

"We will go down to them, but we must not let them think we are in the least afraid of them."

With some anxiety and a decided feeling of insecurity they arose to take the risk. Putting into use all the composure he could command, he deliberately began the descent, turning to assist her Ladyship.

"They are on the ground again, bobbing worse than ever," she whispered, for his back was toward them. In a few minutes, after a descent made more tortuous by the uncertainty of its ending, they found themselves on a level with the huddled natives. Taking her hand in his left and clutching his club nervously in his right, Hugh advanced slowly toward the band. Every nerve in his body was quivering under the strain which his apparent coolness cost. When within fifteen feet of the prostrate figures they halted and Hugh cried out boldly:

"Get up!"

Instead of obeying the command instantly, the little band peeped slyly at the strangers. Then they struggled to their feet, crowding into a bunch, the picture of bewilderment.

"By George, they look at us as if they never had seen white people before," said Hugh. With stately tread he approached the now trembling, shrinking natives, holding his left hand aloft to signify graciousness. Lady Tennys walked beside him, a smile playing on her exceedingly pale face. "My good friends, be not afraid," said he. The brown men looked at each other in deeper wonder than before.

The leader, a perfect giant, stepped forward hesitatingly, fairly pushed on by his comrades. In an awed voice he gave utterance to a most outlandish rattle of sound, the like of which his hearers never had heard. In conclusion he touched his mouth and ears and shook his head solemnly. Hugh, taking the cue, repeated the performance.

"That signifies that we don't understand each other. He sha'n't beat me on the sign language," he said. "I believe this is a great time to work in something dramatic. We can make a hit by simply going among them and laying our hands on their heads. It will be graceful and fetching, I'm sure. First, I am going to see if they are afraid of us." He suddenly threw up both hands and cried "Boo!" in a loud tone. The eyes of the watchers hung out and they jumped like so many mice at the sound. It was so laughable that she was compelled to place her handkerchief over her mouth and turn her head away. "I guess we've got 'em pretty well paralyzed," grinned Hugh. Then he went among them, placing his hands gently upon their woolly heads, Lady Tennys doing likewise. The flesh of the savages fairly quivered at the touch, yet all seemed delighted that the visitors had condescended to lay hands of kindness upon them. They began to chatter and chant softly, all the time eyeing Hugh and his companion with reverence.

"They don't seem to thaw out or show any signs of friendship," said Hugh, very much puzzled. He and his companion walked over to the shade of the rock and calmly sat down to await the next move. They now had no fear of harm at the hands of the simple though savage-looking men, who watched them from a distance jabbering excitedly.

"Hugh, I am firmly convinced that they have never seen white people before. They don't know what we are."

For five minutes they sat and discussed possibilities and probabilities, fully realizing that they were objects of awe to the savages. Finally the tall one left the group and drew near the couple, approaching in fine humility. When he was a dozen feet from them, they arose, extending friendly hands toward him. He dropped to his knees and fairly ground his head upon the rock. Then he arose and came directly to them. Hugh marvelled at his size. Tremendous muscles, cords, knots and ridges stood out all over his symmetrical body. He peered intently at the white man's flesh and then dubiously at his own. When he turned his inspection to Tennys, his eyes riveted themselves upon her clear white face, the most gorgeously beautiful flower he ever had seen. He could not grasp the full glory of that dazzling flower; he was stupefied, helpless before the blue eyes and dazzling smile.

In mute idolatry he at last lifted his puzzled gaze to the sun and then, extending his great arms upward, uttered a few low, guttural appeals to the King of the sky.

"He thinks we are from the sun," said she, keenly ingenious.

"This fellow really seems quite willing to worship us. The best we can do for the present is to set ourselves up as idols. I think I can be a very clever idol with precious little practice. You can be one without an effort. Shall we set up a worship shop among these decidedly willing subjects?"

"But, Hugh, if we go away from the coast we cannot hope to see a white man again; these poor fellows are now, for the first time, looking upon one. Should we not stay here?" she asked, full of fear and perplexity.

"If a white man ever finds this land he will discover us. Besides, we cannot live on this rock forever. It would only be a question of time until we should starve or be killed by wild beasts. I am in favor of retaining the very evident monopoly we have established in this land of nowhere."

"But if they should prove treacherous?"

"There's no mistaking the honesty of their wonder. We are real curiosities, and we have only to follow up the advantage to become regular despots." He was enthused by the possibilities that thronged his imagination.

"I will leave it all to you, Hugh. Do what you think best," she said softly and resumed her seat on the rock.

With his heart quickened by the inspiration in that trusting face, Hugh boldly stepped to the side of the brown giant, deliberately taking his hand to lead him to the edge of the precipice.

There, by signs and gesticulations, he endeavored to tell him that they came from over the sea. From the awed expression on the face of the savage he guessed that he had increased the mystery. It was quite evident that his auditor now believed them to be from the bottom of the sea instead of from the sun. To Hugh it mattered little as long as he could have the wand of power over their heads. He delighted the chief by making him understand that he and his companion would accompany them in the boats. The word was conveyed to his warriors, and a wild chatter of joy went up from among them. They fell upon their faces and groaned in mighty discord.

Within a quarter of an hour the light bark canoes were speeding toward the harbor mouth, big brown arms manning the paddles vigorously. Ridgeway and Tennys sat facing each other in the foremost boat, the chief steering. Their turtle shell was in another boat, and Hugh did not forget the good old spar that lay on the beach below. Hour after hour passed, the oarsmen paddling the same stroke, never tiring, never faltering. The passengers at last began to lose interest in the gorgeous scenery along the coast they were skirting. Where would this startling journey end? When would the indefatigable oarsmen lay down their paddles to rest? When would they be able to procure food and drink?

The sun was sinking toward the water line, the forest along the uneven coast was merging into one vast green shadow, the waters were growing blacker and blacker, and yet the row of canoes continued its wearisome glide toward a seemingly unattainable end. Lady Tennys became so tired and sleepy that her long lashes could not be restrained from caressing her cheeks, nor could her dreamy eyes bear the strain of wakefulness. Hugh, observing her fatigue, persuaded her to turn about in the boat and lie back against his shoulder. Soon she was sleeping soundly, her face protected from the dying sun by a readjustment of her palm-leaf bonnet.

Ridgeway was beginning to fight against the effects of an ungovernable drowsiness when the boat in which they sat suddenly turned toward the beach. Long, powerful strokes sent the little craft whizzing in the new direction. Just as the sun's last rays lost themselves in the night, the prow glided upon the sand and the oarsmen sprang out to carry him and the fair sleeper ashore.

CHAPTER XXII
FLESH SUCCEEDS STONE

Lady Tennys rubbed her eyes and stared blankly about her when Hugh awoke her. The darkness and the strange forms frightened her, but his reassuring words brought remembrance of the unique trip and with it the dim realization that they had landed at last.

If their first landing place was wonderful, this was doubly so. Despite the darkness, they were able to see quite distinctly the general outline of the coast. Two mammoth rocks, as large apparently as the one they had left behind, rose toward the hazy moonlit sky, far in shore, like twin sentinels, black and forbidding. Between them a narrow stretch of sky could be seen, with the moon just beyond. Entranced, they gazed upon the vivid yet gloomy panorama bursting from the shades of night almost as if it were advancing upon them. So immense, so startling, were these vast towering columns, so brilliant was the sky behind them, that the wonder-struck strangers found difficulty in controlling a desire to turn about and fly from the impending rush of mountain, moon and sky. In the first moments of breathless observation it seemed to them that the great rocks were moving toward the sea and that the sky was falling with them, giving the frightful impression that they were soon to be crushed in the ponderous fall. They were exchanging expressions of relief when the big chief came up and prostrated himself at their feet.

Ridgeway touched his shoulder and bade him arise, pointing toward the mounts and their attendant glory. To his amazement the chief uttered an exclamation of satisfaction and abruptly ran back to the boats. In an incredibly short space of time the restless savages were coming up the beach with their canoes on their shoulders, heading straight for the opening through which the moonlight streamed. Two of them formed a "basket," and Lady Tennys, taking her seat upon their hands, and holding timidly to their hard, muscular shoulders, was borne swiftly onward and upward, Ridgeway having some difficulty in keeping pace with the human carriage.

Big rocks told them that they were at the base of the rocky columns and the course of the little band indicated that they were to pass between the towering, almost perpendicular monsters. Suddenly the little cavalcade of the night came to a halt, the boats were thrown down and Hugh arrived at the conclusion that they were to stop until morning. In this he found himself mistaken, for with the very next moment he heard the splashing of water, seemingly beneath his feet. Up to now he had been looking upward at the rift in the rocks. Instead of a rocky gorge he now saw the shimmering of water, and a fresh exclamation of surprise fell from his lips.

"Can this be fairyland?" he cried, completely dazed.

"We must be dreaming, Hugh," murmured she. The party stood at the water's edge, looking up through the miniature cañon, the rushing of distant rapids coming to their ears.

The boats were lowered, and the oarsmen were soon pulling sturdily between the tall twins. These frowning monsters formed a perfect gateway from the sea to the home of the savages. Hugh felt that he was shut off forever from the outside world as he surveyed, with sinking heart, the portals through which they had passed. Soon a second landing was made, this time upon soft, rich soil, instead of crunching sand. It was easy to tell that they were standing on velvety grass, soft, cool and dewy. The boats were made fast, the spar and shell were swung upon broad shoulders, and then the party plunged straight into the wood, Lady Tennys being carried as before.

After ten minutes of rapid walking over a well-beaten trail the band halted, and the chief uttered several piercing cries. From afar off in the still night came an echoing answer and again the march was resumed, the travellers keeping close to the bank of the river. In time they reached an open stretch, across which the escort started, turning away from the stream.

There were fitful flashes of light ahead. Across the little plain came a jumble of flying human beings, two or three bearing torches. They seemed to have sprung from the ground, so abruptly did they appear before the eyes of the dumbfounded strangers in this strange land. The chief went forward rapidly and checked the advancing figures, preparing them for what was to follow. The entire company prostrated itself in good form.

With the horde of stupefied recruits at their heels, the white people at length entered the village, which nestled against the hillside. Hundreds of dark, almost naked, savages rushed from the shadows, the news of the great visitation having spread like wildfire. By the time the halt was made in front of a large, odd-looking structure, her Ladyship was so overcome with excitement that she could hardly stand. Ridgeway caught her as she staggered from her improvised litter. Presently she grew stronger, and with her companion entered what was apparently a palace among the squat, queerly built houses.

The chief ordered torches stuck in the ground, and a bright, strong light filled the interior. They found themselves in a large apartment, twenty by thirty feet in size. A reed or grass roof provided covering. This roof, like those in civilized lands, ran to a high point in the centre, the sides being fully twelve feet from the ground. There were no windows in the walls, but as they did not come within three feet of the roof, there was ample provision for ventilation and light. The entrance to this structure was through wide portals, reaching from ground to eaves. There was no floor save the earth, but there were rugs made from the skins of wild animals. Hugh noticed with a thrill of excitement that among them were tiger and leopard skins. Directly opposite the entrance stood a rough and peculiarly hewn stone, resembling in a general way the form of a man, colossal, diabolical.

"An idol," whispered Lady Tennys in awed tones.

"Perhaps it would be wisdom on our part to kneel before the thing," said Hugh calculatingly.

"I'll do anything you think best," she said reluctantly, kneeling for a moment with him before the idol. Whereupon the chief and his attendants shouted for joy and fell upon their much-used faces. The populace, thronging about the temple, took up the cry, and all night long they chanted praise to the living gods. The weird, ghastly figures flitted from end to end of the mad village long after the chief and his party had left the temple to the sole possession of the new divinities.

"I wonder if they expect us to sit up forever as sedately as that old party over there," mused Hugh, after the savages had withdrawn, greatly to the mystification of their guests. "We're evidently left here to make the best of it. I fancy we are now supposed to be in business as real gods with a steady job in the temple."

"I am beginning to think we have come to a terrible place, Hugh. How fierce and wild these people are! What is to become of us?" asked she, shivering as with a chill. "How horrible it would be if they brought us here as a sacrifice to this beastly idol. Is there no way of escape?"

"Nonsense! We've queered this antiquated old fossil forever. Two real live gods are worth ten thousand stone quarries like that. If you say so, I'll have a few of his worshippers take him down and toss him in the river."

The big room was devoid of furniture save for the rugs and several blocks of stone grouped about the idol. Ridgeway was convinced that they were in the sacred place of worship. Seating themselves rather sacrilegiously upon the stone blocks, they looked about the place with tired, hopeless eyes. The walls were hung with spears, war clubs and other ferocious weapons, evidently the implements of defence to be used by the stone deity in case of emergency.

"Well," quoth Hugh, after the gloomy inspection, "they must think that gods don't sleep. I don't see anything that looks like a berth around here. God or no god, I am going to turn in somewhere for the night. His Reverence may be disturbed if I snore, but I dare say his kick won't amount to much. I'll pile some of these skins over in that corner for you and then I'll build a nest for myself near the door." Suiting the action to the word, he proceeded to make a soft couch for her. She sat by and watched him with troubled eyes.

"Do you think it safe to go to sleep when we don't know what they may do during the night? They may pounce upon us and kill us." Hugh paused in his work and walked to her side.

"Something tells me we are safe with these people. We may as well make the best of it, anyhow. We are in for it, and I'll bet my soul we come out all right. Go over there and sleep. I'll be the first one killed if they attempt violence. Here's a club that will down a few of them before they get the best of me." He took from the wall a great murderous-looking club and swung it about his head.

"I want to be killed first, Hugh, if it comes to that. If you are merciful, you will kill me yourself when you see that it is their intention to do so," she said earnestly.

"Pooh, there's no danger," he said, and went back to his work, impressed by her manner more than he cared to admit. With her chin in her hands she resignedly watched him complete her bed of tiger skins.

"We have desecrated the temple by disturbing the rugs," she said at length.

"I'll have 'em make some hammocks for us to-morrow and we'll hang 'em in each end of the temple. And we'll also have this place divided into two or three apartments, say two sleeping rooms and a parlor, perhaps a kitchen. If necessary, an addition can be stuck on just back of where the idol stands. There'll be great doings around here when Yankee progress takes hold."

"You surely do not mean to ruin their temple! They will be up in arms, Hugh."

"Well, they'll have to endure a great many things if they expect to support such luxuries as we are. If those fellows don't quit falling down and bumping their faces on the ground, I'm going to have a lot of pads made for them to wear when they think there is danger of meeting us. They'll wear their faces out." It did him good to hear her laugh. "Well, your bed is ready, my Lady."

"I am dying for a drink of water. Do you know how long it has been since we touched food and drink?"

"All day! I never thought of it until this minute. I am half famished myself," he cried in dismay. Then he rushed to the door and shouted to some natives who were standing near by eyeing the crude building inquisitively by the light of a single torch. "Hey! you fellows!"

At the sight of his white figure and the sound of his voice, torch and all fell to the ground.

"Get up, you blamed fools," called the white man, walking toward them in exasperation. They arose tremblingly as he drew near, and he managed by signs to make them understand that he wanted food and drink. Away they dashed, and he re-entered the temple. Lady Tennys was laughing.

"What are you laughing at?" he asked in surprise.

"It was so funny to hear you call them fools."

"I hope they understood me. Anyhow, they've gone for the fatted cocoanut or something equally as oriental."

In less time than seemed possible the happy messengers arrived at the door with food enough for a dozen hungry people. The giant chief followed his subjects, and it was through his hands that Hugh received the welcome food. The white people were gratified to find in the assortment rich bananas and oranges, raw meat, peculiar shell fish, berries and vegetables resembling the tomato. At first the natives looked a little dismayed over the disordered condition of the temple, but no sign of resentment appeared, much to the relief of Lady Tennys. The luscious offerings were placed on one of the stone blocks as fast as they were handed to Ridgeway, the natives looking on in feeble consternation.

The chief was the only one to enter the temple, and he started to prostrate himself before the stone idol. He appeared to be at a loss as to what course he should pursue. Hugh promptly relieved him. Shaking his head vigorously, he pointed to the stone image, signifying that there were to be no more salutations bestowed upon it, all homage being due to himself and the lady. The fickle pagan, after a waning look of love for their renounced idol, proceeded to treat it with scorn by devoting himself entirely to the usurpers. He brought cocoanut shells filled with cool water, and the thirsty ones drank.

"We seem to have got here in the fruit, fish, vegetable and novelty season, to say the least," observed Hugh.

"Isn't it wonderful?" was all she could say, her eyes sparkling. Never had he seen her so ravishingly beautiful as now, filled as she was with the mingled emotions of fear, excitement, interest, even of rapture. He could not prevent or subdue the thrill of indescribable joy which grew out of the selfish thought that he had saved her and that she must lean upon him solely for protection in this wild land. Turning sharply from her, he glanced at the tempting feast and unceremoniously dismissed the chief and his followers. The big savage stood undecided for a moment in the centre of the room, wavering between fear of the new god's displeasure and an evident desire to perform some service.

After an instant he boldly strode to a stone block back of and to the left of the image. Seizing it by the top, he gave the impression that he was about to lift the great stone. Instead, however, he merely slid from its position a thin slab, pushing it half way off of its square base. Instantly the sound of rushing water filled the ear, and the unaccountable, muffled roar that had puzzled them was half explained. The block was hollow, revealing a deep, black hole, out of which poured the sound of the hidden stream. The mystified observers could plainly see the water some ten feet below the surface of the earth, gliding swiftly off through a subterranean passage. The chief made them understand that this well was for the purpose of supplying the image with drinking water whenever he needed it.

"That's very interesting," said Hugh to Tennys. "I'll have to see where this water comes from to-morrow. From a practical point of view it is the finest bit of natural sewerage I ever have seen. I'll make arrangements to tap it, if we are to live here."

"You lawless Americans!"

Apparently satisfied, the chief and his staring companions withdrew, devoutly prostrating themselves not to the graven image, but to the living, breathing beings who were awaiting, with an ungodlike appetite, an opportunity to make way with the tempting fruit.

"It is ridiculous to allow those poor things to fall down like that every time they turn around before us," she said, when they were alone.

"We must encourage it. If we are to be idols we can't afford to give our subjects a bit of relief from their religious obligations, and I'm quite sure we are idols or sovereigns, more than likely the former, judging by the snubbing our flinty friend has received."

"If we are to live among these people, Hugh Ridgeway, I, for one, intend to tell them, if possible, of the real God, and to do what I can for a cause I served but feebly in the past. I may be a poor missionary, but I intend to try in my weak way to do some good among these poor, benighted creatures."

"I think we'd better let well enough alone," said he disparagingly.

"Why, Hugh, how can you say that?"

"I haven't thought very much about God since I've been in this land. I've been too busy," he muttered, with no little shame in his face, although he assumed an air of indifference.

"He saved us from the sea," she said simply, with a tremor in her voice. "Surely you remember the prayers you uttered from your very soul on that night. Were they not to God?"

"Begin your missionary work with me, Tennys. I am worse than the savages," he said, not in answer to her question.

Silently and greedily they ate of the delicious fruit, and found new sensations in the taste of more than one strange viand of nature. A calm restfulness settled down upon their tired bodies, and all the world seemed joyfully at peace with them.

Almost overcome by sleep, he managed to toss a few tiger skins on the ground near the door, not forgetting to place his club beside the improvised couch. "Sleep comfortably and don't be afraid," he said. She slowly arose from the block and threw herself on the bed of skins.

"You are so good to me and so thoughtful," she murmured sleepily. "Good-night!"

"Good-night," came his far away voice, as out of a dream.

Outside, the celebration was at its height, but the tired idols heard not a sound of the homage which was theirs that night.

CHAPTER XXIII
THE TRANSFORMATION BEGINS

When Ridgeway opened his eyes, the sunlight was pouring in upon him through the doorway. He looked at his watch, and was surprised to find that it was nearly eleven o'clock. Lady Tennys still slept on her couch of skins; the torches had burned to the ground; the grim idol leered malignantly upon the intruders, and the dream that he had experienced during the night was rudely dispelled. His eyes strayed again to the black, glossy, confused hair of the sleeper in the far corner, and a feeling of ineffable pity for her became companion to the sad wrenches that had grown from the misery of his own unhappiness.

She was sleeping on her side, her face from him, her right arm beneath her head, the dainty jewelled hand lying limply upon the spotted leopard skin. The beautifully moulded figure, slight yet perfect, swelling to the well-turned hip, tapering to the tip of the trim shoe which protruded from beneath the rumpled skirt, affording a tiny glimpse of a tempting ankle, was to him a most pathetic picture. As he was about to turn to the door, she awakened with a start and a faint cry. Sitting half erect, she gave a terrified, bewildered glance about her, her eyes at last falling upon him.

"Are you really here?" she cried, joy rushing to her eyes. "I dreamed that you had fled and left me to be cut to pieces by the savages."

"Dreams go by contraries, and I am, therefore, a very brave man. But come, it is eleven o'clock. Let us see what this place looks like in the sunlight."

Together they went to the wide entrance. A surprise awaited them in their first view of the village by day. Along the base of the circular range of hills stretched the email homes of the inhabitants, but, search as they would, they could discover no signs of life. There was not a human form in sight.

"What the dev--dickens does this mean?" exclaimed he.

"It seemed as if there were thousands of them here last night," she cried.

"Maybe we have lost our worshippers. I wonder if we are to be the sole possessors of this jungle metropolis?"

A mile away they could distinguish the banks of the river, running toward the great stone gateway of this perfect Eden. The plain between the hills and the river was like a green, annular piece of velvet, not over a mile in diameter, skirted on all sides by tree-covered highlands. The river ran directly through the centre of the basin, coming from the forest land to their right.

In some trepidation they walked to the corner of the temple and surveyed the hillside. Rising steeply from the low ground ran the green slope, at the top of which grew huge trees. The village lay at the base of the hills and was over a mile long, a perfect semi-circle of strange little huts, stretched out in a single line, with the temple as its central point.

"There is the beginning of our underground stream," exclaimed he, pointing up the elevation. A fierce little stream came plunging from the very heart of the mound, half way to the summit, tearing eagerly to the bottom, where it disappeared in the ground.

Suddenly the sound of distant shouting--or chanting, to be explicit--and the beating of drums came to their ears. They searched the hills and valley with alarm and dread in their eyes, but there was no sign of humanity. For many minutes the chanting continued, growing louder in volume as it drew nearer. At last Lady Tennys uttered an exclamation and pointed toward an opening in the ridge far to the left of the village. A string of natives came winding slowly, solemnly from this cleft--men, women and children apparently without end.

The white people stood like statues in the doorway, watching the approach of the brown figures. There were fully two thousand in that singular procession, at the head of which strode the big chief, with perhaps fifty native women at his heels.

"His multiplied wife," observed Hugh sententiously.

"Do you think all of them are his wives?" said she, doubtingly.

"It seems to be a heathen's choice to punish himself on earth and avoid it in the hereafter."

Behind the women came five men wearing long white robes and carrying unusually long spears. They were followed by the rabble. At length the weird cavalcade, marching straight across the plain, came to a halt not more than a hundred feet from the entrance to the temple. The chief advanced a few steps, pausing at the edge of a bare, white spot of ground some ten feet square. Then, after a most reverential bow, he tossed a small reddish chunk of wood into the white square. No sooner had the leader deposited his piece of wood than forward came the women, the white-robed men, and then the rag-tag of the population, each person tossing a piece upon the rapidly growing heap. In silent amusement, Ridgeway and Lady Tennys watched this strange ceremony.

"They've been visiting somebody's woodpile," speculated Hugh.

"Perhaps they intend to roast us alive," ventured she.

The small army fell back from the pile of wood, the chief maintaining a position several feet to the fore, a lad behind him bearing a lighted torch. After many signs and presumably devout antics, one of the spearmen took the torch and lighted this contribution from a combined populace. As the thin column of smoke arose on the still, hot air, the vast crowd fell to the ground as one person, arising almost instantly to begin the wildest, most uncanny dance that mortal ever saw. The smoke and flames grew, the dry wood crackled, the spearmen poked it with their long weapons, and the vast brown audience went into a perfect frenzy of fervor.

Not until the pile was reduced to ashes did the smoke dance cease. The spearmen retired, and the big chief came forward with a tread so ludicrously grand that they could scarce refrain from laughter. He carried two short staffs in his hands, the heads of which were nothing less than the skulls of infants. To the disgust of the white people the chief presented to each of them a shudder-inspiring wand. Afterward they learned that the skull-tipped staffs signified death to all who opposed their way. They also learned that the red bits of wood that had gone up in the flame were stained by the blood of a half dozen prisoners of war, executed the night before as a sacrifice to the new gods.

The new monarchs accepted the sceptres gingerly and the wildest glee broke loose in the waiting throng. While they danced and shouted, Hugh inwardly cursed the ostentation that was delaying breakfast.

Impatiently he made the chief understand what was wanted, and that worthy proved an excellent substitute for the genii. He rushed over and bawled a few commands, and a dozen women and men sped away like the wind. A few moments later the chief entered the temple and found

Ridgeway calmly measuring off the ground for the partitions that were to transform one room into three.

So apt was the white man at sign making and so apt was the brown man at understanding that before an hour had passed a dozen strong fellows were at work, carrying out the designs of the new idol, the morning meal having been disposed of in the meantime. Using the same kind of material that comprised the outer walls, a partition was constructed lengthwise through the centre of the temple. The front half was left as a reception hall and living room and the rear half was divided into two apartments, each fifteen feet square. They were to serve as sleeping rooms. These ruthless improvements made it necessary to remove the great stone idol from his pedestal.

"Chuck him out into the backyard," said Hugh. That evening the poor old image, as disgusted as a piece of rock could possibly be, was carried to the river and tossed into the rapids, his successors standing with the multitude on the high bank to witness his disappearance and to hear his unhappy kerplunk! The waters closed over his unhallowed head and the new dispensation began. Back across the little plain to the torch-lit village swarmed the fickle, joyous savages.

"Good Lord," observed Hugh, "what a ferocious crowd it is! They tear their enemies to pieces and yet we have them under our thumbs--for the present at least."

"I believe they are naturally intelligent, and I'm sure we can help them. Do you know what those white robes are made from?"

"Certainly. Cotton."

"It is woven grass. They bleach it. The women do the work down by the river, and the robes worn by their spearmen are really beautiful pieces of fabric."

"I am going to leave my measure for a pair of white grass trousers," said Hugh lightly, "and an umbrella," he added, looking up at the broiling sky.

Together the white usurpers planned many important improvements against the probability of a long stay among the savages. A wonderful system of sewerage was designed--and afterward carried out faithfully. A huge bath pool was to be sunk for Lady Tennys in the rear of her apartment; a kitchen and cold-storage cellar were to grow off the west end of the temple and a splendid awning was to be ordered for the front porch!

Time and patience were to give them all of these changes. Time was of less consequence than patience, it may be well to add. The slaving retinue was willing but ignorant.

The adoring chief gave Tennys a group of ten handmaidens before the day was over, and Hugh had a constant body guard of twenty stalwarts--which he prosaically turned into carpenters, stone-masons, errand boys and hunters.

"You must not try to civilize them in a day," she smilingly protested when he became particularly enthusiastic.

"Well, just see what we have done to-day," he cried. "How can you account for the enforced abdication of old Uncle Rocksy, the transformation of his palace into a commodious, three-room lodging-house, and all such things, unless you admit that we are here to do as we please? We'll make a metropolitan place out of this hamlet in a year if we--"

"A year! Oh, don't suggest such a possibility," she cried. "I'd die if I thought we were to be here for a year."

"I hope we won't, but we may as well look the situation straight in the face. There has been no white man here before us. It is by the rarest chance in the world that we are here. Therefore, it may be years before we are found and taken away from this undiscovered paradise."

The flickering, fitful light of the torches stuck in the ground behind them played upon two white faces from which had fled the zeal and fervor of the moment before, leaving then drawn and dispirited.

"All our lives, perhaps," she murmured.

"With these savages as our only companions, worse than death a thousand times," he groaned, starting to his feet with the vehemence of new despair. "Could anything be worse than the existence that lies before us?"

"Yes," she cried, arising, throwing back her shoulders and arms, lifting her face and breathing long draughts of the cool, pure air. "Yes! The existence that lies behind is worse than the one ahead. No life can be worse than the one from which I have escaped. Welcome, eternal solitude! Farewell, ambition, heart-pangs and the vain mockery of womanhood! To be free is heaven, no matter what the cost, Hugh."

"Do you mean that you would rather live here forever than go back to the old life?"

"If I must stay here to be free, I am willing to live in this miserable village to the very end, rejoicing and not complaining."

"I never associated you with real unhappiness until you uttered that last sentence."

"I should not be selfish, though," she said quickly. "You are so unhappy, you have lost so much. We are to be alone here in this land, Hugh, you and I, forever. I will prove to you that I am more than the frail, helpless woman that circumstances may seem to have shaped me, and you shall have from me all the aid and encouragement that a good, true woman can give. Sometimes I shall be despondent and regretful,--I can't help it, I suppose--but I shall try with you to make the wilderness cheerful. Who knows but that we may be found by explorers within a month. Let us talk about our new subjects out there on the plain. How many of them are there in this village?"

She won him from the despondency into which he was sinking, and, be it said to her credit, she did not allow him to feel from that time forth that she was aught but brave, confident and sustaining. She was a weak woman, and she knew that if once the strong man succumbed to despair she was utterly helpless.

CHAPTER XXIV
NEDRA

The next month passed much more quickly than any previous month within the lives of the two castaways. Each day brought forth fresh novelties, new sensations, interesting discoveries. Her courage was an inspiration, a revelation to him. Despite the fact that their journeyings carried them into thick jungles where wild beasts abounded, she displayed no sign of fear. Jaunty, indifferent to danger, filled with an exhilaration that bespoke the real love for adventure common among English women, she traversed with him the forest land, the plains, the hills, the river, and, lastly, the very heart of the jungle. They were seldom apart from the time they arose in the morning until the hour when they separated at night to retire to their apartments.

Exploration proved that they were on an island of considerable dimensions, perhaps twenty miles long and nearly as wide. The only human inhabitants were those in the village of Ridgehunt, as the new arrivals christened it,--combining the first syllables of their own names. From the tops of the great gate posts, christened by Lady Tennys, far across the water to the north, could be seen the shadowy outlines of another island. This was inhabited by a larger tribe than that which constituted the population of Ridgehunt.

A deadly feud existed between the two tribes. There had been expeditions of war in the past, and for months the fighting men of Ridgehunt had been expecting an attack from the island of Oolooz. Nearly twenty miles of water separated the two islands. The attacking force would have to cover that distance in small craft. Shortly before the advent of the white people, King Pootoo's men captured a small party of scouts who had stolen across the main on a tour of exploration. They were put to death on the night of the arrival in Ridgehunt. A traitor in their midst had betrayed the fact that Oolooz contemplated a grand assault before many weeks had gone. Guards stationed on the summits of the gate posts constantly watched the sea for the approach of the great flotilla from Oolooz. King Pootoo had long been preparing to resist the attack. There were at least five hundred able-bodied men in his band, and Hugh could not but feel a thrill of admiration as he looked upon the fierce, muscular warriors and their ugly weapons.

He set about to drill them in certain military tactics, and they, believing him to be a god whom no enemy could overthrow, obeyed his slightest command. Under his direction breastworks were thrown up along the western hills, trenches were dug, and hundreds of huge boulders were carried to the summits overlooking the pass, through which the enemy must come in order to reach the only opening in the guerdon of the hills. It was his plan to roll these boulders from the steep crests into the narrow valley below just as the invaders charged through, wreaking not only disaster but disorder among them, no matter how large their force. There was really but one means of access by land to the rock-guarded region, and it was here that he worked the hardest during the fourth week of their stay among the savages.

He was working for his own and her safety and freedom. In Ridgehunt they were idols; in the hands of the unknown foe their fate might be the cruel reverse. Pride in the man who was to lead their brown friends to victory swelled in the heart of the fair Briton, crowding back the occasional fear that he might be conquered or slain. She had settled upon the course to pursue in case there was a battle and her protector fell. A dagger made from the iron-like wood used by the natives in the manufacture of spears and knives hung on the wall of her room. When he died, so should she, by her own hand.

Gradually they began to grasp the meaning of certain words in the native language. Hugh was able after many days to decide that the natives knew nothing of the outside world and, furthermore, that no ships came into that part of the sea on account of the immense number of hidden reefs. The island on which they had been cast bore a name which sounded so much like Nedra that they spelled it in that way. In course of time she christened the spots of interest about her. Her list of good English names for this utterly heathen community covered such places as Velvet Valley, Hamilton Hills, Shadburn Rapids, Ridgeway River, Veath Forest and others. Ridgeway gave name to the temple in which the natives paid homage to them. He called it Tennys Court.

Her room in the remodelled temple was a source of great delight to Lady Tennys. It was furnished luxuriously. There were couches, pillows, tables, chairs, tiger-skin rugs, and--window curtains. A door opened into her newly constructed bath pool, and she had salt or fresh water, as she chose. The pool was deep and clay lined and her women attendants were models of the bath after a few days. She learned the language much easier than Hugh. He was highly edified when she told him that his new name was Izor--never uttered without touching the head to the ground. Her name was also Izor, but she blushed readily when he addressed her as Mrs. Izor--without the grand curtsey. The five spearmen were in reality priests, and they were called Mozzos. She also learned that the chief who found them on the rock was no other than the mighty King Pootoo and that he had fifty wives. She knew the names of her women, of many children and of the leading men in the village.

The feeble sprout of Christianity was planted by this good British girl. It had appeared to be a hopeless task, but she began at the beginning and fought with Mercy as her lieutenant. Humanity was a stranger to these people when she found them, but she patiently sowed the seeds and hoped. A people capable of such idolatry as these poor wretches had shown themselves to be certainly could be led into almost any path of worship, she argued.

Late in the afternoon of their thirty-third day on the island the white idol of Nedra swung lazily in her hammock, which was stretched from post to post beneath the awning. Two willowy maidens in simple brown were fanning her with huge palm leaves. She was the personification of pretty indolence. Her dreamy eyes were turned toward the river and there was a tender, eager longing in their depths. Hugh was off in the hills with his workmen and the hour had passed for him to emerge from the woodland on his way to the village.

The shadows of night were beginning to settle upon the baking earth and a certain uneasiness was entering her bosom. Then she caught a glimpse of his figure in the distance. With his swarm of soldiers behind him he came from the forest and across the narrow lowlands toward the river. He steadfastly refused to be carried to and from the "fortifications" in the rude litter that had been constructed for him, a duplicate of which had been made for her. A native with a big white umbrella was constantly at his side and King Pootoo was in personal command of the workmen as "sub-boss." Ridgeway jocosely characterized his hundred workmen as "Micks," and they had become expert wielders of the wooden pick, shovel and crowbar. In the village there were the three hundred tired armorers who had worked all day among the hard saplings in the country miles to the south. It was their duty to make an inexhaustible supply of spears, swords, etc.

As the American came up over the bank of the river Lady Tennys could not repress a smile of pride. The white grass trousers, the huge white hat, and the jaunty military carriage had become so familiar to her that she could almost feel his approach before he came into view. It was always the same confident, aggressive stride, the walk of the master.

Although the sun had dropped behind the twin giants and the haze of the night was on, Hugh's faithful attendant carried the umbrella over his head. The new Izor said, more than once, that, having taught the fellow to carry the protector, he could not unteach him. Were it darkest midnight the umbrella was produced and carried with as much serenity as when the sun broiled and toasted at midday. When the returning band of laborers was half way across Velvet Valley, Tennys, as was her wont, left her hammock and went forth to meet the man beneath the white sunshade. His pace quickened and his face brightened as she drew near. The hatless, graceful figure in white came up to him with the cry:

"Why are you so late? Dinner has been waiting for an hour."

"Pshaw! And the cocoanuts are cold again," he cried with mock concern. She took his arm and they trudged happily through the deep grass on which the never-failing dew was already settling. "But we have finished the fortifications. By George, if those Ooloozers get through that valley they'll be fit to try conclusions with England and America combined. With four hundred men I can defend the pass against four thousand. To-morrow I'll take you over to see the defences. They're great, Tennys."

She dampened his enthusiasm somewhat.

"Won't it be an awful joke if the enemy doesn't come?"

"Joke! It will be a calamity! I'd be tempted to organize a fleet and go over after them. By the way, I have something fine for you."

"A letter from home?" she cried laughingly. "One would think so from the important way in which you announce it. What is it?"

"A pet--a wonder of a pet," he said. "Hey! Jing-a-ling, or whatever your name is, bring that thing up here." A native came running up from the rear bearing in his arms, a small, ugly cub, its eyes scarcely opened. She gave vent to a little shriek and drew back.

"Ugh! The horrid thing! What is it?"

"A baby leopard. He's to be our house cat."

"Never! I never saw an uglier creature in my life. What a ponderous head, what mammoth feet, and what a miserably small body! Where are the spots?"

"He gets 'em later, just as we get gray hairs--sign of old age, you know. And he outgrows the exaggerated extremities. In a few months he'll be the prettiest thing you ever saw. You must teach him to stand on his head, jump through a hoop, tell fortunes and pick out the prettiest lady in the audience, and I'll get you a position with a circus when we go to America. You'd be known on the bills as the Royal Izor of the Foofops and her trained leopard, the Only One in Captivity."

"You mean the only leopard, I presume," she smiled.

"Certainly not the only lady, for there are millions of them in that state."

They had their dinner by torchlight and then took their customary stroll through the village.

"There seems to be no one in the world but you and I," she said, a sudden loneliness coming over her.

"What a paradise this would be for the lover who vows that very thing to the girl he loves."

"Do lovers mean all that they say?" she asked laughingly.

"Very few know just what they say until it is too late. A test on an uncivilized island would bring reason to the doughtiest lover. There's no sentiment in cold facts."

"I don't see why two people, if they loved as you say they can love, should not be perfectly happy to live apart from the world. Do they not live only for each other?"

"That's before the test, you see."

"I have not found existence on this island altogether unendurable," she went on. "I am not in love, I'm cure, yet I am surprised to find myself contented here with you. Then why should not lovers find this a real paradise, as you say?"

"Would you be contented here with any other man as your companion?" he asked, his head suddenly swimming.

"Oh, no!" she cried decisively. "I don't believe I'd like it here with anybody but you. Now, don't look like that! I'm not such a fool as you may be thinking, Hugh. I know the world pretty well. I know how other people love, even though it has never been part of my lot. I'm not quite a hypocrite. I was not presented at court for nothing. You see, you are so good and we are such friends. It never occurred to me before, but I'm sure I couldn't endure being here with any other man I know. Isn't it queer I never thought of that?" she asked, in real wonder.

He looked at her steadily before answering. The flare of the torch revealed a childlike sincerity in her face, and he knew she did not realize the construction he might have been justified in according her impulsive confession. His heart throbbed silently. A wave of tenderness welled within him, bringing with it a longing to kiss the hem of her raiment, to touch her soft, black hair, to whisper gently in her ear, to clasp her hand, to do something fondly grateful.

"Are you quite sure of that?" he asked softly. She looked up into his eyes honestly, frankly, unwaveringly, pressing his arm with a smile of enthusiasm.

"Quite sure. Why not? Who could be better, more thoughtful, braver than you, and for the sake of a woman who, by mistake, owes her life to you? When you have done so much for me, why should I not say that you are the man I like best of all I know? It is strange, perhaps, that it should make any particular difference, but it seems to me no other man could inspire the feeling of resignation and contentment that you do. Really, it isn't so hard to live in the wilderness, is it?"

"Have you never known any one else with whom you could have been contented here?" he asked persistently.

"Oh, I don't know what other men would be like if they were in your place," she said. She appeared deeply thoughtful for some time, as if trying to imagine others of her acquaintance in Hugh's place. "I am sure I cannot imagine any one being just like you," she went on, conclusively.

"No one you may have loved?"

"I have never loved anybody," she cried.

"Do you know what love means?"

"I haven't the faintest conception," she laughed, mockingly.

"I believe you said that to me some time ago," he said.

"I wish I could love," she said lightly. "But I suppose the chance is forever lost if I am doomed to stay on this island all my life."

His smile was understood by the night.

CHAPTER XXV
THE COMING OF THE ENEMY

A fever of queer emotions plagued Hugh's mind as he sought sleep that night. He lay awake on his couch of skins for hours, striving to put from himself the delightful conviction that had presented itself so suddenly. Through all his efforts to convince himself that his impressions were the result of self-conceit or a too willing egotism, there persistently ran the tantalizing memory of her simple confession. When at last he slept it was to dream that a gentle hand was caressing his forehead and loving fingers were running through his hair. For a while the hand was Grace Vernon's, then it was Tennys Huntingford's, then Grace's, then the other's. Its touch brought a curve to his lips.

While he lay awake in these wondering hours and slept through the changing dream, the cause of his mingled emotions lay in the next apartment, peacefully asleep from the moment her head touched the pillow, totally unconscious of the minutest change in her heart or in their relationship, as contented as the night about her.

The next morning he was speculatively quiet and she was brightly talkative as they ate breakfast. He was awake when she took her refreshing plunge in the pool, and heard her conversing learnedly with her attendants, as if they understood all that she said--which they did not. It was then that he thought what a solitude life would be if she were not a part, of it. There was nothing in her manner to indicate that she remembered their conversation of the night before. In fact, it was apparent that she was wholly unconscious of the impression it had made.

Two of her white-robed attendants stood in the doorway while they ate, another industriously fanning them. The flowing white robes were innovations of the past few days, and their wearers were pictures of expressive resignation. Robes had been worn only by Mozzos prior to the revolution of customs inaugurated by the white Izor, and there was woeful tripping of brown feminine feet over treacherous folds.

"Those ghastly gowns remind me that this is the day for our flag raising," said he. "I guess the banner is strong enough to stand the winds that whistle around the tops of the gateposts, isn't it?"

Her thoughts reverted to the white signal that floated from the summit of the big mount at whose base they had been cast up from the sea. Hugh, having completed the meal, went to the end of the room, where, stretched along the wall, hung a huge American flag. Days had been consumed by the women in the manufacture of this piece of woven grass. He had created red stripes from an indelible berry stain. A blue background for the stars was ingeniously formed by cutting out spaces through which the sky could gleam. A strong pole lay on the floor and all was in readiness for the raising of the Stars and Stripes over the Island of Nedra. Their hope was that it might eventually meet the eye of some passing navigator.

"By the way, Hugh," she said, standing beside him, a trace of antagonism in her voice, "who discovered this island, a Briton or an American?"

"Why I--an American, of course! Great Scott! I--I certainly did, didn't I?" he exclaimed, aghast, gradually comprehending that she had a moral claim, at least.

"That is the question," she said simply.

He walked over and sat down rather heavily on one of the stone blocks.

"I saw it from the sea," he stammered.

"And so did I."

For some moments he sat gazing at the flag, actual distress in his eyes. She looked away and smiled faintly.

"I didn't think, Tennys; truly I did not. You have as much right to claim the discovery as I. Why have you not spoken of this before?"

"You seemed so happy over the flag that I couldn't, Hugh," she said, still looking away.

"Poor old flag! It's the first time you ever tried to wave dishonestly or where there was a doubt of your supremacy." He came to her side. "We'll have no flag raising."

"What!" she cried, strangely disappointed.

"Not until we have made a British flag to wave beside this one."

"I was jesting, Hugh, just to see what you would say. The flag shall go up. You--you are the master, as you should be, Hugh."

"You have as much right as I," he protested.

"Then I'll be an American," she cried. "We'll raise our flag."

"But you are not an American."

"Granting that I was the first to see the island, was I not under protection of an American? I have been under American protection ever since. What has Great Britain to do with the situation? I demand the protection of the Stars and Stripes. Will you deny me?" Her eyes were sparkling eagerly. "Could the British have landed had it not been for the American?"

"You really don't care?"

"This is our flag, Hugh," she said seriously. "It will make me unhappy if you continue to take my jest as an earnest. We made it and I shall be proud to have it wave over me."

A few hours later the Stars and Stripes floated high over a new island of the sea, far from the land of its birth.

"How good and grand it looks," she cried as they saw it straighten to the breeze. "After all, it may be waving over its own, Hugh. The United States bought several thousands of islands in this section of the world, I've heard," she added, with a touch of irony.

"It's the flag I love," he cried. "May God let me kiss once more the soil she calls home. Dear America!"

From that day he never looked at the dancing, wriggling stripes without a surge of emotion. Its every flaunt seemed to beckon brave worshippers from far across the sea to the forlorn island on which it was patiently waving.

An uneventful week passed. A Nedrite who had escaped from the Island of Oolooz brought word to King Pootoo that the enemy was completing preparation for a stupendous assault, but a close watch on the sea failed to reveal signs of the approach. Ridgeway and his eager followers were fully prepared for the assault. The prospect was now assuming the appearance of a European war cloud--all talk and no fight. But as King Pootoo insisted in vague earnestness that the informer was trustworthy, precautionary measures were not relaxed at any time. Hugh was now the possessor of a heavy sword made of the metallic-like wood. It had two edges and resembled an old-fashioned broadsword.

"I feel like a Saumeri," he announced.

When he found that fairly sharp blades could be wrought from this timber, he had knives and hatchets made for private use, his own trusty pocket knife being glorified by promotion. He whetted the blade to the keenest possible edge and used it as a razor. Tennys compelled him to seek a secluded spot for his, weekly shave, decreeing that the morals of the natives should not be ruined in their infancy by an opportunity to acquire first-class, fully developed American profanity.

Many of their evenings, delightfully cool in contrast with the intense heat of the day, were spent on the river. The largest canoe of the village was fitted out with a broad, comfortable seat in the stern, upon which it was possible to recline lazily while several strong-armed natives paddled the craft through the shimmering, moonlit waters above the rapids.

One evening, a month after the raising of the flag, they came from the river, the night having been the most perfect they had seen, dark, sombre, picturesque. The moon was hidden behind the banks of clouds, which foretold the coming of rain, yet there was a soft, exquisite glow on land and water, as if blue-black tints were being cast from aloft by some mysterious, experimenting artist among the gods. It had been a quiet, dreamy hour for both. As they walked slowly across the little plain, followed by the oarsmen, they became cognizant of an extraordinary commotion in the village. Pootoo and a dozen men came running toward them excitedly.

"What's up, I wonder?" cried Hugh.

"It is the enemy. I know they have been sighted," she exclaimed breathlessly.

And she was right. Just before sunset the guard at the top of the gatepost had sighted the canoes of the invaders, far to the north. According to the king, to whom the flying messenger had come, there were myriads of canoes and they were headed for a part of the beach about three leagues north of the village. It was the best place for landing along the entire coast and was, besides, the point nearest the home of the coming foe. It was evident that the enemy had miscalculated. They came within eye range of the island before darkness set in. A half an hour later and it would have been impossible to discern the boats in the gloom. By merest chance their arrival was betrayed.

"Thank God, they can't surprise us," cried Hugh after he had learned all. He was mad with excitement, burning with eagerness for the fray.

The possibility of defeat, did not enter his head, so sure was he that he and his warriors could overthrow the invaders. His brain was filled with the hope that he might some day tell the story of this battle to the fellows at his club in Chicago. He could imagine himself sitting with his heels on the window seat, relating to envious listeners the details of the fight in the pass, the repulsing of the enemy, the chase to the shore; the annihilation and--but no time was to be lost in dreaming of the future when the imperative present demanded so much of him.

At his side hurried the distressed, trembling young Englishwoman, her heart almost paralyzed with fear. Two or three times she tried to speak to him; once she timidly, though frantically, sought to grasp his hand to stay him in his excited rush toward the temple. Up to this moment she had been brave, even confident; now a weakness assailed her and every vestige of courage was gone. But one thought filled her mind: the possibility of disaster befalling Hugh Ridgeway.

They reached the temple and he dashed inside, going direct to his room, where the sword and daggers hung. She sank weakly upon one of the big blocks in the long corridor, leaning her head against the partition, breathing heavily, hopelessly. He, unconscious of the pain she was suffering, began to whistle joyously as he bustled about.

"Tennys," he called, "do you know what has become of my shield?"

"It is out here," she answered shrilly, her voice pitched high with the tension imposed. He came forth, tossing his sword on the ground at her feet, hastily taking the shield from a peg in the wall.

"Say, we won't see a live Ooloozer for a hundred years after the fight," he exploded exuberantly. "Is my army out there in front?"

"Hugh," she said piteously, following him about in the hall, "it isn't necessary for you to accompany them."

"Oh, great Scott! I wouldn't miss it for a million. I'm the biggest pig in the puddle," stopping to look at her in amazement.

"But it isn't your--our war, Hugh. Why do you risk so much? They may kill you and then--then what will become of me?"

In an instant his hilarity subsided and deep solicitude came in its stead, every particle of tenderness in his heart asserting itself in response to the rueful appeal. There was a queer rushing of blood to his head, a dizziness, a great thrumming against, the drums of his ears, from all of which sprung, like lightning, the remembrance of his suspicions concerning her feelings toward him.

"You are not worried, are you? Why, there's no danger, not the slightest. We've got them whipped before the fight. I didn't think you'd lose courage. You've been so brave and confident all the time." He took her hands in his own and looked tenderly down into the wavering eyes of blue.

"It is dreadful, Hugh. I never knew how dreadful until now. I cannot bear to see you go out there to-night, perhaps never to come back. I shall die if you go!"

"But I must go, Tennys," he said firmly. "I'd rather die than be a coward. Your fears are utterly ridiculous."

His rather petulant speech caused her to withdraw her hands, her wide eyes sending a glance of wounded pride up into his. That look of reproach haunted him the whole night long. Even in the next moment he sought to withdraw the unintentional sting from his words by the gentle reminder that he would come back to her a victor and that she would be proud of him. Still the hurt eyes looked into his.

"I--I did not mean to interfere, Hugh. You must pay no attention to me. I was selfish and absurdly afraid," she said, a trace of coldness in her voice, her manner entirely altered.

"Any woman might well be afraid at such a time," he said quickly.

"I am not afraid for myself. It is not the kind of cowardice you think it is."

"You just now wondered what would become of you if I were killed," he ventured.

"I know what will become of me if the worst should come. But I must not keep you standing here. There is much for you to do and much for me to do. You shall never again say that I am not brave. Go and fight, Hugh, and when you bring home the wounded I shall have a place to care for them all." All this was spoken rapidly and in high-pitched tones. He moved slowly toward the door, not knowing what to say or how to act at parting.

"I'll be back all right, Tennys," he said at last. "Would you care very much if--if I never came back?"

"Oh, Hugh!" was her wail. "How can you ask? What would it mean to me to be left here all alone? If you would have me brave, do not ask such questions. Go, Hugh. Good-by!"

He grasped her hand, wrung it spasmodically, glanced once in her eyes and was off toward the horde of warriors congregating in the field.

Lady Tennys steadied her swaying figure against the doorpost and looked out upon the preparations for departure. The light in her eyes had died.

CHAPTER XXVI
ON THE EVE OF BATTLE

Ridgeway looked at his watch as he drew up to the torch bearers. It was then ten minutes after ten o'clock. In all probability the entire force of the enemy had landed upon the coast and was already on its way toward the village. He realized that these savages, friend and foe, knew nothing of the finer stratagems of warfare. Their style of fighting was of the cruel kind that knows no science, no quarter. A new commander had come to revolutionize the method of warfare for at least one of the armies. It was to be a case of strategy and a new intelligence against superior forces and a surprised ferocity.

He was somewhat amazed to find that none of his troopers had attempted to leave the village before he was there to lead. This, when he thought of the eagerness and bloodthirstiness of the men, was certainly a fair promise of submissiveness on the field of battle. To be sure, the restraint was almost unendurable to the fierce fellows who had caught up their shields and spears long before he came in from the river. The excitement was intense, the jabbering frightful. Here, there, everywhere danced the frantic warriors, tossing their weapons in the air and screaming with a loyalty that savored very much of impotent rage.

"Heavens, I'd give little for a man's life if he crossed these devils to-night," thought Hugh as King Pootoo detached himself from the horde and raced unmajestically over to meet him, almost, forgetting to prostrate himself in his frenzy. Grossly exaggerated by the flare of the torches, the spectacle was enough to strike terror to the strongest heart. The king subdued himself sufficiently to grasp the meaning of Hugh's signs and set about to bring order out of chaos--a difficult task for even a king. Gradually the excitement subsided and the band stood at rest, awaiting the command to move to the hills across the river. They reminded Hugh of dogs he had seen. We all have held a chunk of meat high above a dog's nose and we have seen him sit in enforced patience, hoping for the fall thereof. And we all know that after a certain time he will throw patience to the winds and leap frantically upward in the effort to secure the prize.

A force of fully one hundred young fellows was to be left in the village as a guard against disaster in case the enemy should force its way through the pass. Lady Tennys was to have a bodyguard, even though it crippled the fighting force at the front. The men comprising this reserve did not relish the plan, but their objections were relentlessly overruled by the white Izor and King Pootoo. With sulky heads they seated themselves as directed near the temple they were to protect with their lives.

It required but a few minutes of time for Ridgeway to find that his little army was ready to move. After some hesitation he went to the temple door to bid farewell to his fellow-castaway. She was still leaning against the doorpost and did not move as he approached.

"We're off now," he said as he came up. "Don't worry, little woman; we'll come home victorious as sure as fate. See these fellows? They are your guard, your own soldiers. You can command them to do as you wish."

"Mine?" she asked slowly, as if not comprehending.

"Yes; they are the Lady Tennys Reserves," he said, smiling. A glad light suddenly broke in her eyes, her face brightened and her whole mien changed from despair to delight.

"Thank you, Hugh. I shall never forget you for this. You will never know how happy I am to have these men to do my bidding. If it is necessary I will show you that a woman of England can fight as valiantly as her brothers, the bravest men in all the world." In her eyes there were tears as she uttered these words,--tears of courage and pride.

"Would that I could have you by my side all through this fight. There is an inspiration in your very gentleness that could make me do prodigious deeds of valor. But, good-by, Tennys! I'll be back for lunch to-morrow!" he cried as he dashed away. He could look into those swimming eyes no longer and restrain a certain impulse that was trying to force him into the liberation of an entirely unnecessary bit of sentiment.

"Good-by, Hugh! Don't be careless. What will the Reserves be worth to me if you are killed? I shall pray for you, Hugh--every minute of this awful night I shall pray for you."

"God bless you," he called back from Velvet Valley, his brain whirling with the wish that he had kissed her and the fear of the result had he made the attempt.

A few minutes later he sent his jacket back to the temple. It was his most valued possession. Had he seen the look of tenderness in her eyes as she hold up the worn, blue jacket; had he seen her kiss the blue cloth impulsively, he would have been thrilled to the bone. But had he been there to observe the startled, mystified blush that rose to her brow when she found that she had really kissed his coat, he might have been as perplexed as she over the unusual act.

With heart beating violently and nerves strung to their highest tension, Ridgeway led the way to the river. He was as confident of victory as if he were returning from the pass with the result out of doubt. Reaching the river, his men plunged into the water and swam across, not waiting for the canoes. He and the king were rowed over, meeting the swimmers as they came up from the bank, dripping and puffing. Again the march was resumed, and within fifteen minutes the band was at the foot of the hills. Here Hugh called a halt.

With Pootoo and a dozen men he went forward to take a look down the long gorge. All torches were extinguished and absolute silence was enforced. The scouting party failed to hear a sound except the cries of night birds and their own heavy breathing. All nature seemed to be resting for the struggle that was to come.

Six fleet fellows were sent over the hills to skirt the edge of the pass for its full length, a mile or more. They were to wait at the opposite end until the enemy revealed its approach and then hurry back with the alarm. Returning to the waiting army, Hugh and the king began the work of assigning the men to their places. Two hundred were stationed in the trenches and behind the breastworks at the mouth of the pass, ready to intercept those of the enemy who succeeded in escaping the boulders and spears from the hilltops. These men stacked their spears behind them and then, at the command of the king, who had been instructed by the Izor, laid themselves upon the ground to sleep. This was an innovation in warfare so great that open rebellion was threatened. The novices in civilized and scientific fighting were fully convinced that the enemy was nowhere in sight and that they would be called when the proper moment came.

Then came the manning of the four hundred boulders on the top of the hills. All along the line of heavy rocks men were stationed with instructions to roll them into the pass when the signal was given, Both sides of the pass were lined with these boulders, The king was as near in ecstasies over the arrangements as one of his nature could possibly be. He prostrated himself a dozen times before the wonderfully clever genius who was in command, twice bumping his head against exceedingly hard rocks that he had been unable to see when he began his precipitous collapse to reverence.

It was after midnight before the army in ambush was ready for the conflict. Hugh was amazed to find the men cool and submissive, obeying every order that he managed in some way to convey to them. With everything in readiness there was nothing to do but to wait for the crisis, so he threw himself on the grass at the top of the highest point on the ridge near the opening to the valley, and tried to sleep.

While he reclined there, thinking of a sweet-faced woman and her Reserves, fully eighteen hundred warriors were stealthily coming up from the sea. Six wakeful sentinels were waiting for them.

CHAPTER XXVII
THE LADY TENNYS RESERVES

The night passed. One, two, three o'clock went by on the trip to sunrise. Hugh dozed at times despite the strain on his nerves. When at last he arose to stretch himself, he saw the faint gray meeting and mingling with the black in the skies, and knew that the crisis was almost at hand.

Swiftly, silently through the darkness came six forms, hurrying from the distant end of the pass with the alarm. They sped into the presence of the king and Hugh just as the first gleam of light began to make itself visible in the east. The messengers had seen the enemy, by that time entering the pass from the north. In an instant Hugh's little army was in a state of wild perturbation. One could have heard the gnashing of teeth had he walked among the groups receiving final orders from King Pootoo. Silence reigned again--the silence of death.

Something that sounded like the heavy breathing of a man came to the ears of the waiters. It was the sweep of naked feet over the pebbly, sandy bottom of the pass, the cautious movement of bodies through the air, sounds growing plainer until they resembled the rustling of grass through which a snake is gliding. To Hugh the intense moments seemed like hours. Would they never come to view? Would the ambush succeed? Why were they so slow? He could have gone ten miles while they were covering the scant mile, he swore in his fever of anxiety.

At last the king pointed excitedly down the dark gulch, and, for the first time, Ridgeway realized that he was facing an enemy in battle. His eyes did not blink, so intently were they glued upon the dim, uncertain objects that moved in the distance. The sword at his side was gripped in a fierce but unconscious grasp. He placed his hand over his throbbing heart; a damp chill seemed to break through every pore in his body.

"In five minutes this place will be hell!" he muttered, and the king looked at him inquiringly.

Slowly the moving mass resolved itself into a thousand entities, swarming towards the opening at the end of the pass. It required all of his coolness and self-possession to control the wild impulse to begin the fight long before the proper moment. To his surprise, not one of his men moved from his position.

In advance of the main body of invaders was a small detachment of scouts. Hugh saw that they would reach the trenches ahead of the army and that the trap would be revealed. His heart almost failed him as he looked down upon that now distinguishable mass crowding up through the gorge. There seemed to be thousands of them, strapping, fierce, well-armed savages. Their spears looked not unlike a field of dancing cornstalks.

It was necessary to check the little advance guard before the plans could go amiss. Ridgeway, suddenly calm and deliberate, despatched the king with instructions to have his men spear the scouts as they came up, driving them back. Pootoo wriggled stealthily to the breastworks below, reaching the position a few moments ahead of the Oolooz squad. Perhaps one hundred yards behind this detail came the swarm of battle men. There was something in the advance that suggested a cat stealing upon an unsuspecting bird.

By this time it was quite light, although sunrise was half an hour away. In the gray, phantom-producing gloom Hugh could see his own men behind the boulders, awaiting his command. A sudden shriek broke on the stillness, causing him to leap as if some one had struck him violently. Then there was a succession of yells and the rushing of feet. He glanced nervously toward the trenches. A dozen Oolooz men were flying back toward the main body, while not a sign of Pootoo or his men was visible. They had delivered a few spears and had dropped back into the trench.

The main body in the pass swayed and jammed in the effort to halt, but the rear pushed forward so clamorously that the whole mass rolled up the ravine fairly into the death trap before it began to understand the meaning of the yells and the sudden retreat of the scouts.

"Now is the time," thought the American. His tall form sprang from behind the tree at the edge of the little cliff. His white face was whiter than ever, his eyes flashed, his long frame quivered. Up went his sword arm and loud came the cry from his lips:

"Fire!"

As if by magic two long rows of immutable boulders wabbled for a second and then thundered down the hillside, while ten score of wild, naked human beings sent up yells of horrid glee to the unveiling dome above.

No pen can describe the flight of those death-dealing rocks as they bounded over the sharp declivities, gaining speed with each revolution, scattering earth, gravel and underbrush with the force of a cyclone, leaping at last with a crushing roar into the very midst of the stupefied army. There was a sickening, grinding crash, an instant of silence, then the piteous wails and groans and the spectacle of a writhing, rolling, leaping, struggling mixture of human forms. Almost as the first volley of rocks left its position to roll upon the vanguard of the ambushed horde, the howling devils on the hill tops were scurrying toward the second row, farther to the right. Down poured this second storm of rocks, increasing the panic below, literally slaughtering the helpless wretches by the score.

Ridgeway looked upon this scene of destruction as if fascinated. He was powerless to move. He had not dreamed that his trap could produce such a havoc. The bottom of the pass was strewn with grovelling, shrieking bodies, trampled beneath the feet of their uninjured but insane companions. Dead and wounded, crushed and maimed, made up the surging humanity in the fatal pass. The rocks had mowed them down. Devastation had come like lightning from the skies. It was horrible!

Closing his eyes, he turned away, utterly sick. A moment later he glanced about, hearing the victorious, eager savages on the heights screeching like madmen. From all sides they were swarming toward him, concentrating for the swoop down the hillside at his command. He was awakened to action, his mind grasped the importance of immediate decision and he was entirely recovered from his momentary palsy. One particular feature of the horrid scene lingered in his memory till his dying day. The surprised Oolooz men, not knowing whence came the foe or the nature of the charge down the hills, had quietly turned their spears to receive the onslaught, expecting men instead of rocks. He never forgot the brief stand they made.

At first he believed that all had been killed--that the battle was over before it began. But even as he turned for another pitying glance below, the recovered foemen started up the hillside, shouting and screaming with rage. The ground was covered with prostrate or crawling forms, yet, to his amazement, there still seemed to be thousands of vigorous, uninjured warriors.

"Good Lord! There are a million!" he shouted. Leaping forward, he swung his sword on high and with every nerve aquiver he cried:

"Fire!"

It was the only command he had taught them. It meant fight, pure and simple. Across the gulch the command could not be heard, but the men over there were only too glad to follow the example set by their comrades, and from both sides a perfect storm of spears hissed through the air.

Up from the rear rushed scores of Oolooz warriors. Despite the vicious attack they crowded steadily up the hillside toward the crest on which stood Hugh and his practically unbroken front. Through some sort of natural generalship they confined their charge to the hills on one side of the pass. Ridgeway saw this with alarm. He knew that they would eventually force their way to the top. Yet the spears from above mowed down the climbing savages like tenpins, while their weapons did little or no damage. With each distinct volley from above the advancing foe fell back, but rallied like heroes. By this time hundreds of them were down; broad daylight made the pass look like a slaughter pen.

Ridgeway ran among his men, urging them to stand firm, to beat back the foe, and they responded with an ardor that was nothing less than fiendishness itself. Their spears were unerringly thrown, but the supply was diminishing; it was the question of a very few minutes before they would be without ammunition. Hugh's hope lay in the possibility that the foe would soon retreat, believing itself unable to cope with an adversary whose numbers were unknown and who held such an advantageous position.

He soon saw that he would have to quickly withdraw his men from the hill after one of the temporary repulses, taking them to the trench at the mouth of the pass. Almost as he was forming this plan, he realized that it would be necessary to carry it out at once.

Far down the pass, beyond his line, the enemy came swarming up the undefended slope, steep as it was, and some of the foremost were already scrambling over the last few feet intervening. He yelled to the men, pointing to the danger spot and then toward the trenches, making a sign immediately thereafter to deliver a telling volley into the struggling ranks.

The savages seemed to understand, and he devoutly thanked God, for they sent a shower of spears into the horde and then dashed helter-skelter in the direction of the trenches where lay the king and two hundred men. Wild yells of triumph came from behind, and long before the descent to the valley was reached by the fleeing white man and his dusky army, the Ooloozers were pouring into the tree-covered summit like so many sheep.

Down the hill sped Hugh and his men. Pootoo saw them coming and waved his spear frantically. As the retreating army rolled headlong into the trenches and behind the breastworks, the enemy arrived at the crest of the hill. Breathlessly Hugh motioned for Pootoo to call the men from the opposite hill into action at once.

A volley of spears shot into and over the trenches, followed by a whirlwind of the long, slender messengers of death, several of them taking effect. Pootoo's men returned the volley from behind the breastworks, but the rampant chargers were not to be checked. Up to the very edge of the trench they rushed, and from that moment it does not lie within the power of the writer to depict the horrors of the conflict in detail. Hugh's men, well protected and well armed, hurled death into the ranks, of the fearless enemy as it crowded to the high breastworks. And out from the mouth of the pass poured the mass of Ooloozers who had not ascended the hill.

Ridgeway, cutting viciously away at the black bodies as they plunged against the wall behind which they stood, felt the spears crash against his shield, heard them hiss past, saw them penetrate the earthworks all about him. At another time he would have wondered how he and his men could hope to withstand such an onslaught. One thing he did have time to observe, and that was the surprise, consternation, even fear that came into the enraged faces of the assaulting savages when they saw him plainly. They were looking for the first time on the face of a white man--the new god of their enemies.

A sudden change in the tide of battle, though brief, transferred the brunt of conflict to another quarter. A withering rain of spears struck the enemy on the flank and rear, and down from the opposite hilltop rushed the mob that had formed the other boulder squad at the beginning of the fight, but who had done nothing after the first charge of the Oolooz men up the hill. They threw themselves upon the enemy and were soon lost in the boiling mass. Gaining fresh courage and a renewed viciousness, the men in the trenches forsook the shelter and poured into the open, Hugh being powerless to check them.

"It is all over," groaned he, when he saw his crazy forces jump into the very centre of the seething mass. With a white man's shrewdness he remained behind the friendly breastworks, a dozen of his warriors fighting by his side. Repeated rushes against his position were broken by the desperate resistance of this small company. Hugh's heavy sword was dripping with blood; it had beaten in the skull of many a foe, had been driven beneath the shields and through the bodies of others. To him it seemed hours instead of minutes since the battle began; his arm was growing tired, his brain was whirling, his body was dripping with perspiration. Still his blood boiled and surged with savage enjoyment; he was now yelling with the same frenzy that filled the wild men; pure delight grew out of the fall of every opponent that went down under his sword.

At last the Oolooz leader, a blood-covered savage as large as Pootoo, led his men up to the breastworks, driving the defenders into the trenches and down the gentle slope. Triumph was theirs apparently, and their yelling was full of it. But inch by inch Pootoo fought them back. Once the king looked helplessly at Hugh, as if praying for him as a god to exert his influence in the unequal struggle. That glance was one of entreaty, surprise, but Hugh could also see disgust in it. It stung him strangely.

Although he had fought and killed more men than any one on either side, perhaps, he had not gone forth from behind the breastworks; he was not out in the thick of it. With a yell of encouragement to the men, he flung himself over the little wall, alighting on the soft body of a corpse. With his supporters at his heels he dashed to the king's side. Inside of two minutes he was struck in the leg by a spear, his hand was cut by a glancing blow from a club and his shield arm was battered so fearfully that it required an effort to hold it in front of his body. Blood streamed into his eyes and down his breast, his arms grew weak, his blows were feeble, his knees trembled, and he was ready to drop. Twice he went to his knees only to stagger to his feet again. Three times Pootoo's mighty club beat down warriors who were about to brain him.

His mind was chaotic, filled with the now certain defeat and the heart-breaking thought that Lady Tennys would be left to the mercies of the victors. Tears were mingling with the blood; his very soul was crying for strength, for hope, for salvation. In his din-stricken ears ran that wail: "What will become of me if you are killed?" Her face seemed to float in front of his eyes, her voice came trembling and lulling and soft through the hellish sounds, piercing the savagery with gentle trustfulness, urging him to be brave, strong and true. Then Grace Vernon's dear face, dim and indistinct, lured him forward into the strife, her clear voice, mingling with the plaintive tones of the other, commanding him to come to her. He must win! He must win!

But the great horde of Oolooz warriors were at last breaking down the smaller force and all seemed lost.

Suddenly new life sprang up among the battered defenders. Joyous yells bespoke a favorable turn of the tide. The enemy fell slowly back, relinquishing the vantage gained. Far behind Ridgeway's fainting form there arose the shouts of fresh factors in the fight.

He fell against the embankment and slowly turned his eyes toward the river. Once more Pootoo's gigantic weapon saved his defenceless head from the blow of an eager antagonist, but the white man knew naught of his escape. His dazed eyes saw only the band of warriors flying over the plain toward the field of battle. Far in their rear came a fluttering white form.

Hardly was he able to realize that help was at hand before the released, ferocious young fellows who had been left behind to guard her Ladyship were plunging over the breastworks all about him.

The Reserves to the rescue!

Exaltation, glorious and strength-giving, flushed through him and he leaped again into the fray. The new hope had come. He was once more battling with a mighty vigor. Fury reigned for a moment and then came the stampede. Down the little valley fled the foe, the conquerors in mad pursuit.

"'THEY HAVE KILLED YOU! LET THEM KILL ME!'"

He was unable to follow, but his heart glowed with joy as he staggered blindly toward the earthworks. As he fell, half fainting, against the bloody bank, the agonized figure in white flew up to the opposite side.

"Hugh, Hugh," she wailed, burying her face in her hands. "They have killed you! Let them kill me!"

"Oh, it's--nothing--" he gasped, trying to smile. "I'm all right, little woman, but--you--got--here--just--in--time! Didn't I say--get--home--for--lunch--or something--like--that?"

And he knew no more.

CHAPTER XXVIII
TO THE VICTOR BELONGS--?

It was a month before Ridgeway was able to leave his couch and to sit beneath the awning in front of the temple. Not that he had been so severely wounded in the battle of June thirtieth, but that his whole system had collapsed temporarily.

After the first terrible fear, Tennys gave herself entirely to the task of caring for him. Night and day she watched, worked, and prayed over the tossing sufferer. In seasons of despair, created by the frequent close encroachments of death, she experienced dreams that invariably ended with the belief that she heard his dying gasps. Until she became thoroughly awake and could hear the movements of the two savages who sat faithfully in the next room with their Izor, her heart was still with a terror so depressing that it well-nigh drove her mad.

The wounds in his legs and side were closed and the great bruises on his back and head were reduced. When he, faint and weak, began to understand what was going on about him, he saw the face of one of the two women over whom he had raved in his delirium. In the hours when death seemed but a step away he had plaintively called for Grace and then for Tennys. A strange gladness filled the heart of the one beside him when he uttered the unconscious appeal to her. Sometimes she found herself growing red over the things he was saying to her in his ravings; again she would chill with the tender words that went to Grace. Then came the day when he saw and knew her. Often in the days of his convalescence she would start from a reverie, certain that she heard him call as he did in delirium, only to sink back and smile sadly with the discovery that she had been dreaming.

The village of Ridgehunt was a great hospital for weeks after the fight. Lady Tennys herself had ordered the dead to be buried in the trenches. For the first time in the history of the island the Oolooz men had been beaten. She spent many hours in telling Hugh of the celebrations that followed the wonderful achievements.

"There is one thing about our friends that I have not told you, Hugh," she said one night as they sat under the awning. "You have been so weak that I feared the shock might hurt you."

"You think of my comfort always," he said gratefully.

"You never knew that they brought a number of prisoners to the village and--and--oh, it is too horrible to tell you."

"Brought them to the village? What for?"

"They intended to eat them," she said, shuddering.

"Great Scott! They are not cannibals?"

"I couldn't believe it until I saw them making ready for their awful feast out there. I shall never be able to eat meat again. Alzam brought me a piece of the horrid stuff. They executed the prisoners before I could interfere."

"Oh, that's too horrible!"

"Sick and terrified, I went among the men who were dancing about the feast they were ready to devour, and, assuming a boldness I did not feel, commanded them to desist. The king was bewildered at first, then chagrined, but as I threatened him ferociously--"

"I should have enjoyed seeing you ferocious."

"He called the brutes away and then I gave orders to have every one of the bodies buried. For several days after that, however, the men were morose and ugly looking, and I am sure it was hard for them to submit to such a radical change."

"Talk about missionaries! You are a wonder!"

"I could not have done it as a missionary, Mr. Ridgeway. It was necessary for me to exert my authority as a goddess."

"And so they are cannibals," he mused, still looking at her spirited face.

"Just think what might have happened to us," she said.

That night as he lay on his couch he was forced to admit that the inconsolable grief that had borne down so heavily upon him at first was almost a part of the past. The pain inspired by the loss of a loved one was being mysteriously eased. He was finding pleasure in a world that had been dark and drear a few short months before. He was dimly conscious of a feeling that the companionship of Tennys Huntingford was beginning to wreak disaster to a supposedly impregnable constancy.

Tears came to his eyes as he murmured the name of the girl who had sailed so blithely from New York with his love as her only haven. He called himself the basest of wretches, the most graceless of lovers. He sobbed aloud at last in his penitence, and his heart went back to the night of the wreck. His love went down to the bottom of the sea, craving a single chance to redeem itself before the one it had wounded and humiliated. Before he fell asleep his conscience was relieved of part of its weight and the strong, sweet face of Grace Vernon passed from his vivid thoughts into vague dreams.

In the next apartment tranquilly slept the disturber, the trespasser in the fields of memory, the undoer of a long-wrought love. He had tried to learn the way to her heart, wondering if she cared for him as he had more than once suspected. In pursuing this hazardous investigation he had learned nothing, had seen nothing but perfect frankness and innocence, but had become more deeply interested than he knew until this night of recapitulation.

One night, two or three after he had thrown off the delirium, he heard her praying in her room, softly, earnestly. Of that prayer one plea remained in his memory long after her death: "Oh, God, save the soul of Grace Vernon. Give to her the fulness of Thy love. If she be still alive, protect and keep her safe until in Thy goodness she may be restored to him who mourns for her. Save and bless Hugh Ridgeway."

The days and weeks went by and Hugh grew well and strong. To Tennys he was not the same Hugh as of old. She perceived a change and wondered. One day at sundown he sat moodily in front of the temple. She was lying in the hammock near by. There had been one of the long, and to her inexplicable, silences. He felt that her eyes were upon him and knew that they were wistful and perplexed.

Try as he would, he could not keep his own eyes in leash; something irresistible made him lift them to meet her gaze. For a moment they looked at each other in a mute search for something neither was able to describe. He could not hold out against the pleading, troubled, questioning eyes, bent so solemnly upon his own. The wounds in her heart, because of his indifference, strange and unaccountable to her, gaped in those blue orbs.

A tremendous revulsion of feeling took possession of him; what he had been subduing for weeks gained supremacy in an instant. He half rose to his feet as if to rush over and crush her in his arms, but a mightier power than his emotion held him back. That same unseen, mysterious power compelled him to turn about and almost run from the temple, leaving her chilled and distressed by his action. The power that checked him was Memory.

She was deeply hurt by this last impulsive exhibition of disregard. A bewildering sense of loneliness oppressed her. He despised her! All the world grew black for her. All the light went out of her heart. He despised her! There was a faintness in her knees when she essayed to arise from the hammock. A little cry of anguish left her lips; a hunted, friendless look came into her eyes.

Staggering to the end of the temple, she looked in the direction he had taken. Far down the line of hills she saw him standing on a little elevation, his back toward her, his face to the river. Some strong influence drew her to him. Out of this influence grew the wild, unquenchable desire to understand. Hardly realizing what she did, she hurried through the growing dusk toward the motionless figure. As she came nearer a strange timidity, an embarrassment she had never felt before, seized upon her and her footsteps slackened.

He had not seen her. A panicky inclination to fly back to the temple came over her. In her heart welled a feeling of resentment. Had he any right to forget what she had done for him?

He heard her, turned swiftly, and--trembled in every joint. They were but a few paces apart and she was looking unwaveringly into his eyes.

"I have followed you out here to ask why you treat me so cruelly," she said after a long silence which she Bought to break but could not. He distinguished in this pathetic command, meant to be firm and positive, the tremor of tears.

"I--I do not treat you cruelly, Tennys," he answered disjointly, still looking at the slight, graceful figure, as if unable to withdraw his eyes.

"What do you call it?" she asked bitterly.

"You wrong me--" he began.

"Wrong you? No, I do not. You saved me from the sea and you have done much for me until within the past few weeks. I had begun to forget that I am here because fate substituted me for another. Hugh, do not let your love for Grace and your regret at not having saved her turn you against me. I am not here because I could have helped it. You must know that I--"

"For Heaven's sake, Tennys, don't talk like that! The trouble is that I do not regret having saved you. That's why you see the change in me--that's why I've hurt you. I cannot be to you what I would be--I cannot and be true to myself," he cried fiercely.

"What do you mean? Why are you so unhappy, Hugh? Have I hurt you?' she asked, coming quite close in sudden compassion.

"Hurt me!" he exclaimed. "You will kill me!" She paled with the thought that he was delirious again or crazed from the effects of the fever.

"Don't say that, Hugh. I care more for you than for any one in the world. Why should I hurt you?" she asked tenderly, completely misunderstanding him.

"You don't mean to, but you do. I have tried to conquer it but I cannot. Don't you know why I have forced myself to be unhappy during the past few weeks? Can't you see why I am making you unhappy, too, in my struggle to beat down the something that has driven everything else out of my mind?"

"Don't talk so, Hugh; it will be all right. Come home now and I will give you some wine and put some cool bandages on your head. You are not well." She was so gentle, so unsuspecting that he could contain himself no longer.

"I love you--I worship you! That is why I am cruel to you!" he burst out. A weakness assailed him and he leaned dizzily against the tree at his side. He dared not look at her, but he marvelled at her silence. If she loved him, as he believed, why was she so quiet, so still?

"Do you know what you say?" she asked slowly.

"I have said it to myself a thousand times since I left you at the temple. I did not intend to tell you; I had sworn you should never know it. What do you think of me?"

"I thought you called it love that sent you to Manila," she said wonderingly, wounding without malice.

"It was love, I say. I loved her better than all the world and I have not forgotten her. She will always be as dear to me as she was on the night I lost her. You have not taken her place. You have gone farther and inspired a love that is new, strange, overpowering--infinitely greater, far different from the love I had known before. She was never to me what you are. That is what drives me mad--mad, do you hear? I have simply been overwhelmed by it."

"I must be dreaming," she murmured.

"I have tried to hide it from myself, but it has broken down all barriers and floods the world for me."

"It is because we are here alone in this island--"

"No, no! Not that, I swear. It would have come sooner or later."

"You are not like other men. I have not thought of you as I see you now. I cannot understand being loved by you. It hurts me to see that you are in earnest. Oh, Hugh, how sorry I am," she cried, laying her hand upon his arm. His heart dropped like lead. He saw that he had been mistaken--she did not love him.

"You are learning that I am not the harlequin after all," he said bitterly.

"There is no one in all the world so good and strong and true."

"You--you *will* love me?"

"You must not ask that of me. I am still Lady Huntingford, a wife for all we know. Yet if I loved you, I would tell you so. Have I not told you that I cannot love? I have never loved. I never shall. Don't look like that, Hugh. I would to God I could love you," she exclaimed. His chin had sunk upon his breast and his whole body relaxed through sheer dejection.

"I'll make you love me!" he cried after a moment's misery in the depths, his spirits leaping high with the quick recoil. His eager hands seized her shoulders and drew her close, so close that their bodies touched and his impassioned eyes were within a few inches of hers of startled blue. "I'll make you love me!"

"Please let me go. Please, Hugh," she murmured faintly.

"You must--you shall love me! I cannot live without you. I'll have you whether you will or no," he whispered fiercely.

She did not draw back, but looked him fairly in the eye as she spoke coldly, calmly, even with a sneer.

"You are master here and I am but a helpless woman. Would you force me to forget that you have been my ideal man?"

"Tennys!" he cried, falling back suddenly. "You don't think I would harm you--oh, you know I didn't mean that! What must you think of me?"

He put his hand over his eyes as if in deep pain, and, turning away, leaned against the tree unsteadily. With his first words, his first expression, she knew she had wronged him. A glad rush of blood to her heart set it throbbing violently.

She could not have explained the thrill that went through her when he grasped her shoulders, nor could she any more define the peculiar joy that came when she took a step forward and placed her hands gently, timidly on his arm.

"Forgive me, Hugh, I must have been mad to say what I did. You are too noble--too good--" she began in a pleading little quaver.

"I knew you couldn't mean it," he exclaimed, facing her joyously. "How beautiful you are!" he added impetuously. He was looking down, into that penitent face and the cry was involuntary. She smiled faintly and he raised his arms as if to clasp her to his breast, come what may. The smile lingered, yet his arms dropped to his sides. She had not moved, had not taken her eyes from his, but there was an unrelenting command in the soft words she uttered. "Be careful. I am always to trust you, Hugh." He bowed his head and they walked slowly homeward.

CHAPTER XXIX
THE OTHER SURRENDER

The first few days and nights after this episode found Ridgeway despairing and unhappy, but as time removed the sting from defeat, his hopes began to flounder to the surface again, growing into a resolution, strong and arrogant. He devoted himself to her tenderly, thoughtfully, unreservedly. There was something subtle in his gallantry, something fascinating in his good humor, something in everything he did that attracted her more than it had before. She only knew that she was happy when with him and that he was unlike any man she had known.

There were times when she imagined that he was indifferent to the shock his pride had received at her hands, and at such times she was puzzled to find herself piqued and annoyed. A little gnawing pain kept her awake with these intermittent fears.

She became expert in the art of making garments from the woven grass. Her wardrobe contained some remarkable gowns, and his was enlarged by the addition of "Sunday trousers" and a set of shirt blouses. They wore sandals instead of shoes. Each had a pair of stockings, worn at the time of the wreck, but they were held in sacred disuse against the hoped-for day of deliverance.

One day, late in September, after the sun had banished the mists from the air and the dampness from the ground by a clear day's process, they wandered down between the gateposts to the beach where they had first landed with Pootoo. The sun was sinking toward the water-line and they sat wistfully watching it pass into the sea. For nearly five months they had lived with the savages, for the greater portion not unhappily, but always with the expectation that some day a vessel would come to take them back to civilization.

"It has not been so unpleasant, after all, has it?" she asked. "We have been far more comfortable than we could have prayed for."

"I should enjoy seeing a white man once in a while, though, and I'd give my head for this morning's Chicago newspaper," he answered rather glumly.

"I have been happier on this island than I ever was in my life. Isn't it strange? Isn't it queer that we have not gone mad with despair? But I, for one, have not suffered a single pang, except over the death of our loved ones."

"Lord Huntingford included," maliciously.

"That is unkind, Hugh. I am ashamed to say it, but I want to forget that he ever lived."

"You will have plenty of time to forget all you ever knew before we die. We'll spend the rest of our days in that nigger village back there. If I should die first I suppose you'd forget me in a week or so. It--"

"Why, Hugh! You know better than that! Why do you say such disagreeable things?"

"I'm not worth remembering very long," he said lamely. She smiled and said the statement threw a different light on the question. Whereupon he did not know whether to laugh or scowl.

"This dear old island," she cried, looking toward the great rocks lovingly. "Really, I should be sorry to leave it."

"When the ship comes, I'll go back to America, and you may remain here if you like and be the only Izor in the business." He said it in jest, but she looked at him solemnly for a moment and then turned her eyes out to sea. She was reclining on her side, her hand supporting her head, her elbow in the sand. He sat five feet away, digging holes in the sand with an odd little walking stick. One of her sandalled feet protruded from beneath the hem of her garment, showing ever so little of the bare, white, fascinating ankle.

"I should despise the place if I had to live here a day without you," she said simply.

"What do you mean?" She did not answer at once. When she did, it was earnestly and without the least embarrassment.

"Can't I make you understand how much you are to me?" she asked without a blush. "You are the best, the noblest man I've ever known. I like you so well that I do not know how I could live if I did not have you to talk to, if I could not see you and be with you. Do you know what I did last night?"

He could only shake his head and tremble with the joy of feeling once more that she loved him and did not understand.

"I prayed that we might never be taken from the island," she said hurriedly, as if expecting him to condemn her for the wish. He rolled over on his back, closed his eyes, and tried to control a joyous, leaping heart. "It was so foolish, you know, to pray for that, but I've been so contented and happy here, Hugh. Of course, I don't expect we are to live here always. They will find us some day." He opened his eyes and hazarded a glance at his face. She smiled and said, "I'm afraid they will."

There was but the space of five feet between them. How he kept from bounding to her side and clasping her in his arms he never knew; he was in a daze of delight. So certain of her love was he now that, through some inexplicable impulse, he closed his eyes again and waited to hear more of the delicious confession.

"Then we shall leave the prettiest land in the world, a land where show and pomp are not to be found, where nature reigns without the touch of sham, and go back to a world where all is deceit, mockery, display. I love everything on this island," she cried ecstatically. He said nothing, so she continued: "I may be an exile forever, but I feel richer instead of poorer away off here in this unknown paradise. How glorious it is to be one's self absolutely, at all times and in all places, without a thought of what the world may say. Here I am free, I am a part of nature."

"Do you think you know yourself fully?" he asked as quietly as he could.

"Know myself?" she laughed. "Like a book."

"Could you love this island if you were here alone?"

"Well, I--suppose--not," she said, calculatively. "It would not be the same, you know."

"Don't you know why you feel as you do about this God-forsaken land, Tennys Huntingford?" he demanded, suddenly drawing very near to her, his burning eyes bent upon hers. "Don't you know why you are happy here?" She was confused and disturbed by his manner. That same peculiar flutter of the heart she had felt weeks ago on the little knoll attacked her sharply.

"I--I--I'm sure--I am happy just because I am, I dare say," she faltered, conscious of an imperative inclination to lower her eyes, but strangely unable to do so.

"You love this island because you love me," he whispered in her ear.

"No, no! It is not that! Please don't be foolish again, Hugh. You will make me very unhappy."

"But you do love me. You love me, and you do not know it," he said, thrilled with exultation. She looked at him wonderingly, a half scornful, half dubious smile flitting over her face.

"I will try to be patient with you. Don't you think I know my own mind?" she asked.

"No; you do not," he said vigorously. "Let me ask you a few questions, and I beg of you, for your own sake and mine, to answer them without equivocation. I'll prove to you that you love me."

"Who is to be the judge?" she asked merrily. She trembled and turned cold as he took her hand in his and--she was not merry.

"First, is there another man in the world that you would rather have here? Answer, dear." The blood mounted to her cheek at the term of endearment.

"Not one," she answered firmly, trying to smile.

"Have you never thought--be honest, now--that you don't want to leave the island because it would mean our separation?"

"Yes, but--but it would be the same with anybody else if I cared for him," she exclaimed quickly.

"But there is no one else, is there?" She looked at him helplessly. "Answer!"

"Oh, Hugh, I--it would not be right for me to encourage you by answering that. Please let us go back to the village," she pleaded.

"Well, I know there is no one else. Tell me that you don't want to leave me because we should drift apart in the big world," he persisted.

"I had thought of that," she said so low that he could barely hear.

"You have prayed that Grace may be alive. What would it mean to you if she should be alive and we should be reunited?"

"I--I don't know," she muttered blankly.

"Would you be willing and happy to give me up to her?"

"I never thought of that," she said. Then a terror leaped to her eyes and her breast heaved as with pain. "Oh, Hugh, what would that mean to me? I could not give you up--I could not!" she cried, clasping his hand feverishly in both of hers.

"Would you be glad to see us married, to see us living together, to see children come to us? Would you be happy if I forgot you in my love for her?" he went on remorselessly, yet delightedly.

"You couldn't forget me," she whispered, faint and trembling now. "You don't mean to say I never could be near you again!" There was dismay in her face and a sob in her voice.

"Oh, occasionally, but in a very formal way."

"I believe I should die," she cried, unable to restrain herself.

"You admit then that you want me for yourself only," he said.

"Yes, yes I do, Hugh! I want you every minute of my life!"

"Now you are beginning to know what love is," he breathed in her ear. His eager arm stole slowly around her shoulders and, as she felt herself being drawn close to him irresistibly, a sweet wonder overwhelmed her. The awakening had come. With singing heart she lifted her hands to his cheeks, bewitched by the new spell, holding his face off from her own while she looked long and yearningly into his eyes. A soft flush crept over her brow and down her neck, her eyes wavered and melted into mirrors of love, her lips parted, but she could not speak. The clasp tightened, his face came nearer, his words sounded like music in her enchanted ears.

"Have I proved that you love me, darling?" "I never knew till now--I never knew till now," she whispered.

Their lips met, their eyes closed, and the world was far, far away from the little stretch of sand.

CHAPTER XXX
WHERE THERE IS NO MINISTER

Six savages lying on the sand far above them saw the strange scene down near the splashing surf and looked blankly at each other. They had never known their Izors to act in that manner, and their benighted minds were troubled.

"Oh, Hugh, those men are looking at us," she protested, after the first moments of joy.

"Let them look," he cried. "You should pity them, dear, for until a few moments ago you were as much in the dark as to the meaning of love as they are now. You were a perfect heathen."

"You are no longer the harlequin. You have become the wizard."

"But it isn't a pantomine," he said.

The shadows were falling and darkness was settling about them as they passed between the giant rocks and into Velvet Valley, his arm around her waist. This new emotion deprived them of the desire to talk. There was a conscious flush in her cheeks, a queer restraint in her voice, a curious timidity in her manner when they sat before the rude table in the temple and partook of food that had never tasted so sweet before; though neither could eat of it. Something had satisfied the grosser appetite; something was tugging and choking the old into submission while the new was crowding into its realm, buoyantly, inflatingly.

They sat in front of the temple until far in the night, revelling in the beauty of the new nature. The whole world seemed different to them as they regarded it through the eyes of love; the moonlit sky was more glorious than ever before; the sombre stillness of the night was more restful; the atmosphere was sweet with the breath of passion; the sports of the savages had a fresh novelty; the torches in front of the king's home flickered with a merrier brilliancy.

All Ridgehunt was awake and celebrating, for it was a festal night. King Pootoo had taken unto himself a new wife, adding one more to the household of his heart. There were dances and sports and all manner of festivities in honor of the event, for it was not oftener than twice a year that the king took a new wife unto his bosom. The white people never knew where the ceremony began. They only knew that on this night of all nights the father of the bride had led her to the king and had drawn with his spear a circle in the soft earth.

Inside of this circle the girl prostrated herself before the groom-elect and the marriage was complete when the royal giant stepped into the wedding ring and lifted her to her feet, leading her to a place among her predecessors, who sat on the ground near by. Then the celebration ran to its highest pitch. Late in the night the weird revelry ceased and the two spectators entered the temple, her hand in his. He led her to the curtained door of her apartment.

"Good-night, dear one," he said softly. She turned her face to his and he held her for an instant to his heart, their lips meeting in a long thrill of ecstasy.

"Good-night," she whispered. He pulled the curtain aside and she slowly entered the room. For an hour afterward he lay awake, wondering what manner of love it was he had given to Grace Vernon. It was not like this.

It was barely daylight when he arose from his couch, dressed and started for a brisk walk over the hills. His ramble was a long one and the village was astir when he came through the woodland, some distance from the temple. Expecting to find Tennys waiting for him, he hastened to their abode. She evidently had not arisen, so, with a tinge of disappointment, he went to his room. Then he heard her, with her women, taking her morning plunge in the pool. The half hour before she made her appearance seemed a day to him. They met in the hallway, he glad and expectant, she shy and diffident. The red that burned in her cheeks turned to white when he kissed her, and her eyelids fell tremblingly with the proof positive that she had not dreamed the exquisite story of the night before.

Later in the morning they called on the king, and that individual promptly prostrated himself. They found the new bride repairing a section of the king's palace that had been blown down by a recent hurricane. Before the white people left, Tennys had the satisfaction and Hugh the amusement of seeing the big chief repairing the rent and the bride taking a rest.

"I've been thinking pretty hard this morning, dear," he said as they walked back to the temple, "especially when I was alone in the forest."

"Can't you think unless you are alone?" she asked, smiling.

"We all think differently sometimes when we are alone, you know. I was just thinking what a dickens of a position we are in for a pair of lovers."

"It seems to me that it is ideal."

"But where is the minister or magistrate?"

"What have they to do with it?"

"Everything, I should say. We can't get married without one or the other," he blurted out. She stopped stockstill with a gasp.

"Get married? Why--why, we have said nothing of getting married."

"And that's just why I am speaking of it now. I want you to be my wife, Tennys. Will you be my wife, dear?" he asked nervously.

"How absurd, Hugh. We may be on this island forever, and how are we to be married here? Besides, I had not thought of it."

"But you must think of it. I can't do all the thinking."

"Lord Huntingford may not be dead," she said, turning pale with the possibility.

"I can swear that he is. He was one of the first to perish. I don't believe you know what love is even now, or you would answer my question."

"Don't be so petulant, please. It is a serious matter to consider, as well as an absurd one, situated as we are. Now, if I should say that I will be your wife, what then?"

"But you haven't said it," he persisted.

"Hugh, dear, I would become your wife to-day, to-morrow--any time, if it were possible."

"That's what I wanted you to say."

"But until we are taken from this island to some place where there is an altar, how can we be married, Hugh?"

"Now, that's something for you to think about. It's almost worried the life out of me."

By this time they had reached the temple. She flung herself carelessly into the hammock, a contented sigh coming from her lips. He leaned against a post near by.

"I am perfectly satisfied here, Hugh," she said tantalizingly. "I've just been thinking that I am safer here."

"Safer?"

"To be sure, dear. If we live here always there can be no one to disturb us, you know. Has it ever occurred to you that some one else may claim you if we go back to the world? And Lord Huntingford may be waiting for me down at the dock, too. I think I shall object to being rescued," she said demurely.

"Well, if he is alive, you can get a divorce from him on the ground of desertion. I can swear that he deserted you on the night of the wreck. He all but threw you overboard."

"Let me ask a question of you. Suppose we should be rescued and you find Grace alive and praying for your return, loving you more than ever. What would become of her if you told her that you loved me and what would become of me if you married her?"

He gulped down a great lump and the perspiration oozed from his pores. Her face was troubled and full of earnestness.

"What could I say to her?" He began to pace back and forth beneath the awning. She watched him pityingly, understanding his struggle.

"Now you know, Hugh, why I want to live here forever. I have thought of all this," she said softly, holding out her hand to him. He took it feverishly, gaining courage from its gentle touch.

"It is better that she should mourn for me as dead," he said at last, "than to have me come back to her with love for another in my breast. Nedra is the safest place in all the world, after all, dearest. I can't bear to think of her waiting for me if she is alive, waiting to--to be my wife. Poor, poor girl!"

"We have been unhappy enough for to-day. Let us forget the world and all its miseries, now that we both love the island well enough to live and die on its soil. Have you thought how indescribably alone we are, perhaps for the rest of our lives? Years and years may be spent here. Let them all be sweet and good and happy. You know I would be your wife if I could, but I cannot unless Providence takes us by the hands and lifts us to the land where some good man can say: 'Whom God hath joined, let not man put asunder.'"

The next day after breakfast she took him by the hand and led him to the little knoll down by the hills. Her manner was resolute; there was a charm in it that thrilled him with expectancy.

"If we are not rescued within a year's time, it is hardly probable that we will ever be found, is it?" she asked reflectively.

"They may find us to-morrow and they may never see the shores of this island."

"But as they have not already discovered it, there is certainly some reason. We are in a part of the sea where vessels do not venture, that is evident," she argued persuasively.

"But why do you ask?"

"Because you want me to be your wife," she said, looking him frankly in the eye.

"I can only pray that we may be found," he said wistfully.

"And in case we are never found?"

"I shall probably die an old bachelor," he laughed grimly. For some moments she was in a deep study, evidently questioning the advisability or propriety of giving expression to what was in her mind.

"Are there not a great many methods of observing the marriage ceremony, Hugh? And are they not all sacred?" she asked seriously.

"What are you trying to get at, dear?"

"I may as well tell you what I have been thinking of since last night. You will not consider me bold and unwomanly, I know, but I want to be your wife. We may never leave this island, but we can be married here."

"Married here!" he exclaimed. "You mean--"

"I mean that the ceremony of these natives can be made as sacred in the eye of God as any in all the world. Nine-tenths or more of all the marriages in the world are crimes, because man, not God, welds the bonds. Therefore, I say frankly to you, Hugh, that I will marry you some day according to the custom of these people, as sacred to me as that of any land on earth."

At first he could hardly believe that he had heard aright, but as she progressed and he saw the nobility, the sincerity, of her declaration, a wave of reverential love swept through his heart. The exaltation of a moment before was quelled, destroyed by a sacred, solemn regard for her. There was a lump in his throat as he bent over and gently took her hand in his, lifting it to his lips.

"Are you sure of yourself, darling?" he whispered.

"I could not have spoken had I not been sure. I am very sure of myself. I trust you so fully that I am sure of you as well."

He kissed her rapturously.

"God bless you. I can hardly breathe for the joy I feel."

"But you do not say you will marry me," she smiled.

"You shall be my wife to-day," he cried.

"I beg your pardon," she said gaily, "but as the bride I am the arbiter of time. If in a year from now we are still here, I will be your wife."

"A year! Great heaven! Impossible! I won't wait that long. Now be sensible, Tennys."

"I am very sensible. While I am willing to recognize the sacredness of the marriage laws here, I must say that I prefer those of my own land. We must wait a year for deliverance. If it does not come, then I will--"

"But that's three hundred and sixty-five days--an age. Make it a month, dear. A month is a long, long time, too."

"A year is a long time," she mused. "I will marry you on the twenty-third of next May."

"Six months!" he exclaimed reprovingly.

"You must accept the decision. It is final."

CHAPTER XXXI
THE WEDDING RING

The six months passed and the strange wedding was near at hand. The underlying hope that they might be discovered and restored to the life that seemed so remotely far behind them was overshadowed, obliterated by the conditions and preparations attending their nuptials. Sincerity of purpose and the force of their passion justified beyond all question the manner in which they were to become man and wife in this heathen land of Nedra.

Wedding garments had been woven in the most artistic and approved fashion. Lady Tennys's trousseau was most elaborate, far more extensive than even the most lavish desires of civilization could have produced.

Their subjects vied with each other in the work of decorating their idols for the ceremony. Never before had native ingenuity and native endurance been put to such a test. Worship was the master workman and energy its slave.

"If they keep on bringing in clothes, dear, we'll have a bargain-day stock to dispose of some time. We'd have to live two hundred years in order to try 'em on and thereby set the fashion in exclusive wedding garments." Hugh made this comment as they stood surveying the latest consignment of robes, which reposed with considerable reverence on the specially constructed tables in the new part of Tennys Court. Amused perplexity revealed itself in the faces of the couple.

"I think this last pair of trousers, if you should ever wear them, will revolutionize the habits of the island. You will look especially killing in green, Hugh."

"That seashell parasol of yours is unique, but I imagine it will be too heavy for you to carry in Piccadilly. I observed that it required two able-bodied men to bring it here, and they seemed immensely relieved when it was off their shoulders--to say nothing of their hands. How do you like this crocodile skin necktie of mine?"

"It is particularly becoming to you--as a belt."

"I'm glad we're to be married soon, Tennys," said he with a grin. "If we put it off a month longer there won't be enough material on land or sea to supply the demand for ready-made garments. As it is, I'm afraid the poor devils will have to go naked themselves until a new crop springs up. I saw one of Pootoo's wives patching his best suit of breech clothes to-day, so he must be hard put for wearing apparel."

"I wonder if it would offend them if we were to distribute what we can't use among the poor."

"I am sure it would please the poor as much as it would please us. They'll all be poor, you know. I have two hundred and eighty-three pairs of trousers and only seven shirts. If I could trade in two hundred and fifty pants for an extra shirt or two, I'd be a much happier bridegroom."

"I dare say they can cut down some of my kimonas to fit you. I have at least three hundred."

"I'd like that blue one and the polka dot up there. They'd make corking shirts. I'll trade you twelve of my umbrellas for one of those grass bonnets of yours. They've been showing too much partiality. Here you've got nearly one hundred suits of pajamas and I have but eleven."

"Yes, but think of the suits of armor they've made for you and not one for me."

"But I wouldn't have time to change armor during a battle, would I? One suit is enough for me. By George, they look worse than football suits, don't they? One couldn't drive a javelin through this chunk of stuff with a battering ram."

Everywhere about them were proofs of the indefatigable but lamentable industry of their dusky friends. Articles inconceivable in more ways than one were heaped in the huge room. Nondescript is no word to describe the heterogeneous collection of things supposed to be useful as well as ornamental. Household utensils, pieces of furniture, bric-a-brac of the most appalling design, knickknacks and gewgaws without end or purpose stared the bewildered white people in the face with an intensity that confused and embarrassed them beyond power of expression.

Shortly after their strange betrothal, Lady Tennys had become a strong advocate of dress reform for women on the island of Nedra. Neat, loose and convenient pajamas succeeded the cumbersome petticoats of everyday life. She, as well as her subjects, made use of these thrifty garments at all times except on occasions of state. They were cooler, more rational--particularly becoming--and less troublesome than skirts, and their advent created great rejoicing among the natives, who, prior to the arrival of their white leaders, had worn little more than nothing and yet had been quite fashionable.

Tennys was secretly rehearsing the marriage ceremony in the privacy of her chamber, prompted and praised by her faithful handmaidens. To her, this startling wedding meant but one thing: the resignation of all intent to leave the island. The day she and Hugh Ridgeway were united according to the custom sacred to these people, their fate was to be sealed forever. It was to bind them irrevocably to Nedra, closing forever to them the chance of returning to the civilization they had known and were relinquishing.

Ridgeway daily inventoried his rapidly increasing stock of war implements, proud of the prowess that had made him a war-god. He soberly prohibited the construction of a great boat which might have carried him and his fair companion back to the old world.

"If we are rescued before the wedding, dear, all well and good; but if not, then we want no boat, either of our own or other construction, to carry us away. Our wedding day will make us citizens of Ridgehunt until death ends the regime. Our children may depart, but we are the Izors of Nedra to the last hour of life."

"Yes," she said simply.

The fortnight immediately prior to the day set for the wedding was an exciting one for the bride and groom-to-be. Celebration of the great event was already under way by the natives. Great feasts were planned and executed; war dances and riots of worship took place, growing in fervor and splendor as the day approached; preparations never flagged but went on as if the future existence of the whole world depended entirely upon the outcome of this great ceremony.

"Yesterday it was a week, now it is but six days," said Hugh early one morning as they set forth to watch their adorers at work on the great ceremonial temple with its "wedding ring." The new temple was a huge affair, large enough to accommodate the entire populace.

"To-morrow it will be but five days," she said; "but how long the days are growing." They sat beside the spring on the hillside and musingly surveyed the busy architects on the plain below.

"How are the rehearsals progressing?" he asked.

"Excellently, but I am far from being a perfect savage. It doesn't seem possible that I shall ever learn how to fall gracefully into that ring. I believe I shall insist that you turn your head at the particular juncture, for I know you'll laugh at me," she said with a great show of concern.

"I don't like that part of the service. It's a shame for me to stand by and to see you tumble at my feet. Firstly, it's not your place; secondly, it's liable to hurt you; lastly, I'd feel a most unmanly brute. Wonder if we can't modify that part of it somehow?"

"I might be carried in on a litter and set down in the ring, or we might stretch a hammock," she said, laughing merrily.

"I'm determined on one point and that is in regard to the pile of soft grass. Pootoo promised to cut a lot of it and put it in the ring. You shan't break any bones if I can help it."

"Pootoo is to be master of ceremonies in every sense of the word, I can see. I am the ward of a king."

At last the day arrived.

They were to enter the ceremonial temple at high noon and in their ears were to be the sound of timbrels and brass, trumpets and drums and the glad though raucous songs of a kingdom.

Early in the day Tennys Huntingford submitted herself to be arrayed for the ceremony by her proud, jealous maidens. She remained alone and obscure in her chamber, awaiting the moment when King Pootoo should come for her. Her gown was of the purest white. It was her own handiwork, the loving labor of months. True, it would have looked odd in St. James or in the cathedral, but no bride ever walked to those chancels in more becoming raiment--no bride was ever more beautiful, no woman ever more to be coveted. Her heart was singing with love and joy; the dreams of months were coming true in these strangely wakeful hours.

Ridgeway wandered nervously through the village, watching the sun as it crept nearer and nearer to the middle of its daily reign--would the minutes never end? Why had the sun stopped in its course across the sky? Why was time so tantalizing?

At last! The sudden clangor of weird instruments filled his ears. He held his hand to his throbbing heart as he turned his gaze toward the door through which she was to come.

Inside the great temple the people of Nedra were singing and chanting with anticipant joy; outside the world was smiling benignly. All Nedra gathered about the circle of earth in which Tennys Huntingford was to cast herself at the feet of her husband and lord for all time.

Hugh had not seen her since the night before, and his eyes were starving for the vision. She came forth, her white hand in the great broad palm of King Pootoo, and she smiled gloriously upon the man who stood below and waited for her to come to him. Together they were to approach the circle. The priests were there to receive them--Hugh first and then his bride; the people were shouting, the instruments were jangling with a fiercer fervor, the sun was passing across the line with his fairest smile and wedding bells were ringing in two red, full hearts.

But even as she came up to him and touched his arm, outside the temple doors, the hand of Fate was lifted and a rigid finger stayed them on the verge.

A mighty intonation, sharp and deafening, came to their ears like a clap of thunder from a clear sky!

Paralysis, stupefaction, fell upon the multitude. There was a silence as of death. Every sound ceased, every heart stood still and every sense was numb. It seemed an hour before Hugh Ridgeway's stiff lips muttered:

"A gun! A ship's gun!"

CHAPTER XXXII
THE CRUISER "WINNETKA"

A moment later pandemonium broke loose. The ceremony was forgotten in the panic that seized the startled savages. There was a rush, a stampede of terror and the great temple was emptied as if by magic. Hugh and his fair companion stood alone in the little plain, staring at the distant gateposts, over which a faint cloud of smoke was lifting, coming up from the sea beyond. The terrified savages had fled to their homes in wildest alarm.

Minutes passed before Hugh could speak again. Power of comprehension seemed to have left them. They were looking dumbly into each other's eyes.

"It *was* a gun--a big gun. Our flag."

Without knowing what they did the two started across the plain, their eyes glued to the great rocks that screened the mystery.

"Can it be the Oolooz men?" she asked.

"The whole Oolooz army, dead or alive, couldn't have made a noise like that. It might have been a volcano breaking through the rocks."

"Then we must not venture down there," she cried, holding back. He threw his big right arm around her waist and broke into a brisk run, taking her along resistlessly.

Together they walked and ran across the plain and through the pass which led to the sea. Far behind straggled a few of the villagers, emboldened by curiosity.

"The rocks seem to be all right," he said, as if a pet theory had been destroyed.

By this time they had passed over the rocks and were upon the sand. Simultaneously they turned their eyes toward the sea, and the sight that burst upon them fairly took the breath from their lungs, leaving them so weak that they staggered. A mile or so out at sea lay a huge ship, white hulled and formidable. There were gun turrets above deck and a swarm of men on board.

Hugh's eyes seemed to turn round and round in his head, his legs began to tremble and his palsied lips parted helplessly, as he pointed to the colors she flew. The American flag fluttered from the mizzen-mast of the great vessel!

Almost crazed by the sight, the castaways, overcoming their stupefaction, forgetting all that had gone before, danced frantically on the sand hill, their ecstasy knowing no bounds.

"Will they see us?" she sobbed, falling at last to the ground in sheer exhaustion, digging her fingers feverishly, unconsciously into the sand.

"Yes, yes! They must see us! We are saved! Saved!" he yelled hoarsely. Then he threw himself beside her, and they were clasped in each other's arms, crying like children. Afterward they could remember only that they saw a boat lowered from the ship. It came toward them, a white uniformed officer standing in the bow. As the boat drew near Tennys began to regain her equanimity. She withdrew hastily from Hugh's arms and arose. With streaming eyes she waved her hands in response to the faraway salute of the officer. Hugh, not so easily restrained, jumped to his feet and shouted:

"Hurrah! Hurrah! God bless you! American sailors! Angels of heaven, every one of you! Hurrah!"

Holding their hands to their temples, the castaways finally calmed themselves enough to look rationally at each other. Their minds began to regain order, their nerves were quieted, their hearts forgot the tumult, and they could think and talk and reason again. In the fierce ecstasy of seeing the long-looked-for rescuers, they had forgotten their expressed desire to live always on the island. Human nature had overcome sentiment and they rejoiced in what they had regarded as a calamity an hour before. Now they realized that a crisis had come.

"Hugh, will they take us away?" she cried, real anguish mingling with triumphant joy.

"Shall we go or stay?" cried he, torn by two emotions.

"It may be the end of our happiness," she whispered, pale as death. "I will stay here forever, Hugh, if you like."

"Do you want to go?"

"I want to go and I want to stay. What shall we do?"

"Go! We shall be happy. Nothing shall part us, darling."

"But Grace? What if she is alive?" she asked faintly.

"God grant she is. I'll throw myself at her feet and she shall be made to understand," he said, but a nameless chill crossed him.

"You would break her heart," moaned she. "Our poor, poor wedding day."

"There will be another glad and joyous day," he said, trying to find heart.

"I will go where you go, Hugh," she said.

A few long sweeps of the oars and the white boat, with its blue trimmings, shot upon the beach, and the officer leaped forward to meet the waiting pair.

"I am Ensign Carruthers, United States cruiser *Winnetka*, Captain Hildebrand commanding. We saw your flag and were considerably mystified," he said, doffing his cap to her Ladyship. But Ridgeway, forgetting politeness, dignity and reserve, rushed up and grabbed him by the hand, mad with the exuberance of joy.

"Saved! Saved! Saved!"

Carruthers, dumbfounded, looked from one to the other of the now frantic couple. He saw white people dressed in most unusual garments, the woman possessing a gloriously beautiful face and the air of royalty, the man bushy haired and stalwart, every inch a gentleman and an American.

"What does this mean?" he demanded.

"You are the first white man we have seen in more than a year," cried Hugh.

"We have seen none but savages," added she, tears of happiness starting afresh down her cheeks.

"You were wrecked?" exclaimed the sailor, appalled.

It was an incoherent recital that the two poured into his ears, first one, then the other talking excitedly, but it was not long before he was in possession of all the facts.

"You were on the *Tempest Queen*," he cried, doubting his ears.

"Was no one saved?" they cried breathlessly.

"The captain and five or six passengers, I think, were picked up, almost starved, in a boat, some days after the wreck. All others were lost."

"Who were the passengers?" asked Hugh, trembling with eagerness.

"I don't recall the names."

"Was there a Miss Ridge among them?"

"Was Lord Huntingford saved?"

"I can't say as to the lady, but I know that Lord Huntingford was lost. I remember the papers were full of headlines about him and his young wife. His dead body was picked up by a steamer. She was not found."

"She has just been found," said Hugh. "This it Lady Huntingford."

The *Winnetka* was on a three years' cruise. Her engines had broken down a few days before, during a storm, and she was carried out of her course. The machinery being repaired, she was now picking her way toward Manila. The sailors were sent back to the warship, with information for the commander, and Carruthers accompanied the joyous couple to the village. The natives had seen the ship and the white men, and there was intense excitement among them.

Then came the struggle for Hugh and Tennys Huntingford. For an hour they wavered and then the die was cast. Back to the old world!

When it became known that the Izors who had done so much for them were to leave the island on the big, strange thing of the deep, the greatest consternation and grief ensued. Chattering disconsolately, the whole village accompanied the belongings of the Izors to the beach. Lady Tennys and Ridgeway went among their savage friends with the promise to return some day, a promise which they meant to fulfil.

"I'll have missionaries out here in a month," vowed Hugh, biting his lips and trying to speak calmly through the grip that was choking him involuntarily.

King Pootoo, the picture of despair, stood knee-deep in the water. As the sailors pushed off, he threw up his hands and wailed aloud; and then the whole tribe behind him fell grovelling in the sand. Two white-robed figures flung themselves in the water and grasped the gunwales as the boat moved away. The sailors tried to drive them off, but they screamed and turned their pleading faces toward their mistress.

"Please take them in," she cried, and strong arms drew the dusky women into the boat. They were Alzam and Nattoo, the devoted handmaidens of the beautiful Izor. Trembling and in fear of dire punishment for their audacity, they sank to the bottom of the boat. Nor did they cease their moaning until they were on the broad deck of the *Winnetka*, where astonishment overcame fear.

Slowly the boat moved away from the island of Nedra, just one year after its new passengers had set foot on its shores. High upon the top of the tall gatepost fluttered the frayed remnants of an American flag. The captain pointed toward it, removed his cap proudly, and then there arose a mighty cheer from the men on board the man o' war.

CHAPTER XXXIII
APPARITIONS

The *Winnetka* passed Corregidor Island and dropped anchor in Manila harbor on the morning of June 1st. On the forward deck stood Hugh Ridgeway and Tennys Huntingford. They went ashore with Captain Hildebrand, Ensign Carruthers, the paymaster and several others. Another launch landed their nondescript luggage--their wedding possessions--and the faithful handmaidens. The captain and his passengers went at once to shipping quarters, where the man in charge was asked if he could produce a list of those on board the *Tempest Queen* at the time she went down.

"I have a list of those who left Aden and of those who were rescued. Did you have friends on board?"

"Yes, we had friends," answered Hugh, in a choking voice. "First, let me see a list of the lost." The clerk found the book containing the list, alphabetically arranged, and placed it on the desk before the trembling man and woman. Both had an insane desire to rush from the office and back to the *Winnetka*, where they could hide from the very knowledge they were seeking. In their hearts they were wishing for the solitude and happiness of the Island of Nedra. The clerk, observing their anxiety, considerately offered to read the names to them.

"No, I thank you; I'll look," said Hugh, resolutely turning to the pages. Lady Tennys leaned weakly against the counter and looked through blurred eyes at the racing lines of ink. Hugh rapidly ran his fingers through the list, passing dozens of passengers they had known. As the finger approached the "R's" it moved more slowly, more tremblingly. "Reed--Reyer--Ridge!" "Hugh Ridge, Chicago, Illinois, U.S.A." He grew sick when he saw his own name among those who were dead.

"She was saved," he murmured, for there was but one Ridge there.

"Look for Vernon," whispered his companion.

"Van Camp--Valentine--Wilson." It was not there--nor was Veath's!

"Are they on the list?" asked the clerk.

"Let me see the names of those who were saved," said Hugh bravely, joy and anxiety welling to the surface like twin bubbles.

"Two pages over, sir."

Over went the pages so ruthlessly that the scribe was in trepidation lest they should be crumpled beyond redemption. Hugh read aloud in an unnatural voice:

"Costello--Hamilton--Ridge--Shadburn--Veath."

His hand fell upon the page and his head dropped forward till his lips touched the name that danced before his eyes.

"Here it is! Here it is!" he shouted, hugging the book.

"Thank God!" cried she, tears rushing to her eyes. Together they read and re-read the name, scarcely able to believe that she was truly one of the few to escape. "And Henry Veath, too. Oh, Hugh, it is a miracle--a real miracle!"

"Old Veath saved her! I knew he would if he had a ghost of a chance. Tennys, Tennys, I can't believe it is true." He was beside himself in his excitement. Captain Hildebrand, the clerk, and the other attachés looked on with happy smiles. In this moment of relief they forgot completely that, in leaving the island, they had been filled with a sort of dread lest they should find her who might come between them.

"We must find Veath," went on Hugh rapidly. "Is he in Manila?"

"He is in the Government Building, sir," answered the clerk. Already Hugh was edging toward the door, holding Lady Tennys by the arm. "Is Mr. Veath a relative?"

"No; he's more than that. He's a friend. We were on the *Tempest Queen* together when she went down."

"You were--on--the--what did you say, sir?" gasped the clerk.

"He doesn't know who we are, Hugh."

"That's so. Add two more names to the list of saved and scratch 'em off the other. Put down Lady Huntingford and Hugh Ridge."

The clerk's eyes bulged. Every man in the office came forward in amazement.

"It's the truth," volunteered the *Winnetka's* captain. "I picked them up last week."

"Where's the cable office? I must send a message to Miss Ridge. When did she sail for the United States?"

"She hasn't sailed, sir. Her name is Vernon, and she's been waiting in Manila for news of you ever since. Get some water there, Cleary! He's going to faint." Ridgeway collapsed against the counter, his face going deadly pale. Lady Tennys sank into her chair, huddling limply as if to withstand a shock, while from her stricken face two wide blue eyes centred themselves hopelessly on her lover.

"Needn't mind the water. I'm all right," stammered Hugh, moving away with legs as stiff as rods. "Where is she now?"

"At the home of her uncle, Mr. Coleman. There were seven of them saved, after being buffeted about by the sea for three days in the boat in which they left the wreck. When they were picked up by the *Sea Gull*, they were almost dead with hunger, thirst and madness. It seems Miss Vernon had written her uncle before sailing; and the letter, coming by way of San Francisco, got here two or three weeks before she was expected. Afterward, Mr. Coleman got the government to send ships out to find the wreck. It was many weeks before Miss Vernon was fully recovered."

"Thank you," muttered he. "Come, Lady Huntingford, we will go to a hotel." She arose and silently followed him to the door. The men in the office glanced at each other, completely mystified, Captain Hildebrand as much so as any one.

For a long time the occupants of a certain carriage looked straight before them as if bereft of the power of speech or comprehension. A great abyss of thought confronted them; they were apparently struggling on the edge, utterly unable to grasp a single inspiration or idea.

"She's been waiting a year, Tennys. Do you know what that means?"

"Yes, Hugh; I know too well. She has prayed and hoped and loved, and now you are come to her. It means that she will be happy--oh, so happy!" murmured his white-lipped companion, cold as ice.

"But I can't go to her and tell her what we know. It would kill her. I can't go to her--it is impossible! I'd die if she looked at me," he groaned.

"You must go to her," she said intensely. "She will know you have been rescued. She will thank God and wait for you to come to her. Think of that poor girl waiting, waiting, waiting for you, filled with a joy that we can never know. Oh, I will not have you break her heart. You shall go to her!"

"I cannot, I tell you! I cannot tell her that I love you! That would be worse than any cruelty I can imagine."

"You are not to tell her that you love me. I release you, Hugh. You were hers first; you are hers now. I would kill myself rather than lake you from her. Go to her--go to her at once. You must!" She was nervous, half-crazed, yet true nobility shone above all like a gem of purest ray.

"Don't force me to go, Tennys," he pleaded, as she left him to go to her room.

"Go now, Hugh--go if you love me," she said, turning her miserable face from him.

"But what is to become of you--of me?" he protested.

"We must think only of her. Go! and bring her to see me here! I want to tell her how happy I am that she has found you again;" and then she was gone.

The dominant impulse was to rush after her, grasp her and carry her back to the waves from which he had unwittingly saved her. Then the strong influence that she had exerted over him, together with the spark of fair-mindedness that remained, forced him to obey the dictates of honor. He slowly, determinedly, dejectedly re-entered the carriage and started toward the end.

CHAPTER XXXIV
THE COURSE OF TRUE LOVE

Ridgeway had been directed to the home of Mr. Henry Coleman. He was never able to describe his emotions as he drove through the streets toward that most important place in all the world at that hour. The cab drew up in front of the rather pretentious home and he stepped forth, dazed and uncertain, his knees stiff, his eyes set. Had some one shouted "Run!" he would have fled with his resolution.

Every window in the home seemed to present Grace Vernon's glad face to his misty eyes; she was in there somewhere, he knew, waiting as she had been waiting for a whole year.

Slowly he mounted the steps and stood before the screen door. After what seemed an hour of deliberation, during which he sought to resurrect the courage that had died, he timidly tapped on the casement with his knuckles. The sound could not have been heard ten feet, yet to him it was loud enough to wake people blocks away. There was no response and his heart, in its cowardice, took a hopeful bound. No one at home! He turned to leave the place, fearing that some one might appear to admit him before he could retreat. At the top of the steps he paused, reasoning that if no one was at home he could at least rap again. His conscience would be easier for the extra effort. He rapped once more, quite boldly. A man appeared in the doorway so suddenly that he caught his breath and put out his hand to steady himself.

The screen flew open and Henry Veath grasped him by the arms, fairly dragging him into the hallway.

"Hugh! Hugh! Is it really you?" For a moment he stood like one suddenly gone mad.

"Henry, I can't believe it!" gasped Ridgeway. Both of them stood looking at one another for more than a full minute. "What a wonderful escape!" fell hazily from the newcomer's stiff lips.

"How did you escape?" cried the other in the same breath. Pale as ghosts they wrung each other's hands spasmodically, dazed and bewildered.

"Where is Grace?" demanded Hugh.

"She is out just at present," said the other slowly and with an effort. "Come in and sit down. She will be here presently." He staggered as he drew back.

"Has--has my sister given up all hope of ever seeing me again?" said Ridgeway. Their hands were still clasped.

"Miss Vernon feared that you were lost, Hugh," said Veath. A cold perspiration was showing itself on his brow. "She has told me all. How ill and white you look. Sit down here and I'll get you some wine."

"Never mind, old man. I'm well enough. When will she return? Great heaven, man, I can't wait!" He sank limply into a chair. His companion's heart was freezing.

"Be calm, old friend. She shall be sent for at once."

"Break it to her gently, Veath, break it to her gently," murmured Hugh.

Veath excused himself and left the room. In the hall, out of Hugh's sight, he stopped, clenched his hands, closed his eyes and shivered as if his blood had turned to ice. Presently he returned to the room, having gone no farther than the hall.

"I have sent for her," he said in a strange voice.

Grace was coming down stairs when Veath admitted Hugh. Startled and almost completely prostrated, she fell back, where Veath found her when he went to announce the news. Finally, with throbbing heart, she crept to the curtain that hung in the door between the parlors and peered through at the two men. Ridgeway was standing in the centre of the room, nervously handling a book that lay on the table. His face was white and haggard; his tall, straight figure was stooped and lifeless. Veath stood on the opposite side of the table, just as pale and just as discomposed.

"Does she often speak of me?" she heard Hugh ask hoarsely. The other did not answer at once.

"Frequently, Hugh, of course," he said finally.

"And--do--you--think she--she loves me as much as ever?" There was fear in his voice; but poor Grace could only distinguish pathetic eagerness. Veath was silent, his hands clasped behind his back, his throat closed as by a vise. "Why don't you answer? Does she still love me?"

Grace glanced at the drawn face of Henry Veath and saw there the struggle that was going on in his mind. With a cry she tore aside the curtains and rushed into the room, confronting the questioner and the questioned.

"Grace!" gasped the former, staggering back as if from the effect of a mighty blow. Through his dizzy brain an instant later shot the necessity for action of some kind. There stood Grace, swaying before him, ready to fall. She loved him! He must clasp her to his heart as if he loved her. This feeble impulse forced him forward, his arms extended. "Don't be afraid, dear. I am not a ghost!"

Veath dropped into a chair near the window, and closed his eyes, his ears, his heart.

"Oh, Hugh, Hugh," the girl moaned, putting her hands over her face, even as he clasped her awkwardly, half-heartedly in his arms. He was saying distressedly to himself: "She loves me! I cannot break her heart!"

Neither moved for a full minute, and then Hugh drew her hands from her eyes, his heart full of pity.

"Grace, look at me," he said. "Are you happy?"

Their eyes met and there was no immediate answer. What each saw in the eyes of the other was strange and puzzling. She saw something like hopeless dread, struggling to suppress itself beneath a glassy film; he saw pitiful fear, sorrow, shame, everything but the glad lovelight he had expected. If their hearts had been cold before, they were freezing now.

"Happy?" she managed to articulate. "Happy?"

"Yes, happy," he repeated as witlessly.

"Don't look at me, Hugh. Don't! I cannot bear it," she wailed frantically, again placing her hands over her eyes. His arms dropped from their unwilling position and he gasped in amazement.

"What is it, Grace? What is the matter? What is it, Veath?" he gasped. She sank to her knees on the floor and sobbed.

"Oh, Hugh! I am not worthy to be loved by you." He tried to lift her to her feet, absolutely dumb with amazement. "Don't! Don't! Let me lie here till you are gone. I can't bear to have you see my face again."

"Grace!" he cried blankly.

"Oh, if I had been drowned this could have been avoided. Why don't you say something, Henry? I cannot tell him." Veath could only shake his head in response to Ridgeway's look of amazed inquiry.

"Is she mad?" groaned the returned lover.

"Mad? No, I am not mad," she cried shrilly, desperately. "Hugh, I know I will break your heart, but I must tell you. I cannot deceive you. I cannot be as I once was to you."

"Cannot be--deceived me--once was--" murmured he, bewildered.

"While I mourned for you as dead I learned to love another. Forgive me, forgive me!" It was more than a minute before he could grasp the full extent of her confession and he could not believe his ears.

Gradually his mind emerged from its oblivion and the joy that rushed to his heart passed into every vein in his body. At his feet the unhappy girl; at the window the rigid form of the man to whom he knew her love had turned; in the centre of this tableau he stood, his head erect, his lungs full, his face aglow.

"Say you will forgive me, Hugh. You would not want me, knowing what you do."

"For Heaven's sake, Hugh," began Veath; but the words choked him.

"So you love another," said Hugh slowly, and cleverly concealing his elation at the unexpected change in the situation. He was not without a sense of humor, and forgetting, for the moment, the seriousness of her revelation, he could not resist the temptation to play the martyr.

"My dear girl," he went on with mock gravity, "I would sacrifice my life to see you happy! Whoever he may be, I give you to him. Be happy, Grace;" and with decided histrionic ability concluded heart-brokenly: "Forget Hugh Ridgeway!"

A portrait of a buxom lady hanging on the wall received the full benefit of his dejected glance; and she could have told the unhappy lovers that the wretched man had winked at her most audaciously.

"When are you to be married?" he resumed solemnly.

"To-night," she choked out, then added quickly:

"But I won't, Hugh--I won't marry him if you say--"

"Not for the world! You must marry him, Grace, and I'll bless you," he interrupted quickly, even eagerly. Then there came a new thought: "Tell me truly, do you love him better than you loved me?"

"I love him better than the world!"

"Thank God!" exclaimed the discarded lover devoutly. "Give me your hand, Henry, old man--there is no one in all the world whom I'd rather see get her than you. You saved her and you deserve her. Take her and be good to her, that's all I ask; and think of me once in a while, won't you? Good-by."

Without waiting for an answer he broke away, as if starting for the hall.

"Please don't go away like that!"

The cry of anguish came from Grace, and she threw herself sobbing on Veath's breast.

Hugh turned like a flash. Contrition and the certainty of his power to dispel her grief showed plainly in his face.

"Don't cry, Grace dear," he begged, going over to them. "I was only fooling, dear. I'm not a bit unhappy." Grace looked up wonderingly at him through her tears. "You must take me for a brute," he stumbled on penitently. "You see--you see--er--the fact is, I'm in love myself." He did not know he could be so embarrassed. Veath actually staggered, and the girl's tear-stained face and blinking eyes were suddenly lifted from the broad breast, to be turned, in mute surprise, upon the speaker.

"What did you say?" she gasped.

"I'm in love--the very worst way," he hurried on, fingering his cap.

"And not with me?" she cried, as if it were beyond belief.

"Well, you see, I--I thought you were drowned--couldn't blame me for that, could you? So--I--she was awfully good and sweet and--by George! I'd like to know how a fellow could help it! You don't know how happy I am that you are in love with Veath, and you don't know how happy it will make her. We were to have been married a week ago but--" he gulped and could not go on.

Grace's eyes were sparkling, her voice was trembling with joy as she cried, running to his side:

"Is it really true--really true? Oh, how happy I am! I was afraid you would--"

"And I was equally afraid that you might--Whoop!" exploded Hugh, unable to restrain his riotous glee a second longer. Clasping her in his arms, he kissed her fervently; and all three joining hands, danced about the room like children, each so full of delight that there was no possible means of expressing it, except by the craziest of antics.

"But who is she?" broke out Grace excitedly, as soon as she could catch her breath.

"And where is she--can't we see her?" put in Veath, slapping Hugh insanely on the back.

"She's a goddess!" burst out Hugh, grabbing his cap and running out of the room, shouting hilariously: "Follow on, both of you, to the hotel, and see me worship at her shrine!"

CHAPTER XXXV
HISTORY REPEATS ITSELF

Hugh lost no time on the way back to the hotel. The lazy driver awoke his lazy horse and, to the intense amazement of both, the vehicle held together during the return trip. At least a dozen rattling bumps over rough places in the street caused the driver to glance apprehensively over his shoulder in the unusual fear that his fare and the cab had parted company. For the first time in ten years he was sufficiently interested to be surprised. It astonished him to find that the vehicle stuck together as a whole.

On the way back, Hugh suddenly bethought himself of his financial condition. He was attired in a suit of clothes belonging to Mr. Carruthers and the garments fitted him well. In one of the pockets rested his small leather purse. When he plunged into the sea on that memorable night a year ago it contained a half dozen small American coins and some English money, amounting in all to eleven dollars and thirty cents. Carefully he had treasured this wealth on the island and he had come away with the principal untouched. Now, as he jogged along in the cab, he emptied the contents of the purse upon the seat.

"Eleven thirty," he mused. "A splendid dowry. Not enough to buy the ring. No flowers, no wine--nothing but pins. My letter of credit is at the bottom of the sea. Borrowed clothes on my back and home-made clothes on hers. I have a watch, a knife, and a scarf pin. She has diamond rings and rubies, but she has no hat. By Jove, it looks as though I'll have to borrow money of Veath, after all."

Lady Tennys was in her room, strangely calm and resigned. She was wondering whether he would ever come back to her, whether she was ever to see him again. Her tired, hopeless brain was beginning to look forward to the dismal future, the return to England, the desolate life in the society she now despised, the endless regret of losing that which she had never hoped to possess--a man's love in exchange for her own. She kept to her room, avoiding the curious stare of people, denying herself to the reporters and correspondents, craving only the loneliness that made the hour dark for her.

It seemed to her that she had lived a lifetime since he went forth to find the girl who had waited so long for him.

Then came the rush of footsteps in the hall. They were not those of the slow-moving servants, they were not--a vigorous thumping on the door was followed by the cry of a strong, manly, vigorous voice. Her head swam, her heart stood still, her lips grew white and she could utter no sound in response.

He was coming at last to commit her to everlasting misery.

The door flew open and Ridgeway bounded into the room. Before she could move, he rushed over and drew her limp form from the chair, up into his strong embrace. She heard a voice, tender and gladsome, as from afar off, singing into her ear.

"Look up, darling! This is to be our wedding day--yours and mine! You are mine--mine!"

The glad light slowly struggled back into her eyes, but it was as if she had come from a death-like swoon. He poured into her dull ears the story of the visit to Grace Vernon, but he was compelled to repeat it. Her ears were unbelieving.

"Grace is coming here with Henry Veath," he said in the end. "By Jove, I am happy!"

She held his face close to hers and looked deep into his eyes for a long, long time.

"Are you sure?" she whispered at last. "Is it all true?"

"They'll be here in half an hour; but I haven't told them it was you they are going to see. She loves Veath--loves him more than she ever cared for me. I don't blame her, do you? Veath's a man--worthy of any woman's love and confidence. Tennys, do you know what I've been thinking ever since I left them fifteen minutes ago? I've been calling myself a cad--a downright cad."

"And why, may I ask?"

"Because Veath isn't one--that's all."

"But you are a man--a true, noble, enduring one. The year just gone has changed you from the easy, thoughtless boy into the strong man that you are, just as it has made of me a woman."

"I am no longer the harlequin?" he interposed eagerly.

"The harlequin's errand is accomplished, dear. The spangles and glitter are gone. Pure gold has come in their stead. It won't wear out. God has worked out this end for all of us. In His own good time He rectifies our errors and points the new way."

"I am but a year older than when I began."

"It isn't time that makes the man."

"It's opportunity, after all. I wasn't a man when I dragged Grace Vernon away from home; I was a fool--a callow boy in--"

"That was a year ago, Hugh, dear. What was I two years ago?"

"A rich man's wife. I was a rich man's son."

"You were the rich man's son by chance. I was a rich man's wife from choice."

"History repeats itself with variations, dearest. Although I have but eleven dollars and thirty cents in my purse, I have a million at home. You don't mind, do you?"

"I suppose it was foreordained that I should always marry from choice," she said with her most entrancing smile.